HOW TEXTILE COMMUN

HOW TEXTILE COMMUNICATES

From Codes to Cosmotechnics

Ganaele Langlois

BLOOMSBURY VISUAL ARTS
LONDON • NEW YORK • OXFORD • NEW DELHI • SYDNEY

BLOOMSBURY VISUAL ARTS
Bloomsbury Publishing Plc, 50 Bedford Square, London, WC1B 3DP, UK
Bloomsbury Publishing Inc, 1385 Broadway, New York, NY 10018, USA
Bloomsbury Publishing Ireland, 29 Earlsfort Terrace, Dublin 2, D02 AY28, Ireland

BLOOMSBURY, BLOOMSBURY VISUAL ARTS and the Diana logo
are trademarks of Bloomsbury Publishing Plc

First published in Great Britain 2024
Paperback edition published 2025

Cover design by Holly Capper
Cover image © photohampster/Adobe Stock

Bloomsbury Publishing Plc does not have any control over, or responsibility for,
any third-party websites referred to or in this book. All internet addresses given
in this book were correct at the time of going to press. The author and publisher
regret any inconvenience caused if addresses have changed or sites have
ceased to exist, but can accept no responsibility for any such changes.

A catalogue record for this book is available from the British Library.

A catalog record for this book is available from the Library of Congress.

ISBN: HB: 978-1-3503-8434-7
PB: 978-1-3503-8694-5
ePDF: 978-1-3503-8435-4
eBook: 978-1-3503-8436-1

Typeset by RefineCatch Limited, Bungay, Suffolk

For product safety related questions contact productsafety@bloomsbury.com.

To find out more about our authors and books visit www.bloomsbury.com
and sign up for our newsletters.

To my family

CONTENTS

ILLUSTRATIONS

ACKNOWLEDGEMENTS

This book is deeply indebted to the generosity and kindness of many people all over the world. When I was conducting fieldwork research for this book, I always found myself bumbling into many spaces without a clue of what was going on—a typical side-effect of spending too much time in academia. I am very grateful for the patience of all my interlocutors including Jenny Boucher, Mauricio Navarro, Yuki Seo, Hiroko Karuno, Nobuko Hiroi, Jorie Johnson, Hiroyuki Shindo, Miyuki Sano and Aurore Thibout. Special thanks as well to Gallery Kei and Kawashima Textile School in Kyoto, the Musée des textiles et arts décoratifs in Lyon, the Centre d'enseignement de la dentelle au fuseau du Puy en Velay, and Alianza Arkana in Yarinacocha.

To friends at the Contemporary Textile Studio Co-op in Toronto—Rachel MacHenry, Sharon Epstein, and Munira Amin: thank you so much for your support, mentorship, and advice throughout the years.

Many thanks to the academic community for their support in helping me present and publish earlier chapters of the book: Sarah Sharma, Baruch Gottlieb, Liam Cole Young, and Rianka Singh.

Finally, this research would have not been possible without the financial support of the Social Science and Humanities Research Council of Canada and York University.

An earlier and more compressed and truncated version of Chapter 3 was published as: Langlois, G. (2019). "Distributed Intelligence: Silk-Weaving and the Jacquard Mechanism." Special Issue on *Many McLuhans*. Edited by Sarah Sharma, in the *Canadian Journal of Communication* 44 (4): 555–566. An earlier version of Chapter 6 was published as: Langlois, G. (2022). "Forgotten Media: Textile and Shipibo-Conibo Cosmovision." In *Re-Understanding Media*. Edited by Sarah Sharma and Rianka Singh. Durham, NC: Duke University Press. Parts of Chapter 7 were published as: Langlois, G. (2022). "Cosmomedia: Natural Dyes in Japan." *Into the Air* Special Issue. *Media Theory* 5 (2), 289–306.

Open access was funded by York University, Canada.

INTRODUCTION: TEXTILE AS COMMUNICATION

Winding Back

On April 24, 2013, 1,129 garment factory workers were killed and another 2,515 injured in the collapse of the Rana Plaza in Savar, Bangladesh. The reasons for the building's collapse—illegal construction, criminal ignorance of building and occupation codes, the sacrifice of workplace health and safety for higher productivity—became headline news. In Toronto, where I live, reactions to the disaster were particularly acute: the workers at the Rana Plaza were making clothes for Joe Fresh, a local success story of a Canadian brand that had become a big player in the global market of "affordable" (read: fast) fashion, competing with the likes of Zara and H&M for hip clothes at bargain prices (Strauss, 2013; Safi and Rushe, 2018; *CBC Radio*, 2019). The Rana Plaza disaster disrupted, for a while, the common western perception of cheap clothes as guilt-free, cheerful commodities. Where I live—in downtown, multicultural yet hyperconsumerist Toronto—there re-emerged a common awareness of the hidden story embedded in our everyday clothing: one of corporate greed, over-consumption, and the destruction of both human lives and the environment (Thomas, 2021). In the wake of the deadliest garment factory accident in history, there was thus a willingness (albeit momentary) to decipher fast-fashion garments—to uncover the actual meaning of a simple piece of fabric, to realize that such pieces of fabric symbolized and materialized destructive environmental, economic, political and social processes. Textile garments, in other words, ceased to be perceived as personal objects of consumption and were revealed as communicative objects that epitomized virally transmitted and entrenched global inequalities.

Textile indeed communicates, and in many ways. Nowadays and for many, it mostly communicates by propagating commodity fetishism through the global fashion market: advertising, marketing and the fashion industry imbue textile with meanings of enjoyment, pleasures and luxury that hide away the actual abysmal conditions of its production: environmentally unsustainable production; heavy pollution, from fiber dusts in factories and the millions of liters of dye chemicals polluting rivers to the endocrine disruptors coating our clothing; worker exploitation; and the active promotion of global systemic inequalities to maintain low prices (O'Connor, 2017). But textile used to, and still does in many settings, communicate social bonds related to family, cultural values, community, and existence in the world. Textile, as Yuko Tanaka in *The Power of the Weave* (2013) so powerfully and elegantly puts it, acts both at the level of the intimate and the global: newborns are welcomed into the world by being wrapped in cloth that mimics the mother's skin; and in many cultures we soothe ourselves by wrapping up in a soft, warm piece of cloth. One of the most poignant uses of textile as a medium of communication is *boro* (Tuzuki, 2009). Practiced in rural and remote areas of Japan, where textile fibers were scarce up until after WW2, *boro* ("rags") was born out of necessity: it involved the careful recycling of fabric (a similar process exists in India and is called Kawandi). A jacket, for instance, would be patched with scraps of textile and reinforced with over-stitching. When it started falling apart, it would in turn be cut up into scraps to sew or patch other clothes. Scraps too worn to be sewn or stitched together would be used as bedding filler or rags. Tanaka provides important insight into *boro* as a form of communication. A *boro* piece is the trace of unique, often locally woven textile objects that were completely erased when textile became an industrial commodity, providing a window onto local economies and habits. In essence, *boro* is a patchwork of different times and existences—it is a quiet, subtle mode of cultural transmission that nevertheless fostered a unique aesthetic. Indeed, *boro* clothes sell for a fortune now, and are displayed as artworks worldwide, while inspiring many in the Do-It-Yourself scene to upcycle used clothing through creative mending (Holroyd, 2016; McLaren and McLauchlan, 2015; Diddi and Yan, 2019; König, 2013). It is a powerful idea that one would wear not just a jacket, but a presence that carried generational traces: one would be surrounded by ancestors, and in a very material way. Meaning, and this is the refrain of this book, comes to matter and matter comes to be meaningful. *Boro* thus "bears witness to the people who wear and use it" and "is charged with their life essence" (Tanaka: 171). The practice creates temporal links—it makes possible both retention and protention (Stiegler, 2013), that is, the materialization in the present of past existences, and therefore their projection into a future yet to be made.

At the same time, the practice of mending establishes a unique kind of relationship between the human and the non-human. Tanaka explains that *boro* entailed that "cloth was a living thing, and as such it had a lifespan and should be kept alive until that time came" (2013: 167). The idea that textile could be considered as *living* is more than just provocative. Indeed, textile does not fall neatly into a category of what we consider "the living" in the standard sense of the biological; from an actor-network perspective, however, it has agency that evolves through time (Latour, 2007). Artificial life is a popular topic these days, and it usually conjures up images of synthetic machines and high-end computing power. But looking at textile as a form of artificial life, as a living hybrid interface of encounter—and as something that had to be nurtured and protected through its life span—opens up our horizon about the relationships between the human and the non-human. Through *boro*, the neat boundaries between nature and culture, human and non-human are blurred. More importantly, *boro* reminds us that artificial life has a long history, and that it relied on a set of technically mediated relations between humans and the world. This insight stands in stark contrast to the contemporary discourses of artificial life as providing an *escape* from the limitations of biology and materiality, from the limitations of life and the world we live in. *Boro* as artificial-life-making was about the creation of new temporalities, memories, futures and lines of existence, relations that endured through the cycle of human life and death. What is key to note here is a kind of relationship with artificial, fabricated, technological objects that takes into account their particular life and changing agencies. Rather than thinking about technical agencies as de facto surpassing human capacities and therefore being stronger, the practice of *boro* embraces technological decay. The cycles of *boro*, from reinforcing to patching together to layering to stuffing, follow textile as it degrades, as its threads get thinner and eventually fall apart. To account for the decay of fabricated actants as enabling important modes of cultural expression and transmission: this is completely unimaginable in our western technological mindset oriented as it is toward immortality and incapable of thinking about degrowth in the first place.

With *boro*, we have one of the most profound types of communication: one that makes both collective and individual existence possible by tying us, binding us, wrapping us to others and to the world, both physically and imaginatively; one that gives us pasts to bring to our presents and presents to project into futures. With *boro* as well, we have communicative objects, borne out of necessity and meant to be continuously used, that do not last. And thus with *boro*, as with any other forms of textile in existence before the arrival of modernity, capitalism and colonialism, we have a medium of communication that, for material as well as cultural purposes, had to be continuously practiced by many. And far from being a quaint low-tech craft, textile as a communication medium required that humans constantly extend themselves with technical tools in order to transform materials into meaningful patterns in ways that we can barely understand today.

In this book, I start by asking: what was lost when the western world abandoned textile as a medium of communication and made it a mass industrial commodity? My answer is: a capacity to practice and craft temporal and intersubjective ties that matter, that transform and imbue the worlds we live in with strange and new, yet familiar and comforting meanings. And further, in not only abandoning and forgetting about, but also violently erasing textile as a communication medium altogether to replace it with textile as an unsustainable and unjust commodity, we ensured that only one dystopian future could emerge, which now has become a non-future altogether: the impossibility of human life on a healthy planet. I show in this book that when most of the world ceased to see textile as a medium of communication, we lost unique ways to craft collective modes of existence, modes that are not simply relevant for establishing a history of the past, or rather of the immense cultural plurality and rich intercultural and pluriversal dialogues of the many pasts where textile was practiced; but modes that are incredibly relevant today to address the question of what comes after the failures of modernist attempts to fully control the world via technology, of capitalist logics that can only exploit and destroy, and of the continuous neo-colonial subjection and violent erasure of humans, non-humans and environments. To practice textile as a medium of communication today, then, means to necessarily engage in a politics of survival and beyond that, in a politics of life in the midst of catastrophes (Tsing,

2017), a pharmacology of productive engagements and imagination. And in this book, I highlight both past and contemporary practices of textile as a medium of communication (as distinguished from textile as craft, which is much more common), in European, Asian, South American and Indigenous and non-Indigenous contexts. Let me be clear: this book is not an exercise in purification (Shotwell, 2016), ultimately arguing for the reconstruction in the present of a mythical past when textile was unsullied by power. Rather, this book is about how textile as a medium of communication engages with both power as creative freedom and expression, and power as control, offering ways to navigate life in compromised, and troubled times and to "stay with the troubles" (Haraway, 2016). The case studies presented here all have in common the mobilization of textile to forge new ways of being in destabilized worlds and how *we*—those of us caught and deeply entangled in these troubled and compromised times—can develop new politics of living together.

Textile as a Medium

It does seem quite outlandish to declare that a simple stitch can be a political act and pact, but this is only so if one, like me, suffers from media amnesia and obliviousness. I came to textile purely by chance; I was looking for an artistic outlet, a hobby. In a vague attempt to find balance in my working life, I signed up for the wrong (and non-refundable) screen-printing course: textile instead of paper. And thus I had to push past my deep-seated aversion for all things related to the needle and thread, which stemmed from being a very, very impatient child. More importantly, the notion that textile is about communication above all else is not something I came up with (see, for instance, Andrew, 2008). I first heard it mentioned during a workshop led by textile researcher Yoshiko Wada in 2015 at the Contemporary Textile Studio in Toronto. Wada's statement had a dual impact on me: one, I could only but agree with it, and two, I was left wondering why I, as a communication and media studies scholar, had never thought about textile in this way, but only as art, craft and design. What was it that made me oblivious to textile as a medium of communication? But I am not the only media scholar to suffer from this: why is it that one of the oldest communication media ever to exist—textile—never received the same kind of attention in the field of western communication and media studies as others such as writing, television or the internet? Of course, any media history courses in North America will mention that the Incas used knotted ropes known as Quipus, which are proto-databases (Hyland, 2017; Graham 2014); that knitting is similar to binary code; that textile craft cultures today are forms of political expression and cultural resistance. In addition, the articulation of fashion, advertising and everyday life is well acknowledged in the field (Barthes, 2013; Nistor, 2016). But all these accounts tend to selectively use textile when it behaves most closely to the media that we in the west are more familiar with: writing, printing, and digital media. A more systematic study of textile as a medium of communication acknowledging that it functions in ways that are radically different from what we understand as communication media has yet to be fully investigated. This book offers an analysis of the singular aspects of textile as a medium of communication, showing that it is ephemeral yet deeply material, that its meanings cannot be reduced to analysis of signs alone, and that the kind of mathematical thinking it entails has nothing to do with western digital technologies, that it ultimately is about the power to weave together worlds.

I say that media studies by and large ignore it, but at the same time the *communicative* capacities of textile are taken for granted in the many fields that have focused on textile as a site of analysis: Textile and Fashion studies, of course, but also Fine Arts, Craft, Design, Anthropology and Archeology (Bachmann and Scheuing, 2006; Gordon, 2014; Jefferies et al., 2015; McDougall, 2011; Postrel, 2020). Textile and Fashion studies have long pointed out the many communicative aspects of textile as code and cultural interface (McCracken and Roth, 1989; Foxhall, 2017; Atkins 2005). Anthropology has long seen textile as a form of language (Tedlock and Tedlock, 1985). Also, feminist engagements with arts and science have long shown how textile enables radical and alternative ways of thinking, practicing, and applying digital codes (King, 2012); and textile centers such as The Textile Futures Research Community (University of the Arts, London), Textile + Materiality (Milieux, Concordia University) and MIT's Fabric Innovation Hub develop new smart textiles that make use of the newest information and communication technologies. The many metaphors drawing on textile suggest some kind of deep communication and communion still embedded in our collective psyche: we often talk about the "fabric of life" to express the interconnectedness of all living beings, and use weaving metaphors to express the coming together of disparate forces, that is to say, the overcoming of difference to create unity, including reaching some kind of ultimate meaning through, for instance, "weaving the web of destiny" (Glusica, 2016: 132). This book further explores these communicative aspects of textile: intimate yet universal, sensorial yet symbolic, fleeting yet traversing times and spaces, material yet spiritual, physical yet abstract, artificial yet deeply linked with environments, affective, yet logical and mathematical.

Textile, as opposed to other media, is both medium and communication: the distinction between technical support for storage and transmission and the message being transmitted co-emerge through the process of making, of weaving, of knitting. As T'ai Smith (2018) explains: "the conceptual and structural matrix are built through the same material processes." And as I show throughout this book, even textile ornamentations such as painting, and embroidery have to take into account this very quality of textile as the co-emergence of materials, techniques and message. In exploring these paradoxes and unique qualities of textile, I show how they extend and enrich conceptualizations of communication and media and, in so doing, I want to further explore an intractable paradox of communication: that it can be so ethereal, yet profoundly and concretely shape worlds and modes of existence. To do so, I not only explore how textile as a medium transforms how we traditionally understand cultural semiotics, material culture and digital technology, but also add another fundamental communicative aspect of textile that has received much less, if any, attention in the field so far: textile as *cosmotechnics*, a term inherently bound to textility itself, as I touch on below.

The most common understanding of textile as communication is as a support for the transmission of signs (Andrew, 2008). But even this semiotic function of textile is amorphous, and covers all kinds of semiotics. There are, of course, the visual signs and slogans that adorn clothing and send out all kinds of messages (Hudson and Hudson, 2003). As fashion studies tell us, moreover, textiles have a profound effect on identities through their interplay between bodies and visual designs such as symbols, colors, shape and so on (Lipovetsky, 1994). Thinking about textile as signification already requires examining the relationship between the symbolic and haptic properties of textile (Schoeser, 2012), between the visual and the tactile. At the same time, as it is intimate by covering and touching our skins, textile also plays a crucial role in broadcasting social bonds and cultural identities: textiles can be heavily coded to indicate social status and community belonging (Buckridge and Nettleford, 2009). The widespread acknowledgement that culturally specific clothing and textile, especially Indigenous ones, need to be protected as they are too often the site of cultural appropriation highlights the complex and important sociopolitical role of local textile worldwide. But most textile does not just behave like mainstream forms of cultural semiotics: patterns, embroidery, woven fabric and so on do not simply represent something. They enter the realm of the echoing mark, of repetition, rhythms, refrains and in so doing the visual and haptic information they carry has meaning effects that are much more open-ended, changing, and subject to all kinds of both symbolic and material rearticulations. As I show in this book, this capacity of textile is found in many places, in the homes of European women embroiderers and in the weaving spaces of Quechua artisans and enables the crossing of temporal and spatial distances.

It follows from this that we need, in turn, to focus on the question of information embedded in textile. Anybody engaging in critical analysis of digital technologies has encountered many references to textile (Smith, 2018; Monteiro, 2017). These references usually question the general bias toward digital media technologies as being radically and revolutionarily new. In particular, the parallel between digital binary code and the binary code of knitting and weaving notations surfaces over and over again in research-creation around digital technologies (Egenhoefer, 2008; Harlizius-Klück, 2017). Along these lines, the Jacquard mechanism designed to partially automate weaving has been heralded as a precursor to software and data processing (Essinger, 2007). There is a nascent recognition that the kind of mathematics practiced through textile in different parts of the world differs significantly from the western conception of mathematics (Splitstoser, 2022; Friedman, 2020), which in turn begs a more full-fledged, systematic analysis of textile as a digital technology that has been in existence since prehistoric times, and long before the arrival of what traditionally counts as the beginning of "media"—alphabetical writing. There are two threads emerging from this that I examine in this book: one that information behaves differently with textile in that it articulates in specific ways the abstract and the material through both intellectual processes and embodied gestures in practices of making and through the materials being used. Specifically, information in textile does not follow the western trajectory of abstract information: its mathematical underpinnings always rely on a keen sense of material transformation within specific contexts and environments, which is something that is particularly apparent in Indigenous textile practices that continue to exist today. It follows then, that textile radically opens the door to re-envisioning the field of communication and media studies from a decolonial perspective. It invites us to think more carefully about digital cultures—how mathematical processes have fostered modes of cultural expression that are organized in radically different fashions and for radically different effects than our current dominant digital cultures. In particular, I show in the book how the conception of the textile maker as engaged in profound mathematical thinking negates mainstream positioning of textile-making as a low-tech, low-skill activity. On the contrary, the textile-maker emerges as a central figure able to combine the material and the abstract, to bind worlds and beings together.

Through the figure of the maker, the politics of textile come even more to the fore: that textile as a medium of communication allows us to open up to a plurality of worlds and temporalities and to engage in meaningful dialogue among these radically different worlds—Western, Asian, Indigenous and so on. Such politics should be understood as, following philosopher Yuk Hui (2016), *cosmotechnics*. Broadly put, cosmotechnics is about the relationship between cosmopolitics and technics, between the politics and ethics of relations with environments and the practices of making that mobilize material and symbolic capacities in order to produce conditions of existence. The contemporary global textile industry is infamous for its complete disregard of people and the environment, being one of the worst polluters on the planet and well known for sustaining itself on poor working conditions and low wages. By contrasting this with non-industrial textile as a medium, we find a discrepancy between two technological models: one (industrial) that asserts itself through a complete disregard of the environment and people and that corresponds to the legacy of industrial capitalism, the logics of which have spread globally. The other (non-industrial) model that I focus on in this book is about the appropriate relationships with environments: it involves a practical ethics and material thinking about one's place in a specific cosmos, and the right kind of associations and networks with other humans and non-humans that can be developed from this. A more global approach to the history of textile would, I argue, see it as the history of the struggle between these two models of technology and making, and their constant friction. Caught up in this friction are questions concerning not only technology, but more fundamentally of technics, of how we relate to the world, to the very world of worlds—questions of *cosmotechnics*. It comes as no surprise that cosmotechnics, in an age of human-produced climate change and species extinction, is literally a burning issue. The current dominant version of technology corresponds to a vision of the cosmos where the human is the agent capable of exerting total control on the environment and nature, which are seen as disposable materials. Based on this epistemological premise, and combined with capitalist logics of ever-increasing profits through the constant transformation of every relation into a marketable one, this model of dominant technology has been heralded as universal. As Yuk Hui explains, one of the key tasks is to question the universalizing tendencies of this dominant version of technology and the epistemologies that sustain it. If technics are practices of knowing and engaging with the world, then to think about cosmotechnics is to acknowledge that there are many cosmoses and that therefore the relations between humans and environments are multiple and open to experimentation. And textile as a medium that was practiced by so many and still continues to survive in many non-western contexts, is an important site for delineating a politics of potential relationships that would give us new futures.

Textile-Making as Mediating

As I convey in these pages, textile as a medium is deeply tied to the question of making and the politics of our relationships with other humans and non-humans that emerge through them, what Donna Haraway calls, when exploring Navajo Weaving, *sympoeisis*—"making-with" (2016: 89–97). Making-with is not solely a human activity of transformation of inert materials—rather making is multiple, compositional, and distributed among humans, non-humans and more-than-humans, what Karen Barad would call an apparatus for intra-actions. In other words, the maker cannot exist but in a relational web with other non-humans and more-than-humans that work, as well, in creating textile objects. I focus in this book on making processes rather than finished textile pieces in order to bring to light how hand-making textile assembles, enacts and expresses relationships between humans and non-humans. In so doing, and in reference to Karen Barad (2007), I hope to make it clear to readers that my understanding of communication encompasses both the planes of meaning and that of matter, and that textile-making interfaces between the level of materialization and that of abstract expression. Under the shortcuts of "handmade" or "non-industrialized" textile that I use throughout the book is a series of complex and intertwined processes: first off are the bodily processes of making, which require a coordination between hands, general posture, gestures, sensations, attention, cognition, reflexes and intellect. Second are the technical tools and processes that arrange these human bodies, extend, abstract and externalize them and thus offer new creative capacities. Finally, there are the materials themselves—the plant or animal fibers and threads, finished textile pieces, and the dyestuff that possess their own agencies, histories and characteristics and allow for forms of expression. It is how these three spheres—humans, technical tools, and materials, which are already made up of different components and processes and have each their own complexities and relationalities—are made to relate to and thus transform each other in specific contexts, that creates effects that go beyond the production of textile objects.

Such assemblages, I argue in this book, offers their own mediation processes, in the way that John Durham Peters thinks about media as "forms of life" (2015: 23). In the same vein, this book follows a recent turn in communication media studies that shifts attention away from media systems and media objects to look at mediation, which Sarah Kember and Joanna Zylinska define as:

> . . . a key trope for understanding and articulating our being with, and becoming with, the technological world, our emergence and ways of interacting with it, as well as the acts and processes of temporarily stabilizing the world into media, agents, relations and networks.
>
> Kember and Zylinska, 2014: xv

This book echoes this conceptualization of mediation by questioning in particular the cosmotechnical dimension embedded in these attempts at "stabilizing" the world: that the moments of making are not simply about internal assemblages, but about the coming together of disparate elements, humans and nonhumans, organic and technological, that are put in relation with each other. Specifically, this book shows how non-industrialized textile-making constitutes planes of mediations through which potential forms of living together, not only with humans, but also with non-humans, emerge. Some of these forms continue to exist and solidify as they become systems of making, as they are both symbolized and materialized as textile objects that in turn circulate within local, national and global networks. Many, however, struggle as they are in turn dismantled or encounter other logics (capitalist, modernist and neocolonial) that make their existence difficult, if not downright impossible. These fragile planes of mediation that are constituted at the moments of making are typically under-studied, because making has been so subsumed to the industrial model, which (a) removed the complex human assemblage of hands, posture, sensations and thoughts; (b) automated technical tools and processes; and (c) kept only a few materials able to withstand the speed and force of new automated tools. In the industrial process nothing is left to chance, and in so doing there is closing off of potentialities in order to maximize capitalist goals. As I explain throughout the book, the moments of making by hand, while they might seem at first just repetitive and mundane, activate different potentialities, and it is by paying attention to these potentialities that new relations and modes of being together emerge.

It might seem then that my analysis might be more appropriate to craft studies, which is after all, where the politics of making come to the fore (Sennett, 2009), especially with regard to the relationship between traditional conceptions of craft and contemporary digital technologies (Crow, 2008; Harrod, 2007; McCullough, 1998). However, I argue throughout the book that there are deep conversations that take place when making non-industrialized textile, conversations that usually happen without words, but that connect, exchange, create agreements and alliances among humans, and between humans and non-humans, and cross time and space to bind us to a cosmos. And it is through these exchanges that formulations of modes of existence, of embodied ethics, of ways of being to each other and in the world come into being. In so doing, I further the already existing insight into textile-making as a multimedia activity, as Sadie Plant (2016) declares when she describes the conversations, meetings, friendships and moments of cultural transmission that happens when mostly women traditionally gather together to make textile. But these multimedia conversations, I argue, are not just human activities layered on top of making: for many who engage with textile as a medium, to make is to organize the relationships between human and non-human, to find some form of meaningful collaboration that requires the coming together of many processes, some microscopic and biological, some cosmological, some traditional, others radically creative and revolutionary. The erasure of making by hand is not only the loss of ways of doing, but also the loss of important forms of communication and mediation.

The question of textile-making as mediation requires rethinking some common divides between media technologies understood as dealing with immaterial information, and other technologies that are in charge of material extraction and transformation. In that regard, this book is indebted to Bernard Siegert's concept of cultural techniques (2015). Siegert uses this concept to move beyond an understanding of media as second-order techniques aimed at producing meaning rather than something tangible. Likewise limiting, other technologies (e.g., agricultural and industrial technologies) would be cast as first-order techniques in that they are operational: they deal with the transformation of matter and work directly on the real. Siegert asks us rather to examine the continuum through which the dichotomy between the real and the symbolic comes to emerge and persists. In so doing, cultural techniques present a much richer version of mediation: the co-articulation of technologies working with materials and technologies working through abstraction operates the transitions from real to symbolic and from symbolic to real and in so doing establishes a horizon of possibilities of existence. Combined with the concept of cosmotechnics, the cultural-techniques approach encourages us to look at how textile-making forges relationships with the world, with environments, and between humans and non-humans and in so doing articulates and actualizes ethical processes.

Textile-Making and Power

Aspects of making have been central to communication and media studies: I am thinking of the relationships between human bodies and technical tools which is core to both the Toronto School of Communication and in Friedrich Kittler's work. And while there are other theoretical frameworks that pay attention to this very relationship between bodies and techniques—specifically of Leroi-Gourhan (1985) and Simondon's work (2017)—the Toronto School of Communication is fundamental for tracing how the relationship between bodies and technical tools as extensions give shape to modes of power. For Innis (2008), the study of Eurocentric media was the study of empires, from the rise of European empires through the colonial land-grab of resources to the mobilization of mass media as tools to assert a capitalist mode of productivity over social life. However, my exploration of textile as a medium in this book does not limit itself to questions of dominant powers. Rather, it brings to the fore the capacity for textile as a medium to engage in power plays, specifically in interfacing between power as control, power as composition and power as potential. And in focusing on such plays of power, I highlight that for all their usefulness, the Toronto School of Communication and the critical traditions of communication and media studies that emerged from it suffer from a specific bias: that of reducing questions of media and power to western-centric media and power formations. I share the common critical conceptualization of media power as the capacity to exert effects at a distance on both humans and their environments through the deployment of systems for producing, storing, retrieving and distributing information. However, the field in general primarily focuses on how and which media technologies articulate themselves into—are transformed and in turn shape—the capacities for dominant power formations to organize all aspects of life and to mobilize resources through time and space. While the usefulness of such an approach to understand the relationships between media and dominant power is undeniable, the risk is to see dominant media as the only media in existence—a position of limited critical potential indeed, especially as the demand to formulate alternatives to a dominant system that can only sustain itself by eventually destroying the very possibility of life could not be more pressing.

In my analysis, I keep a central insight from the Toronto School: that bodies—including sensations, affects, and cognitive processes—refashioned through media technologies are key to understanding the relationship between media and power (McLuhan and Zingrone, 1995). Friedrich Kittler goes further: through the refashioning of the relationships between bodies and media also emerge impersonal dynamics that operate a media teleology where human bodies and capacities are increasingly broken apart and subsumed into increasingly complex and abstract technological systems (1999). In the works of Innis, McLuhan and Kittler, there is a recurring argument that massive shifts in power, in social organization, in infrastructure of knowledge and action, are brought about by this seemingly small, but profound reconfiguration of bodies and technical tools for information storage, retrieval and distribution. Kittler refers to Nietzsche's radical philosophical metamorphosis as he started using a typewriter, where typing on hard keys promoted short burst of thoughts—his famous aphorisms—as opposed to long hand-written treatises. Analog media technologies mobilize human hands, minds, postures and the senses in different ways than writing/drawing on paper, from typing to clicking on a shutter button while staring through a lens, to manipulating dials while listening and so on. Hand gestures with digital media technologies continue translating back and forth sensory input and thought into action via interacting with keyboards and mice, clicking or swiping right and left: such hand and tool assemblages actualize power and enact power effects. Interestingly, textile makes an appearance in these discussions. A notable intervention with regards to hapticity and media making is Stephen Monteiro's *Fabric of Interface* (2017) which pays close attention to the tactile-textile metaphors and practices that surface with digital technologies, considering how "haptic activities" that are similar in textile and digital work are inscribed within networks of exploitation of women's labor. This follows critical feminist work by Wendy Chun (2013), Lisa Nakamura (2014) and N. Katherine Hayles (2005) among others who have long highlighted how women's manual labor has long been part and parcel of digital infrastructures, but has also been constantly devalued and its power erased. As Monteiro (2017) and Sadie Plant (2016) show as well, there is a historical pattern of capitalism's appropriation and devaluation of women's manual labor, from domestic craft (including textile work) to the present day assembling of digital components (Nakamura, 2014). The involvement of hands in making overall, within the kind of ideologies of technological progress that are dominant today, is taken as a sign of lack of sophistication and efficiency. In such ideologies, to make by hand is to showcase one's absence of power.

This book challenges such ideologies by going beyond questions of labor and labor power (especially women's labor and disempowerment) in textile to examine different contexts of textile-making by hand: domestic of course, but also highly professionalized and male-dominated, as well as Indigenous and artistic. I follow T'ai Smith (2014) in that regard: textile has often been "gendered" and therefore devalued as a technical, mathematical and artistic medium. In particular, I argue that the question of making exceeds that of labor, which focuses on the production of something (an object or service). Making by hand is a mode of communication where the human-technological assemblage has to answer to the third type of actant: materials. And, as I argue in this book, there is a specific mode of power that emerges from the encounter between bodies, techniques and materials: a power of composition, which is the opposite of power as control. The Toronto School of Communication paid close attention to materials as sources of power— think for instance of Harold Innis distinguishing between different writing supports such as clay, papyrus, stone and parchment codex and the kind of expansionist strategies they enabled. Today, the environmental turn in media studies as exemplified by John Durham Peter's *Marvelous Clouds* (2015) further explores a material turn to media that pays attention to elemental entities such as air, fire, water and earth as mediators that yield non-human and super-human power. By mobilizing the capacities of different entities and materials, physical and chemical processes—not only fibers turned into thread and then woven, but also natural materials used for dyeing and applying colors—as well as further ornamentations, textile-making is by necessity an engagement and composition with such non-human powers. As Tim Ingold argues, textile thus challenges the hylomorphic model that operates in all dominant technological systems, that is, the "imposition of form upon the material world, by an agent with a design in mind" (2010: 91). Opposing this model, Ingold defines *textility* in making: not the imposition of form on inert substance through force, but the weaving together of materials in accordance with their own pliancy, resistance and agencies. Similarly, Anni Albers in *On Weaving* insists on the importance of tactility in making to understand the unique properties and agencies of materials (Albers et al., 2017: 44). A significant part of this book is devoted to exploring how making textile is a mode of communication with materials, which requires a deep understanding of how non-human agents such as fibers, chemicals and so on interact with each other, often through some form of elemental mediation. Often, the textile maker is but one element in a long and layered chain of collaboration rather than the single creative authority. Obviously, this kind of *communication-with* which becomes *compositional power* is based on a kind of making that is at odds with the technological systems that produce most of the textile we consume today. Indeed, one history of textile is about the constant drive to control and suppress textility. And yet, the dominant global textile industry has never quite been able to get rid of textility altogether, despite its best effort to do so over the past 250 years. Sewing in particular cannot easily do without humans, because the shifting tensions and minute adjustments required to sew pieces of fabric together necessitate a type of coordination between attention and gestures that only humans can provide. Even if they are among the most exploited working force in the world, textile workers are indispensable to the textile industry. This, combined with the survival of non-industrialized textile-making processes to the present day, make textile a unique site for understanding the relationship between textile as what links humans to non-human power, and in so doing creates cosmological compositions.

I further argue throughout the book that textile-making is an interface for these two forms of power: to make textile is to actualize power dynamics, be they dynamics of control and mastery, or in turn freeing flows of creative invention and reinvention. And in terms of the politics of textile, I argue that it is necessary to pay attention as to how makers not only engage with power as composition, but also deal with power as control. And I show that as much as textile in general has been appropriated by a model of power as capitalist, colonial and modernist control, moments of making are not just the actualization of this dominant type of power, but also its suspension: textile-making is an interface of connections, disconnections and reconnections between material, social, economic and political dynamics and therefore the site where new connections can take place. Textile-making, in other words, means engaging with the *power of potentialities*, of what could, and should and needs to be.

Decolonizing Media and Communication

By looking at textile as a medium as it is practiced in the present in many Indigenous and non-western groups, I develop a decolonial perspective to media studies. It should be noted that my decolonial approach addresses the specific obliviousness, mentioned earlier, that western media studies suffer from. I follow Lisa Gitelman's argument (2015) that decolonizing media not necessarily requires looking at how non-western cultures adopt and use existing dominant western-centric media, but primarily recognizing that there are and have been non-western media that have been either destroyed, rendered invisible or glossed over (Mignolo, 2012). And in looking at textile in particular, my goal is to further expand this critical project, by exploring what is outside, at the margins, pushed away, repressed, made invisible by these dominant power formations and yet still haunts them. I look for such instances of forgetfulness and erasure in the past, in domestic and high-end textile practices in France, in pre-Columbian practices that extend to the present day, and in the unique context of Japan. In so doing, the book's decolonial approach offers the following critical interventions: in questioning the history and teleology of media, and in showing how mediation helps us rethink power from "power over" to composition with non-human beings, entities and elements.

The first critical decolonial intervention within which the book operates is to explore textile as a digital medium that involves both hands (digits) and high-end mathematical thinking (digital cultures), something that feminist media studies and media archeology approaches have long pointed out. I show that this understanding not only revalues domestic women's practices, but that it also radically challenges both the place attributed to the invention of the alphabet as the origin of media, and how we think about digital media as a radically new and western invention. To discover a plurality of digital cultures that did not separate between the material and the virtual, and that engaged in the production and storage of data by mobilizing and extending human capacities for thought, mathematics and creative imagination offers a much needed corrective for rethinking the potential of the digital outside the dominant matrix of power. In so doing, I focus in particular on what has prevented western critical media theory from considering the plurality of media forms that have existed worldwide.

The second decolonial intervention that the book operates lies in showing how non-industrialized textile practices have endured to the present day and have sometimes found ways of existing in a context that in turn relentlessly appropriates, destroys, or pushes away that which does not fit into this dominant matrix of power. I define this dominant matrix of power by borrowing first from Mignolo and Walsh, who in *On Decoloniality* (2018) explore the matrix of modernity and colonialism, and to which I add capitalism (Coulthard, 2014). While Mignolo and Walsh (2018) building on Quijano (2007) focus on the articulation of modernity and colonialism—the moral, scientific and technical superiority of so-called white man—it is also clear that colonialism became inseparable from capitalism, that is, from the ruthless exploitation of human, non-humans and their environments for purposes of ever-expanding profit. Textile plays a singular role in the historical development of the matrix of power: the history of cotton, for instance, is inseparable from a long history of technical appropriation and ruthless exploitation of human beings all the way to mass enslavement. And yet in pre-colonization India, cotton was used with unparalleled technical and artistic prowess and sophistication. Similarly, indigo dye is inseparable from the triangular slave trade of the sixteenth through nineteenth centuries at the same time as it is one of the most revered colors in many cultural groups from Asia, Africa, South East Asia to South America, enabling deep forms of cultural transmission that have continued for millennia. In its current form, the majority of textile produced today continues the longstanding ruthless exploitation and destruction of humans and their environments. But textile also exceeds its articulation within dominant power, particularly when it is still practiced in non-industrial ways. Today, contemporary non-western textile arts and craft are valued the world over as important sites for creating new political, social and economic relationships. And yet as we will see in the foregoing pages, the revival of textile craft also leads to its capture by dominant power through cultural appropriation. Textile has therefore been the intense subject of the modernist, colonial and capitalist matrix, which transformed it from a medium of intercultural, cross-cultural and sociopolitical exchange to an industrialized, mass-commodified system that epitomizes all that is wrong with the never-ending, and always expanding search for profit and its attendant ruthless and unsustainable exploitation. Still, some forms of textile have never been completely captured, surviving in the margins, as modes of resistance and otherness. In that regard, the history of textile is a long history of the struggles against this dominant matrix, including the formulation of other modes of being. To the universalizing tendency of the dominant matrix of power, textile offers pluriversal (Escobar, 2018) communication, that is, a way for worlds that are radically divergent (Stengers, 2018) to continue to exist and communicate to other worlds. Such textile practices formulate and transmit ways to exist outside and potentially *delink*, in the words of Walsh and Mignolo (2018) and Amin ([1985] 1990), from this dominant matrix of power. Delinking, on the ground, has multiple forms—it cannot be reduced to establishing a closed, autarkic system that would keep non-industrialized textile practices away from the infrastructures, people, technologies, and practices that have been subsumed by the dominant matrix of power. Rather, all the case studies presented in this book are about non-industrialized textile being mobilized to encounter and necessarily engage with infrastructures, people and practices from this dominant matrix of power. Be it Indigenous textiles being sold to tourists and consumers all over the world via digital networks or Japanese indigo practices that are gathering the interests of textile practitioners in North America and Europe, to women in the early twentieth century dealing with the ambiguous legacy of embroidery and lace-making as both patriarchal power and source of economic independence, the case studies in this book show how engaging with aspects and actants within the dominant matrix of power and entering into some form of dialogue with them is a form of delinking. In that regard, I follow closely Édouard Glissant's reflection on poetic thought under the totalizing universalization efforts of the French colonial empire: "beneath the fantasy of domination, it sought the really liveable world" (1997: 28).

Third, the decolonial approach that I develop in this book also follows Alliez and Lazzarato's argument (2018) that historically, European colonization and capitalist expansion has been both inward and outward. Many technologies, worldviews, practices, languages and cultures within Europe were erased as the capitalist-colonial project took hold, and the book focuses with one such instance of how creative lines of flight were subsumed to industrial capitalist logic in the case of silk-weavers in Lyon. As well, the transformation of textile as cultural practice to textile work as a mode of exploitation and domination is not limited to workers and slaves in colonized North America, South America and India, but also internally as part of patriarchal processes of controlling women (Federici, 2004) and groups deemed divergent by the dominant system. Such continuity of experience makes it possible, in turn, to imagine lines of resistance and reinvention that cross over a plurality of worlds: the world of French domestic workers in the nineteenth century, the world of Shipibo-Conibo women in twenty-first-century Amazon, the world of diasporic communities in the Northern coast of Peru, the world of indigo artists the world over. The decolonial framework that I develop through the book recognizes of the existence of many worlds, many ontologies and therefore many epistemologies, following works such as *A World of Many Worlds* (de la Cadena and Blaser, 2018) and *Design for the Pluriverse* (Escobar, 2018). I show as well how such "divergence" between worlds (Stengers, 2018) requires critical engagement that avoids attempt to unify plurality into one world, one ontology or one epistemology that ultimately works to reject and nullify that which does not fit into a dominant framework. Rather, this book engages in what Viveiros de Castro calls "controlled equivocation" (2004)—a process of comparison that recognizes, includes and integrates heterogeneity and difference, a process that overall embraces destabilization of dominant epistemologies and ontologies as a mode of critical inquiry and insight. In that regard, I follow Marisol de la Cadena's definition of cosmovivir as the "proposal for a partially connected commons achieved without cancelling out the uncommonalities among worlds because the latter are the condition of possibility of the former: a commons across worlds whose interest in commons is uncommon to each other" (2015: 286). If anything, the paradoxical qualities of textile mentioned earlier serve as a critical guiding point here: that critical thought can accommodate and embrace divergence in its work of creating relational solidarities. Further, in thinking about the historical role of textile as that which was originally developed in parallel by many groups that had nothing in common, and that which subsequently organized exchanges among these groups, I highlight how we can think about textile as a pluriversal medium, that is, a medium where many worlds can co-exist and exchange.

Fourth, the decolonial framework that I adopt necessitates a reconsideration of what critical thinking and analysis means. My epistemological strategy starts with self-reflexivity: what about my blind spots as a communication and media scholar trained in Europe and North America? Where do I encounter what I cannot understand given the critical and analytical tools at my disposal, and how do these moments of not knowing, or rather, *un-knowing*, open up the space for Indigenous and non-western epistemologies to come to the fore? And further, what do they say about the need to rethink what communication stands for, once we take into account such previously ignored mediating capacities? Textile-making hybridizes, expands, transforms, puts in contact humans and non-humans both near and far, in the past, present and future, all by working with hapticity and visuality, with the rubbing of fingers against fibers, with materializing abstract mathematical thoughts as patterns, with the prehension of what cloth would feel like against the skin, with, quite simply, the capacity for making what is foreign and external intimate. What I find especially important in such textile processes is the capacity to create new connections, new potentials, to foster spaces of indeterminacy that are not vague, but rather allow for the flourishing of new imaginaries and practices about how to relate to the world. In so doing, I want to highlight the immense intellectual richness that comes with processes of unlearning (Azoulay, 2019) as part of delinking from the dominant matrix of power. I would not define the decolonial approach in this book as particularly new: in that regard, I follow Azoulay's reminder that:

> Unlearning is a way of disengaging from political initiatives, concepts, or modes of thinking, including critical theory, that are devised and promoted as progressive and unprecedented. Instead, it insists that finding precedents—or at least assuming that precedents could be found—for resistance to racial and colonial crimes is not the novel work of academic discovery.
>
> Azoulay, 2019: 23

Fifth, if anything, the decolonial approach that I propose here not only investigates what has been pushed away as an important medium of communication worldwide—textile—but it is also a critical realignment exercise. How to rethink and reshape the critical conceptual tools (Deleuze and Guattari, 1996) to the decolonial work of un-knowing and delinking in the context of the global crisis is the actual challenge here. As Déborah Danowski and Eduardo Viveiros de Castro show in *Ends of the World* (2016), such crisis opens up continental critical thought to American Indigenous knowledge. Many have pointed out the crisis of subjectivity and the crisis of meaning that accompanies contemporary forms of capitalism (Bifo, 2015; Sampson, 2020). Bernard Stiegler (2018) has long highlighted as well the crisis of critical thinking and western philosophy and the difficulties of navigating the "new barbarism" of post-truth, new fascisms, constant warfare, and violent polarization. Through the critical concept of the pharmakon as that which poisons but also offers a cure, Stiegler long argued for a renewal of critical thinking and philosophy as caring with and through the crisis (2018). The crisis, then, requires us to look inwards as well as outwards. With regards to inward (that is, western) looking, Lisa Lowe, in the *Intimacies of Four Continents* (2015) masterfully shows how narratives of liberal freedom that emerged in the eighteenth and nineteenth century are inseparable from colonialism and the slave trade, forcing us to reconsider how the liberal project has both built on and erased its own systemic violence up to the present day. In turn, delving into the "space of loss" fostered by the intimate relations between "slavery, genocide, indenture and liberalism" provides "the space of a different kind of thinking"—the "what could have been" (ibid.: 40–41) where new forms of justice, politics and solidarities can emerge. And with the scholarship and activism that is bringing to the fore not only the systemic role of violence in the development of western thought, but also the unrelenting need to care for immense pain and loss from Indigenous genocides and the slave trade, comes another realization: that the crisis that we face today might be unprecedented for the western world and western thought, but it is not new from an Indigenous perspective. As Danowski and Viveiros de Castro point out:

> Be as it may, what we hinted above, that indigenous people have something to teach us when it comes to apocalypses, losses of world, demographic catastrophes,

and ends of History, means simply this: for the native people of the Americas, *the end of the world already happened*—five centuries ago. To be exact, it began on October 12, 1492.

Danowski and Viveiros de Castro, 2016: 104

Non-industrial textile-making, I argue throughout the book, is a mode of engaging with such deep end-of-the-world crises. The continuation of millennial traditions of textile-making in Peru and other parts of the world is a testament to a unique force of survival, resilience, and reinvention. Crucially perhaps, it pierces the universalizing, globalizing bubble of the dominant matrix of power and its accompanying despair to show that there have been and are other ways of being. Further, the adaptation of Indigenous textile-making practices to specific contexts—by incorporating new tools, techniques, and materials—highlights how continuity and innovation can be in dialogue with each other in order to formulate engagements with the world. Looking at non-western textile practices thus participates in looking outward and reaching out to non-western knowledge and practices.

Which leads to the sixth and final aspect of the decolonial framework developed in the book: non-industrial textile-making should not be understood as an object or site of analysis on which to project a decolonial theory. Rather, it should be understood as an epistemology of the south (Santos, 2018), as a mode indeed, of critical action. Let me illustrate why such a statement is needed: one day I was visiting Shipibo-Conibo women painting their intricate designs on textile, which are further described in Chapter 6. I was accompanied by a couple of staff members from a local NGO, who generously offered to set up and act as translators for an interview with a Shipibo-Conibo textile artist. As I started asking questions, it became clear that my very kind and patient interlocutor was bored: she'd been asked these kinds of questions many times by other researchers, her answers were generic. And the unfairness of the situation could not be clearer: why was I taking her away from her textile work and tasking her with trying to explain meanings that are usually not verbalized but rather expressed through textile? It was much more appropriate to focus on observations of making. This book in that regard is an attempt to translate into academic words non-industrial textile-making as critical thought and praxis—a destabilizing exercise for the academic framework that is, I find, needed to further develop decolonial epistemologies. I relied on haptic analysis, close observation of making gestures, and as much as possible, learning textile practices myself, as I further explain below. While many forms of textile-making, especially domestic ones, are considered tedious and repetitive, often indeed requiring automatic coordination between hands and minds, they are nevertheless profound modes of engagement with the world: to deny them the status of epistemological inquiries in and of themselves would be a profound betrayal. Further, in reaching out to non-industrialized textile practices as practices of mediation, of production of intimate yet collective and cosmological knowledge, this book shows a continuity between critical practices of textile-making in very different contexts: the high-end silk weaving shops as well as domestic women's textile work in France, in conjunction with Peruvian Indigenous textile practices and millennial textile traditions in Japan. Western textile practices that were devalued or misunderstood in the west are highlighted in a new light by looking at non-western textile practices and vice-versa, revealing a common non-verbal yet potent struggle against capitalist monotechnologism and its accompanying processes of exploitation and devaluation of making by hand.

Book Overview

To approach these communicative qualities of textile, I will focus on textile before and beyond its mass industrialization and mass commodification by examining unique networks of practices and affiliations in France, Peru and Japan. I see this book as a journey in rediscovering textile and in so doing, of moving beyond the abysmal failures of the dominant matrix of power. In the west, where I am from, our contemporary perceptions and habits around textile can be described as amnesic. We cannot even remember how only a few generations ago textile would be viewed and valued as a significant investment of time, effort and care: textile was a daily preoccupation, from selecting a durable piece of cloth to sewing and maintaining it. Textile asserted a certain kind of unavoidable presence as a site of material concern and care. The nineteenth-century industrial revolution turned textile into one of the first machine mass-produced global commodities, a trend that has only accelerated since. Textile today is largely, to borrow from Agamben, a neocolonial, neoliberal dispositif (2009), a heterogenous and ever-adapting network of technologies to extract and transform raw materials all over the world, of workers and the labor regulations (or rather, lack of thereof) that govern them, of abstract discourses that advertise textile commodities and set up their branding, of economic and financial institutions that set the (low) value for the millions of textile commodities that are produced and sold every year. Amid all of this, we find ourselves as consuming subjects. It does not matter that clothes will not last long these days: after all they will be discarded fast, as they become unfashionable. As for home textiles, there are so many cheap options now that the idea of bedsheets lasting a lifetime does not even make sense. Plentiful cloth is convenient and for many it is a mark of progress. For women especially, not having to care for textile means being free from the demands and pressures of domesticity, from scrubbing stains off and darning socks, and to become something other than unpaid domestic workers. Switching from one subject position (the unpaid domestic laborer) to another (the consumer) has mostly been seen as a mark of progress and liberation.

To be sure, when I was conducting research for this book and mentioned to people in Europe and North America that it would explore textile as a medium of communication, many of my interlocutors were at first puzzled. However, such an idea would start making sense in a very personal way, and many people recalled the haptic relationships their grandparents had with textile. A friend of mine told me stories about frustrating shopping excursions with her grandmother. A teenager in the 1990s, she was quite proficient at deciphering brands and recognizing which piece of clothing would be the best for fitting into the high school scene. Her grandmother, on the other hand, would feel the fabric by rubbing it in her fingers, rejecting cheap nylon that looked nice and shiny but felt uncomfortable against the skin. My friend's grandmother would also pay particular attention to the seams, explaining how poorly done and badly constructed a garment was, despite its fashionable appearance. Many of my other interlocutors similarly recalled how a grandparent would run their hands along fabric, appreciating high quality wool-suiting, for instance. Textile used to be read by hand, and it was indeed a useful skill to be able to feel in clothing the relative strength and qualities of the materials that went into making a piece of fabric, and the different level of expertise, craft and technique that went into making something durable. This kind of material reading (Mida and Kim, 2015; Casey and Davies, 2020), which has almost disappeared in the west as the over-production of textile means that their durability is no longer a concern, is not simply a relic of the past, but an indication of how communication also takes place in very material ways, and with non-human interlocutors. To feel a beautiful piece of fabric in that way means to tacitly understand a chain of collaboration, where the making process involves combining the capacities of different materials, physical, chemical and artistic processes, not only of fibers turned into thread and then woven, but also dyed, transformed, adorned and so on. Haptic reading constitutes a departure point for us, at the receiving end of a piece of textile, to go back and both trace moments of rupture and unravel the embodied meaningfulness of textile as that which always and constantly surrounds us and enables us to relate to the world and to others (Paterson and Dodge, 2016).

I focus on the haptic as a way to bridge the profound rupture that happened with the mass production of textiles as cheap and easily discardable commodities. It is also a way of exploring the technical mediations at multiple levels that help us come to being through our relationships with others and with the world—what Bernard Stiegler (2013) called transindividuation: personal and intimate, but also collective and cosmological. It should be clear at this point that I am not trying to replicate other approaches to understanding the meaningfulness of textile based on archeological, archival and historical research, which offer a staggeringly wide and rich array of accounts of the role played by textile as a medium of transindividuation in many parts of the world and throughout history. While I lean heavily on these accounts, especially with regard to understanding socioeconomic contexts and subject positions, my intent is to not only explore what textile used to mean in the past, but to probe what its remnants and traces mean for our present. In that regard, I follow media archeology (Parikka, 2012) and its invitation to undertake experimental analysis of old, discarded, failed and minor media technologies as a way to challenge dominant media systems of technologies, knowledge and power. Following Zielinski and Druckrey (2008), discarded or ignored media (in my case, textile) offer new ways of relating to the past and the future, spurring new lines of flight and new creative connections. Overall, building on Stiegler's exploration of our relationships with past and future as mediated through technologies (1998), I want to show how coming to term with the collective amnesia discussed above by rediscovering non-industrial textile opens up new potentials for existing in the present and building common futures together. Such potentials are always already complex and sometimes contradictory, and the exercise might very much feel like unraveling a tangled ball of yarn. Perhaps this image is most fitting: the need to unravel multiple and diverse threads in order to be able to eventually weave them together.

This book is an unravelling indeed—I originally started with one thread, and then bifurcated to other threads that I encountered in this process of pulling apart. This book is therefore not an entire history of textile—there are countless fascinating studies of historical and contemporary textiles, some of which will be published in the forthcoming multi-volume *Bloomsbury Encyclopedia of World Textiles* (Co-chief editors: Janis Jefferies and Vivienne Richmond). But to examine textile as a communication medium, and as one that has been forgotten and pushed aside necessarily requires a systematic introspection into the limitations of communication and media studies research as it has been developed in Europe and North America. I first interrogate how media are conceptualized, typically as technologies that deal with abstracted information. In contrast, the making of non-industrial textile necessarily requires embodied practice and awareness of materials in order to produce complex abstract information, thus blurring the divide between media technologies as dealing with abstraction in contrast to other technologies dealing with the transformation of materials. This necessarily opens up another key question: what, then, constitutes communication in such a mediated environment? And here, I move away from a representational focus on communication to insist that communication is the process of building common worlds, and that this requires not only shared ethics and vision, but also collaboration with non-human agents and entities, from the hair of animals to sun and water. I show in particular how acts and objects of communication become meaningful not just by carrying information, but by enabling coming and becoming together, an emergence and co-emergence of multiple beings. In so doing, I am heavily indebted to Deleuzian and Guattarian frameworks, particularly their framework on what they call "a-signification," which looks at processes through which modes of being and horizons of existence emerge from specific communicative assemblages of heterogenous elements, processes and dynamics, from the biological to the ideological, from the small gesture to global systems of production. Through showing that non-industrial textile involves profound and complex communicative practices where textile mediates by bringing together many humans and non-humans together, and by enabling the recording of these encounters and their reconfigurations, I hope to highlight some of the ways we can move forward in the building of better common worlds.

My starting point is the encounter between communication and textile, and how the history of textile in Europe and North America can be revisited through Harold Innis's concept of media as technologies that organize information transmission through space and time, and how textile fulfilled such functions up until its mass industrialization, but in ways that differ from dominant western media technologies such as writing, printing, analog and digital media

(Chapter 1). This historical and theoretical overview gives way to a series of "agential cuts" (Barad, 2007): case studies where encounters with textile practices and makers allowed me, as a researcher, to experience the radically transformative expressive and creative capacities of non-industrial textile as it gathers and connects together materials, humans, objects, technologies, as it starts in a specific places, but eventually travels through spaces and pasts, presents and futures to reconfigure modes of beings and modes of being touched and transformed. Rather than organize the book geographically according to the regions for the case studies (France, Peru, Japan), my approach is to engage with continuities of experience between worlds and periods which, at first do not have much in common. Chapter 2 continues the themes developed in Chapter 1 and examine how non-industrial and Indigenous textile-making has found ways to survive within and alongside the dominant matrix of power. It focuses on the long legacy of Pre-Columbian textiles in Peru, and how the Quechua community in the Cusco region works to create a space for their textiles that delineate their cosmovision and indigeneity in a context of mass tourism. Indigenous textile become a way of engaging with the dominant matrix of power, and to map its contradictions and limitations. Through this, we see textile as a medium of power play, which survives and thrives despite and through its continuous engagement with dynamics that would ultimately empty it of its transformative potential.

The next duet of chapters focuses in turn on delinking as the (re)configuration of digital techniques, mediation and creativity. Chapter 3 explores the Jacquard mechanism for weaving, which has often been recognized as the device that linked together industrial automation with automated information processing: it is seen as a precursor of the digital age in that it showed how digital information processing could assist material productivity. My analysis of the Jacquard mechanism troubles linear accounts of technological development as the coupling of automated production and information processing: rather, it shows how the Jacquard mechanism spurred a new kind of creativity that built on and expanded the digital imaging capacities of textile. Such a media-archeological approach shows alternate histories of digital media, and helps contextualize the mediating capacities of textile: how by articulating together materiality, technique, automation and information, it spurred new horizons of creative imagination. In other words, delinking can lurk as the potential at the very heart of the dominant matrix of power. Chapter 4 continues exploring textile-making as delinking, and turns towards the diasporic experience of Quechua groups as they move from the Andes to the Northern coast of Peru, and how their textile-making practices for local and international markets allows for the crossing of multiple abysses: temporal, spatial, and colonial. It highlights how Indigenous digital techniques and mathematical thinking spurs new creative flights that gesture towards textile as the site of new entanglements.

Chapter 5 and 6 follow up on this theme of materializing imagination by exploring the relationship between textile-making and the crafting of existence. Chapter 5 turns to domestic textile work in France in the period from World War 1 to 1950s by focusing on textile objects, tools and techniques from the Auvergne region. It examines the relationships between textile-making and women's subjectivities under a patriarchal order, and shows that domestic textile practices are an ambiguous means to exert control over women, but also means for women to reinvent themselves, refashioning themselves as makers rather than subjects to craft new agencies. The quiet domestic world of needlework becomes an interface where new potentialities of existence can emerge. Chapter 6 moves to examine how Shipibo-Conibo women from the Amazon region are reinventing their own textile practices to formulate a politics of encounter with the western world in a way that destabilizes western pre-conceptions of what politics is and should look like. I end with Chapter 7 on textile and the indigo tradition in Japan, to further explore the politics of encounter that textile enables, especially with regard to the question of world-making, which engages not only with humans and culture, but with non-human agencies and environmental politics as well.

The choice of these specific sites and regions by no means aims to establish some kind of hierarchy or superiority. Indeed, the weaving and natural dyes traditions of Mexico for instance are as complex, rich, and a source of cultural and economic resistance and revival as Quechua weaving in Peru. Furthermore, that Indigenous embroidery patterns are subject to economic and cultural appropriation is far from unique to the Shipibo: the case of Zapoteca embroidery in Oaxaca, Mexico, often appropriated by western fashion houses, has been well documented. Similarly, indigo traditions abound the world over, beyond Japan, from the Miao people's time-consuming hammering of indigo-dyed cloth to create black shimmering garments adorned with intricate colorful embroideries to the Yorubas' (Nigeria) cassava-starch intricate resist patterns on indigo, and many more. Finally, the epicenter of the struggles over the industrialization of textile production can be located in the United Kingdom rather than France. The choice of France, Peru and Japan was driven by a series of encounters that suggest how decolonial delinking and unlearning can happen through paying close attention to the mediations enabled by non-industrialized textile practices. There are however two regions that are crucially missing from this book: Africa and South Asia. The textiles from the Indian empire were among the first commodities to be traded the world over. The technical innovations, aesthetic sophistications and sheer array of cultural imagery developed through Indian textiles fill entire libraries. It is unfortunate that a planned case study for this book, which involved a collaborative artistic project with embroiderers in Pakistan, unfortunately has been pushed back because of various delays in assembling an international team, the most recent of which is the Covid pandemic. The vast array of textile techniques and practices on the African continent and their crucial importance for crafting identities is well established (Gillow, 2009). Unfortunately opportunities for observing traditional textile techniques in Africa, particularly with regards to the revival of local Indigenous cotton and the use of natural dyes, were delayed by a wide variety of factors, from timing to eventually running out of funding. Overall, I focused specifically on selecting places where projects were under way to open up domestic textiles to external markets, be it a design team that sought to foster new markets for traditional and Indigenous textile techniques, an NGO that interfaced between

Indigenous communities and public and private institutions to preserve traditional ways of life while building economic and health infrastructures through the marketing of textile craft to global markets, or textile scholars, artists and teachers dedicated to presenting and explaining their own textile work to a global audience. Most of the people doing this kind of work are incredibly busy—developing textile communities, designing products and finding new markets requires an enormous amount of work, not only creative, but also organizational. It is also highly dependent on external funding, and seeking local, national and international grants and investors to fund many aspects of the work—from technical equipment to training, materials, promotion and exhibitions and travel to international design shows—is incredibly time-consuming, on top of organizing work on the ground. Welcoming an outsider researcher is usually often neither feasible nor a priority, especially when one regularly works twelve to fourteen hours a day. I was lucky enough to encounter interlocutors who were intrigued enough by my research to welcome me into their own projects, and I am incredibly grateful for them to have made time for me, and even luckier when complex schedules eventually lined up so that my visit was possible. Overall, I relied heavily on pre-existing networks to approach textile makers, and I am incredibly grateful for the time my interlocutors—designers and textile makers—spent expressing and explaining the unseen mediations that take place through non-industrialized textile-making. I am bilingual in French and English, and many of my interlocutors spoke English. I can understand written and oral Spanish although I cannot speak it well, and had to rely on translators at times, both for Spanish, but mostly for Japanese. Importantly though, it was the observations and recording of making processes that is at the core of the book, where I map different making-assemblages, and how in turn these making-assemblages are stabilized via discursive, distributional and economic infrastructures. It was important to observe processes but also to pay attention to the everyday exchanges that took place among the makers and between makers and designers, and to how the makers related to each other, to their kids who accompanied them and so on. But my observations were not only of the makers only, but also equally on the textile objects slowly appearing before my eyes. Such objects were interlocutors as well, for the makers who worried and fussed over them, as well as for my research process. My interviews with textile designers, artists and scholars involved textile objects as key interlocutors as well: almost always, the interview would start with my human interviewee(s) and I looking at textile objects together, either at somebody's home, workshop or at a museum, and once a shared tacit understanding of how important these objects were was established, conversation could ensue, which often would take the form of looking at more textile objects, digging through one's textile collections, or opening drawers at museums. Often, by the end of the interview, the space would be covered with beautiful textiles that we would then carefully fold away. As much as I could I also tried to learn some basic techniques, especially backstrap weaving, on top of having experimented with indigo dyeing for many years as well as embroidery and painting on textile. I unfortunately could only observe the Jacquard mechanism, as it takes quite intensive training to master. My own experiments with making served as a reminder of not only the haptic qualities of textile, but also of textility itself: textile resist, demands attention, and textile materials are often stubborn. Control in this case is more about reaching a fragile equilibrium, and at times welcoming resistance as a mode of non-verbal communication. In becoming more and more aware of this, I eventually gesture towards a politics of making that does not try to translate making into existing political or critical discourses—be they western or Indigenous ones. I move towards making as non-verbal political thought and action in and of itself, as a politics of potentiality that does not necessarily fit readily into or illustrate existing political discourses and infrastructures. I argue that critical work does not have to force such translation, but to see how these non-verbal political gestures in and of themselves, rearrange, even if only fleetingly, the world around them.

Finally, a word about my positionality as a researcher. I am by all external account a middle-age, middle-class white woman born in France, who was able to choose to emigrate to and settle in Canada. My whiteness is a result of the genetic lottery—I am half-Vietnamese. Because of this, I have been a privileged witness to macro and micro forms of anti-Asian racism since I was a child, and developed a keen awareness of power differentials. As well, I have personal and deep knowledge of the continued violence of colonialism, both external and internalized: my generation of siblings were purposefully not transmitted the Vietnamese language, and very little of its culture, because back in 1970s France, assimilation was seen as the only way forward. Questions of loss and abysses that I mention at length in the book are also, therefore, quite personal. Overall, I am the product two opposite camps: colonizers and colonized, exploiters and exploited. This legacy is not an easy one, but it has made me critically aware of how colonial and capitalist power works, and the devastations big and small that it can bring. This positionality, which is quite common in this global world, drives a commitment for crafting solidarities across the abyss. It is for this reason that for instance, I look at networks of NGOs, designers and Indigenous textile-makers: such assemblages that straddle western and Indigenous worlds are deeply risky in courting, using and disturbing existing neoliberal infrastructures in order to bring about something different—new ways of communicating, exchanging, relating to each other and to the world. For me, this is important political work, albeit dangerous, slow, careful and fragile.

References

Agamben, Giorgio. (2009). *"What Is an Apparatus?" And Other Essays*. Translated by David Kishik and Stefan Pedatella. Stanford, CA: Stanford University Press.

Albers, Anni, Nicholas Fox Weber, Manuel Cirauqui, and T'ai Smith. (2017). *On Weaving*. New expanded edn. Princeton, NJ: Princeton University Press.

Alliez, Eric, and Maurizio Lazzarato. (2018). *Wars and Capital*. Translated by Ames Hodges. South Pasadena, CA: Semiotext.

Amin, Samir. (1990). *Delinking: Towards a Polycentric World*. London: Zed Books. (Original published in French, 1985).

Andrew, Sonja. (2008). "Textile Semantics: Considering a Communication-Based Reading of Textiles." *TEXTILE* 6 (1): 32–65. https://doi.org/10.2752/175183508X288680.

Atkins, Jacqueline, ed. (2005). *Wearing Propaganda: Textiles on the Home Front in Japan, Britain, and the United States, 1931-1945*. New Haven, CT: Yale University Press.

Azoulay, Ariella. (2019). *Potential History: Unlearning Imperialism*. London: Verso.

Bachmann, Ingrid, and Ruth Scheuing, eds. (2006). *Material Matters: The Art and Culture of Contemporary Textiles*. Toronto: YYZ Books.

Barad, Karen. (2007). *Meeting the Universe Halfway: Quantum Physics and the Entanglement of Matter and Meaning*. Durham, NC: Duke University Press.

Barthes, Roland. (2013). *The Language of Fashion*. Edited by Andy Stafford and Michael Carter. Reprint edn. London: Bloomsbury Academic.

"Bifo" Berardi, Franco. (2015). *And: Phenomenology of the End*. South Pasadena, CA: Semiotext.

Buckridge, Steeve O., and Rex Nettleford. (2009). *The Language of Dress: Resistance and Accommodation in Jamaica, 1750-1890*. Kingston, Jamaica: University of the West Indies Press.

Cadena, Marisol de la, and Blaser, Mario. (2018). *A World of Many Worlds*. Durham: Duke University Press.

Casey, Sarah, and Gerry Davies. (2020). *Drawing Investigations: Graphic Relationships with Science, Culture and Environment*. London: Bloomsbury Visual Arts.

CBC Radio. (2019). "6 Years after Rana Plaza Collapse, Many Fashion Giants Still Unwilling to Make Changes, Says Industry Expert." April 26, 2019. https://www.cbc.ca/radio/thecurrent/the-current-for-april-26-2019-1.5111980/6-years-after-rana-plaza-collapse-many-fashion-giants-still-unwilling-to-make-changes-says-industry-expert-1.5111984.

Chun, Wendy Hui Kyong. (2013). *Programmed Visions: Software and Memory*. Illustrated edn. Cambridge, MA: The MIT Press.

Coulthard, Glen Sean. (2014). *Red Skin, White Masks: Rejecting the Colonial Politics of Recognition*. Minneapolis: University of Minnesota Press.

Crow, David. (2008). "Magic Box: Craft and the Computer." *Eye Magazine* 70. https://www.eyemagazine.com/feature/article/magic-box-craft-and-the-computer (accessed January 4, 2023).

Déborah Danowski and Viveiros de Castro, Eduardo. (2016). *The Ends of the World*. Translated by Rodrigo Guimaraes Nunes. Malden, MA: Polity.

de la Cadena, Marisol, and Mario Blaser, eds. (2018). *A World of Many Worlds*. Illustrated edn. Durham, NC: Duke University Press.

de la Cadena, Marisol. (2015). *Earth Beings: Ecologies of Practice across Andean Worlds*. Illustrated edn. Durham, NC: Duke University Press.

Deleuze, Gilles, and Félix Guattari. (1996). *What Is Philosophy*? Translated by Hugh Tomlinson and Graham Burchell. Rev. edn. New York: Columbia University Press.

Diddi, Sonali, and Ruoh-Nan Yan. (2019). "Consumer Perceptions Related to Clothing Repair and Community Mending Events: A Circular Economy Perspective." *Sustainability* 11 (19): 5306. https://doi.org/10.3390/su11195306.

Egenhoefer, Rachel Beth. (2008). *Virtual Knitting: Knitting in Virtual and Physical Space.* https://www.rachelbeth.net/work-virtual-knitting.

Escobar, Arturo. (2018). *Designs for the Pluriverse: Radical Interdependence, Autonomy, and the Making of Worlds.* Durham, NC: Duke University Press.

Essinger, James. (2007). *Jacquard's Web: How a Hand-Loom Led to the Birth of the Information Age.* Oxford: Oxford University Press.

Federici, Silvia. (2004). *Caliban and the Witch: Women, the Body and Primitive Accumulation.* Illustrated edn. New York: Autonomedia.

Foxhall, Lin. (2017). "The Fabric of Society: Recognising the Importance of Textiles and Their Manufacture in the Ancient Past." *Antiquity* 91 (357): 808–11. https://doi.org/10.15184/aqy.2017.76.

Friedman, Michael. (2020). "Introduction: On Weaving Practices and Geometry." In Virtual Event. https://www.matters-of-activity.de/en/activities/2241/?preview.

Gillow, John. (2009). *African Textiles: Color and Creativity Across a Continent.* London: Thames & Hudson.

Gitelman, Lisa. (2015). "Media Studies from Scratch." Research talk given at York University, Toronto.

Glissant, Édouard. (1997). *Poetics of Relation.* Translated by Betsy Wing. Ann Arbor: University of Michigan Press.

Glusica, Katie. (2016). "The Seen and Unseen: Weaving as a Metaphor for Wave/Particle Duality." *Leonardo* 49 (2): 130–37. https://doi.org/10.1162/LEON_a_00920.

Gordon, Beverly. (2014). *Textiles: The Whole Story.* Reprint edn. London: Thames and Hudson.

Graham, Richard. (2014). "A 'History' of Search Engines: Mapping Technologies of Memory, Learning and Discovery." In *Society of the Query Reader*, 105–20. Amsterdam: Institute of Network Cultures.

Haraway, Donna J. (2016). *Staying with the Trouble: Making Kin in the Chthulucene.* Durham, NC: Duke University Press.

Harlizius-Klück, Ellen. (2017). "Weaving as Binary Art and the Algebra of Patterns." *TEXTILE* 15 (2): 176–97. https://doi.org/10.1080/14759756.2017.1298239.

Harrod, T. (2007). "Otherwise Unobtainable: The Applied Arts and the Poetics and Politics of Digital Technology." In *Neocraft: Modernity and the Crafts.* Edited by Sandra Alfoldy, 225–40. Halifax, NS: The Press of the Nova Scotia College of Art and Design.

Hayles, N. Katherine. (2005). *My Mother Was a Computer: Digital Subjects and Literary Texts.* Chicago: University of Chicago Press.

Holroyd, A. Twigger. (2016). "Perceptions and Practices of Dress-related Leisure: Shopping, Sorting, Making and Mending." *Annals of Leisure Research* 19 (3), 275–93.

Hudson, Ian, and Mark Hudson. (2003). "Removing the Veil?: Commodity Fetishism, Fair Trade, and the Environment." *Organization & Environment* 16 (4): 413–30. https://doi.org/10.1177/1086026603258926.

Hui, Yuk. (2016). *The Question Concerning Technology in China: An Essay in Cosmotechnics.* Falmouth: Urbanomic Media.

Hyland, Sabine. (2017). "Writing with Twisted Cords: The Inscriptive Capacity of Andean Khipus." *Current Anthropology* 58 (3): 412–19.

Ingold, Tim. (2010). "The Textility of Making." *Cambridge Journal of Economics* 34 (1): 91–102. http://www.jstor.org.ezproxy.library.yorku.ca/stable/24232023.

Innis, Harold A. (2008). *The Bias of Communication*. 2nd edn. Toronto: University of Toronto Press.

Jefferies, Janis, Diana Wood Conroy, and Hazel Clark, eds. (2015). *The Handbook of Textile Culture*. London: Bloomsbury Academic.

Kember, Sarah, and Joanna Zylinska. (2014). *Life after New Media: Mediation as a Vital Process*. Reprint edn. Cambridge, MA: The MIT Press.

King, Heidi. (2012). *Peruvian Featherworks: Art of the Precolumbian Era*. New York: Metropolitan Museum of Art.

Kittler, Friedrich. (1999). *Gramophone, Film, Typewriter*. Translated by Geoffrey Winthrop-Young and Michael Wutz. Stanford, CA: Stanford University Press.

König, Anna. (2013). "A Stitch in Time: Changing Cultural Constructions of Craft and Mending." *Culture Unbound* 5 (4): 569–85. https://doi.org/10.3384/cu.2000.1525. 135569.

Latour, Bruno. (2007). *Reassembling the Social: An Introduction to Actor-Network-Theory*. New York: Oxford University Press.

Leroi-Gourhan, Andre. (1985). *Le geste et la parole I: Technique et langage*. Paris: Albin Michel Littérature.

Lipovetsky, Gilles. (1994). *The Empire of Fashion: Dressing Modern Democracy*. Princeton, NJ: University Press Princeton.

Lowe, Lisa. (2015). *The Intimacies of Four Continents*. Illustrated edn. Durham, NC: Duke University Press.

McCracken, Grant D., and Victor J. Roth. (1989). "Does Clothing Have a Code? Empirical Findings and Theoretical Implications in the Study of Clothing as a Means of Communication." *International Journal of Research in Marketing* 6 (1): 13–33. https://doi.org/10.1016/0167-8116(89)90044-X.

McCullough, Malcolm. (1998). *Abstracting Craft: The Practiced Digital Hand*. Reprint edn. Cambridge, MA: MIT Press.

McDougall, Ruth. (2011). *Threads: Contemporary Textiles and the Social Fabric*. South Brisbane, Qld: Queensland Art Gallery.

McLaren, A., and S. McLauchlan. (2015). "Crafting Sustainable Repairs: Practice-Based Approaches to Extending the Life of Clothes." In *Product Lifetimes and the Environment (PLATE) Conference Proceedings*, 17–19 June 2015. Edited by T. Cooper, N. Braithwaite, M. Moreno, and G. Salvia, 221–28. Nottingham: Nottingham Trent University. http://www.ntu.ac.uk/plate_conference/proceedings/index.html.

Mida, Ingrid, and Alexandra Kim. (2015). *The Dress Detective: A Practical Guide to Object-Based Research in Fashion*. London: Bloomsbury.

Mignolo, Walter. (2012). *Local Histories/Global Designs: Coloniality, Subaltern Knowledges, and Border Thinking*. Princeton, NJ: Princeton University Press.

Mignolo, Walter D., and Catherine E. Walsh. (2018). *On Decoloniality: Concepts, Analytics, Praxis*. Durham, NC: Duke University Press.

Monteiro, Stephen. (2017). *The Fabric of Interface: Mobile Media, Design, and Gender*. Illustrated edn. Cambridge, MA: The MIT Press.

Nakamura, Lisa. (2014). "Indigenous Circuits: Navajo Women and the Racialization of Early Electronic Manufacture." *American Quarterly* 66 (4): 919–41. https://doi.org/10.1353/aq.2014.0070.

Nistor, Laura. (2016). "Fashion as a Communicative Phenomenon Agenda Setting for Research Project on Youth's Clothing Consumption." *Acta Univ. Sapientiae, Communicatio* 3: 73–79.

O'Connor, Morgan. (2017). "The Monster in Our Closet: Fast Fashion & Textile Waste on the Rise." *Center for EcoTechnology* (blog). October 11, 2017. https://www. centerforecotechnology.org/fast-fashion-textile-waste/.

Parikka, Jussi. (2012). *What Is Media Archaeology?* Cambridge, UK: Polity.

Paterson, Mark, and Martin Dodge, eds. (2016). *Touching Space, Placing Touch.* London: Routledge.

Peters, John Durham. (2015). *The Marvelous Clouds: Toward a Philosophy of Elemental Media.* Chicago: University of Chicago Press.

Plant, Sadie. (2016). *Zeros and Ones: Digital Women and the New Technoculture.* Rev. edn. London: Fourth Estate.

Postrel, Virginia. (2020). *The Fabric of Civilization: How Textiles Made the World.* New York: Basic Books.

Quijano, Aníbal. (2007). "Coloniality and Modernity/Rationality." *Cultural Studies* 21 (2–3): 168–78. http://www.tandfonline.com/doi/full/10.1080/09502380601164353.

Safi, Michael, and Dominic Rushe. (2018). "Rana Plaza, Five Years on: Safety of Workers Hangs in Balance in Bangladesh" *The Guardian*, April 24, 2018. http://www. theguardian.com/global-development/2018/apr/24/bangladeshi-police-target-garment-workers-union-rana-plaza-five-years-on (accessed July 11, 2023).

Sampson, Tony D. (2020). *A Sleepwalker's Guide to Social Media.* Cambridge: Polity.

Santos, Boaventoura de Sousa. (2018). *The End of the Cognitive Empire: the Coming of Age of Epistemologies of the South.* Durham: Duke University Press.

Schoeser, Mary. (2012). *Textiles: The Art Of Mankind.* Illustrated edn. New York: Thames and Hudson.

Sennett, Richard. (2009). *The Craftsman.* New Haven, CT: Yale University Press.

Shotwell, Alexis. (2016). *Against Purity: Living Ethically in Compromised Times.* Minneapolis: University of Minnesota Press.

Siegert, Bernhard. (2015). *Cultural Techniques: Grids, Filters, Doors, and Other Articulations of the Real.* Translated by Geoffrey Winthrop-Young. New York: Fordham University Press.

Simondon, Gilbert. (2017). *On the Mode of Existence of Technical Objects.* Translated by Cecile Malaspina and John Rogove. Minneapolis: University of Minnesota Press.

Smith, T'ai. (2014). *Bauhaus Weaving Theory: From Feminine Craft to Mode of Design.* Illustrated edn. Minneapolis: University of Minnesota Press.

Smith, T'ai. (2018). "Textile, A Diagonal Abstraction: Glass Bead in Conversation with T'ai Smith—Glass Bead." *Glass Bead.* 2018. http://www.glass-bead.org/article/ textile-diagonal-abstraction/?lang=enview.

Splitstoser, Jeffrey. (2022). "Mathematics and Textiles Special Issue." *Textile Museum Journal* 49.

Stengers, Isabelle. (2018). "The Challenge of Ontological Politics." In *A World of Many Worlds.* Edited by Marisol de la Cadena and Mario Blaser, 83–111. Durham, NC: Duke University Press.

Stiegler, Bernard. (1998). *Technics and Time, 1: The Fault of Epimetheus.* Translated by Richard Beardsworth and George Collins. Stanford, CA: Stanford University Press.

Stiegler, Bernard. (2013). *What Makes Life Worth Living: On Pharmacology.* Cambridge: Polity.

Stiegler, Bernard. (2018). *Qu'appelle-t-on Panser ?: 1. L'immense régression.* Paris: Les Liens qui libèrent.

Strauss, Marina. (2013). "Canada's Joe Fresh among Brands Made in Collapsed Bangladesh Building." *Globe and Mail*, April 24, 2013. https://www.theglobeandmail.com/news/

world/canadas-joe-fresh-among-brands-made-in-collapsed-bangladesh-building/
    article11540359/ (accessed January 11, 2021).
Tanaka, Yuko. (2013). *The Power of the Weave: The Hidden Meanings of Cloth*. Tokyo:
    International House of Japan.
Tedlock, Barbara, and Dennis Tedlock. (1985). "Text and Textile: Language and
    Technology in the Arts of the Quiché Maya." *Journal of Anthropological Research* 41 (2):
    121–46. http://www.jstor.org/stable/3630412.
Thomas, Dana. (2018). "Why Won't We Learn from the Survivors of the Rana Plaza
    Disaster?" *The New York Times*, April 24, 2018. https://www.nytimes.com/2018/04/24/
    style/survivors-of-rana-plaza-disaster.html (accessed January 11, 2021).
Tsing, Anna Lowenhaupt. (2017). *The Mushroom at the End of the World: On the Possibility
    of Life in Capitalist Ruins*. Reprint edn. Princeton, NJ: Princeton University Press.
Tuzuki, Kyouiti. (2009). *Boro: Rags and Tatters from the Far North of Japan*. Tokyo: Aspect
    Corp.
Viveiros de Castro, Eduardo. (2004). "Perspectival Anthropology and the Method of
    Controlled Equivocation." *Tipití: Journal of the Society for the Anthropology of Lowland
    South America* 2 (1). https://digitalcommons.trinity.edu/tipiti/vol2/iss1/1.
Zielinski, Siegfried, and Timothy Druckrey. (2008). *Deep Time of the Media: Toward an
    Archaeology of Hearing and Seeing by Technical Means*. Translated by Gloria Custance.
    Cambridge, MA: MIT Press.

Part I

COMMUNICATIVE POWER

Chapter 1

UNRAVELING TEXTILE FROM COMMODITY TO COMMUNICATION

A Plural Medium

The goal of this chapter is to show that textile needs to be understood as a medium of communication with a fascinating complexity in its own right. There is no single origin to textile: wherever suitable fibers were available, textile techniques to process said fibers into threads and fabric emerged. Textile, then is plural, and while there are common techniques (e.g., weaving) found everywhere there is textile, these techniques were developed within specific material, political, socio-cultural and spiritual contexts. At the same time as it was always plural, textile objects functioned as a medium of exchange across cultures, and for a long time in Europe there was intense desire for foreign textiles exhibiting unknown techniques and materials. Eventually, the incorporation of these techniques and materials served to formulate, in turn, culturally specific textile objects. It is important to note in that regard that textile carried a unique potential to make worlds that have nothing in common exchange and communicate with each other. Eventually and by the end of the book, I argue that this means that textile has exhibited the capacity to be a pluriversal medium: a medium where not only many worlds fit, to refer to the Zapatista slogan, but also a medium where many worlds (de la Cadena and Blaser, 2018) can flourish and exchange with each other. But, before we can get to this point, let's first focus on the historical communicative capacities of textile.

Historically, textiles were not only key cultural techniques acting at the same time as modes activity in and engagement with the world and means of expression (Siegert), but also ways to exert geopolitical and economic power through commerce (Postrel, 2020). The production and distribution of textiles constituted some of the first global systems of exchanges of goods and ideas, and they still play a crucial role today as a means of expressing the complex webs of global relations that weave together cultures, modes of expression, webs that have progressively been dominated by colonial and capitalist logics. There are indeed many histories of textile as medium: some of them see textile as part of a global system of flows of commodities, information and power; others reveal how textile solidified the cohesiveness of groups, communities and societies by becoming a means to store and express cultural values and important information; and others still that focus on how textile established social differences among group members. It is somehow not a surprise therefore that textile has been an interface for key political struggles that sought to challenge colonial and capitalist rules.

Seemingly disparate, these histories nevertheless point to the role of textile as a polyvalent medium: not only a carrier of values and identities but crucially as a channel for power relations. In this chapter, I explore how textile communicates by intervening at multiple and sometimes paradoxical levels: at the geopolitical level, at the socioeconomic level and at the cultural level; at the collective, individual and intimate levels. Crucially, textile layers together these many levels, enabling new articulations, directions and possibilities. In other words, to think about textile as a medium of communication means to think beyond whatever meanings individuals can assign to it, and rather to explore how it both fosters new connections between all these disparate and heterogenous planes. For this reason, looking at textile as a communicative medium provides a critical entry point to understand the dynamics between power and social change.

This chapter focuses in particular on three specificities of textile as communication that embody what is different between textile and our more familiar, western-centric communication and media systems. First, despite its visual characteristics, making textile is not like writing a letter or drawing a picture—both forms of communication that work through the transmission of linguistic and visual-representational signs. Rather, textile mobilizes the senses in multiple and complex ways. Second, to fully understand textile as communication, we need to rethink what it means to communicate. Communication means the expression of an engagement with the world, that is, an assertion of a relationship with the world, and this is something that is hard for the post-industrial reader, accustomed to consuming textile rather than making it, to understand. That is to say, communication is not simply about transmitting information, but more importantly about enacting modes of relations to and with the world. Therefore, communication is not only about the transmission of some kind of content, but rather about the expression of relationships. While content transmission and expression of relationships sometimes overlap, the latter expands far beyond the former, and it is only through understanding this that one can start understanding the historical and contemporary potentials of textile as medium. Finally, understanding textile as engagement with the world means that textile, along with many other communication systems, reshapes social relationships at the individual, collective and global level. In that regard, textile expresses relationships of power, but because it weaves itself with socioeconomic, subjective and political dynamics in ways that are meaningfully different from traditional communication technologies, it allows for new ways of engaging with power formations.

Textile as Communication Medium: Historical Pointers

Until its automated mass production during the nineteenth-century industrial revolution, textile was a communication medium, used to carry cultural values and serving as a memory device and transmitter of all kinds of information in ways that bound people together through space and time (Innis, 2008). To fully understand this, we must first overcome a basic bias in our perceptions of textile, namely, that it is related to woven fabric meant primarily for keeping bodies warm and protected.

The history of everyday textile in that regard is a long and rich one that is masterfully explained in Elizabeth Barber's *Women's Work: The First 20,000 Years* (1994). Barber explains that fiber and textile crafts appeared between 20,000 and 30,000 years ago in the middle of the Upper Paleolithic era, with evidence from that period that "some genius hit upon the principles of twisting handfuls of little weak fibers together into long, strong thread" (43). We can imagine that ropes would quickly become memory and communication tools on top of providing much needed material support. Ropes can be thin and lightweight, and extremely portable. Easy to manipulate, ropes are useful tools to store information: if I need to remind myself to do something, I can do that by tying a knot on my rope, just as in more recent times one would tie a knot on their handkerchief as a cue to

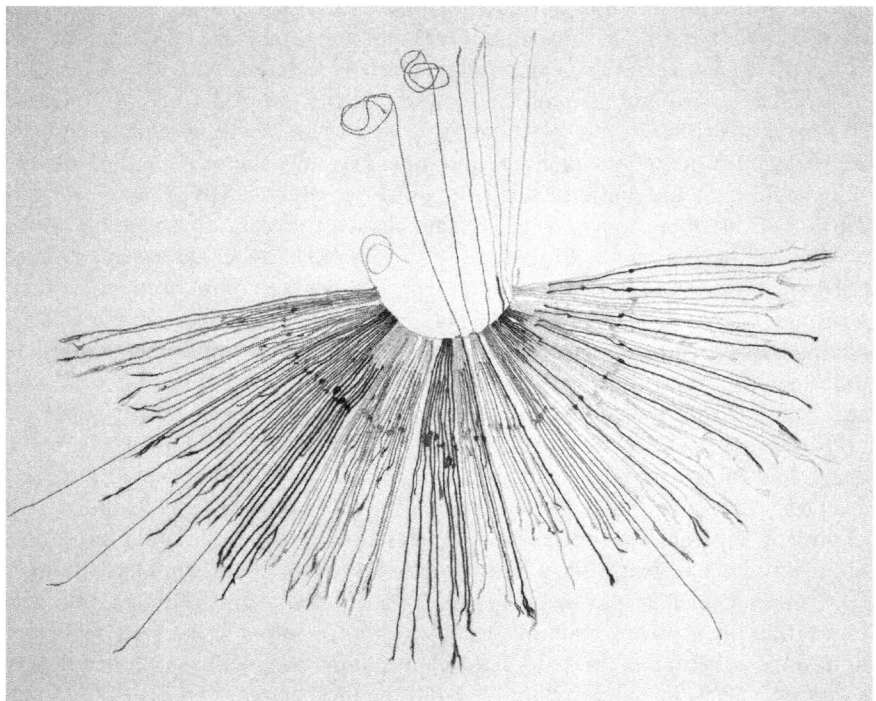

Figure 1.1 Inka *Khipu* (Fiber Recording Device), *c.* 1400–1532. Peru, Inca Period, 15th–16th century. Cords, knotted and twisted; cotton and wool; overall: 113 × 137.2 cm (44½ × 54 in.); mounted: 119.4 × 143.5 cm (47 × 56½ in.). The Cleveland Museum of Art, Gift of John Wise 1940.469, Courtesy of the Cleveland Museum of Art.

remember something. A simple rope can be knotted in different ways, thus allowing for some kind of code to emerge. Historically, knot-based codes were developed in various places around the world through the use of ropes and knots to store not only personal information, but also all kinds of socially relevant and important information related to ownership, social status or weather patterns, tax records and so on. South American *quipus* in particular are historical evidence of the use of combinations of ropes and different knots to encode information (Hyland, 2017). *Quipus* (Figure 1.1) are fascinating objects: made of very simple colored fiber materials, they encode complex information using a colored numerical system, which has led some to describe them as proto search engine and databases (Graham, 2014). Widely used as tools for administration purposes during the times of the Incas, *quipus* were replaced by writing and other western recording systems after the Spanish conquest of the Andes. Similarly, while there is still evidence of knots used as memory devices in South America, China, Hawaii and among Indigenous groups in North America, such uses of textile tend to have fallen into oblivion and replaced by western-based types of communication systems during colonization.

As one can imagine, the road from these first coarse threads to the diversity of textiles available up until nineteenth-century industrialization is a long and complex one that involved continuous and multiple technical innovations, as well as new social organizations of labor, all of which were dependent on both available material resources and geopolitical contexts. Textile scholar Tomoko Torimaru (2018) explains that in many places, the use of ropes for carrying weight eventually led to the invention of weaving. A round rope is sturdy for sure, but it digs into the skins of humans and domesticated animals—hence the need to come up with flat ropes that distribute weight while resting against the skin. To create flat ropes, strands of fibers are made to interlap with each other rather than being twisted together, forming indeed, a proto-weaving. Ropes are quintessential cultural techniques (Siegert, 2015): they serve domestication and transportation purposes, but they also, with different color combinations and patterns, can be used to indicate property and belonging, acting both in the real and in the symbolic realms and enacting the transition between reality and culture. Fishing nets have also been credited as one of the origins of knotted textiles, such as knits, crochets, and gauze. It is difficult to pinpoint exactly when woven cloths first appeared, but there are a few instances of both cloth and remnants of looms from the Neolithic period in present-day Iraq, from approximately 7000 BCE. As one can imagine, extracting durable and pliable textile fibers from plants (e.g., cotton, linen from flax), animals (e.g., sheep, camelids) or insects (e.g., silkworms) took time, skill and technical innovation, and so did spinning these raw fibers into fine threads ready for knitting, crocheting, or weaving (e.g., cotton, linen and silk). As Barber recalls, sheep needed to be carefully bred "over thousands of years" in order to obtain "some varieties that had a fair amount of wool, which molted every year in the spring" (1994: 97).

Prior to industrialization, the making of everyday textile was time-consuming and was therefore done by many, both men and women. As Barber argues, there emerged a gender separation between domestic textile work and textile work outside of the home in weaving workshops and so on: tasked with breastfeeding, women tended to stay at home and organize textile work around child-rearing duties while men were freer to work outside of the domestic sphere. The demand for everyday textile was important, and spinning was a constant. Today, in many places in South America, people still carry with them hand spinners so that whenever they have a moment when their hands are free, they can spin threads. Spinning was a constant activity in Europe, mostly for women (hence the origin of "spinster"), regardless of class (cf. the tale of Sleeping Beauty). The invention of the mechanized spinning wheel (in India between 500 and 1000 CE) and its spread (in Europe throughout the fourteenth century) helped, but it did not erase the need for constant thread production for everyday life. Weaving was also the subject of many technical innovations, with many kinds of looms being developed until the industrial mechanized loom—from the backstrap loom used from prehistoric times onward to the Jacquard loom (1804) featured later in this book.

The initial demand for textile was partly about needs: skin protection and shelter, mainly. However, textile has never simply been about survival and fulfillment of material needs—it was a tool to transmit multiple kinds of social and cultural information. Early examples from Africa show that fibers (e.g., thread) combined with other materials (e.g., colored beads) served to create jewelry (necklaces) and garments (belts) that would express the social status of the person wearing them: where one was from, whether one was married, or looking for a spouse and so on (Carey, 1986). Barber posits that such were the first uses of textile in Europe as well: the kind of textile produced in Neolithic times was not appropriate to cover a body with but was rather used as informational ornamentation in the form of belts and skirts. Textile, in that sense, encoded

Figure 1.2 Child's sleeping mat (*boro* Shikimono), late 19th century. Courtesy of Cooper Hewitt, Smithsonian Design Museum and Wikimedia Commons. 2017.

information and inscribed the status of a person in the world. The discovery of natural dyes around 4000 BCE further allowed for woven textile itself to be subjected to all kinds of manipulation through the creation of color patterns. Even today, specific techniques for dyeing and weaving textile express particular cultures. Think for instance of batik primarily associated with Indonesian culture, which entails the use of wax to create what is called resist patterns that are then filled in with dye, or the Scottish tartans that express clan affiliations. We can still find plenty of contemporary examples all over the world of cloth and garments that are culturally specific and constitute a core practice for group identity-building—indeed, there are still so many of them that it would not be possible to list them all here. For instance, ethnic Hmong, originally from Southeast Asia, are divided into groups that are named after their main textile craft: Black Hmong dye

Figure 1.3 Detail of Sashiko Kimono. Indigo-dyed plain-weave cotton, quilted and embroidered with white cotton thread, mid-19th century. Courtesy of the Metropolitan Art Museum, New York and Wikimedia Commons.

their cloth with indigo to obtain an almost black color, and Flower Hmong work with colorful embroideries. Textile not only served as a mnemonic device or to signal social status, but also for spiritual purposes: monks' robes identify those who have abandoned secular life; religious clothes also show the hierarchies among religious group (e.g., black cassocks for priests, red cassocks for cardinals in Catholicism).

Textile arts and crafts fulfilled both material and aesthetic needs as well. In Japan for instance, the simple stitches used for mending and strengthening cloth— the practice of *boro* mentioned in the introduction (Figure 1.2)—evolved into embroidery patterns, giving birth to Sashiko embroidery techniques (Figure 1.3). Mending, in a nutshell, became an artistic practice that expressed a particular cultural aesthetic. The transition from *boro* to Sashiko shows the multiple purposes of textile as cultural technique, from the mundane, everyday context to more special-occasion contexts. Perhaps, therefore, what is most interesting in the very plurality of meanings in textile, is that textile has always been a way to weave together the everyday and the sacred, the individual and the social, the mundane and the spiritual, the personal and the social. In short, it is not simply that textile has many uses, but that it allows for these many uses to be layered together, articulating and connecting different temporalities and modes of experience that are usually kept separate from each other.

Two Common Understandings of Communication through Textile: As Representation and Information

The commodification of textile through its industrialization and mass production explains why postindustrial societies have generally discarded textile as a mode of communication. However, this does not fully explain why textile has been mostly pushed aside in the field of communication studies. There are several reasons for this: first, compared to more durable forms of communication that can be stored and archived, textile does not provide for a lasting support for communication in most climates except desert ones, even with sustained care. Furthermore, the kind of textile used for administrative purposes, such as the *quipu* mentioned above, were subject to destruction during the Spanish conquest, to protect information from being stolen by the colonizers. In the same vein, many non-western textile-based communication practices were destroyed or disappeared as they were replaced by Eurocentric communication technologies during colonization. With little historical evidence remaining, it is difficult and painstaking to imagine the historical place of textile in many societies around the world, and only the very specialized field of ethnology has both the tools and methods available for such reconstruction. That textile was typically meant to be used and subjected to constant wear and tear, rather than carefully stored in specialized archives compounds the problem. Indeed, unlike with paper, there are very few remnants of preserved textile as a technology that has been around worldwide since prehistoric times.

The second reason for not recognizing textile as a means of communication is linked to the sheer multiplicity of textile techniques and practices. Compared to more traditional communication technologies, which usually tend to coalesce around a set of standards and norms to gain a global reach, the cohesiveness of textile, as reduced to a set of standardized techniques commonly used all over the world, only dates back to its mass industrialization throughout the nineteenth century. Indeed, we usually see communication technologies such as radio, television or the internet develop as global technologies through the standardization of their protocols, codes, techniques and practices. The history of textile is different in that regard: for ages it existed in a "state of indeterminacy" (Fuller and Goffey, 2009), allowing for countless techniques and creative innovations from prehistory up until most of the nineteenth century, many of which have now been forgotten. The sheer number of techniques one can use to transform a single piece of fabric— dye its fibers plain or in complex patterns through binding it (e.g., *ikat*), apply a resist paste, paint on it, silk-screen it, embroider it, sew it into different shapes and forms, apply other decorative materials to it and so on—show that textile cannot be contained under a coherent code. Further, up until industrialization, there was an immense variety of fibers that were used. There were many different specimens of the cotton plant for instance, each with different qualities, until one type of cotton was bred to withstand the power loom. Similarly, there are quite a few species of silkworms available apart from the most common, Bombix Mori. One can also think of the multiple kinds of bast fibers available in different regions all over the world: banana leaves in Southeast Asia, ramie, and so on. The sheer variety of textiles that can be produced as well, from a thick wool knit to a transparent silk gauze only highlights this dispersal of textile, which in turn fosters many forms of communication (Weiner and Schneider, 2013).

The third reason for not thinking about textile as communication is that it does not fit with our common, and I would argue limited, understanding of what communication is. Typically, when we say that something communicates, we mean that it transmits some kind of information. Traditionally, such information is packaged into a narrative, because narratives are easier for us to remember and understand than, say, a set of raw data. This kind of understanding of communication is built on the assumption that orality was the main mode of communication prior to the invention of the alphabet, and that creating stories was the main way we passed along the kind of information that would allow individuals and communities to survive and thrive (Ong, 2012). For this reason, we in western contexts usually narrow down the question of communication to the distribution of linguistic signs (words), representations (images), or recorded input (e.g., sound recording), all of which we are taught from early in life to recognize and understand by applying to them socio-cultural grids of interpretation. Thus, there is an inherent bias when we narrow our thinking about communication to informational inputs, linguistic signs and representations that fit into pre-existing cultural codes of interpretation.

Textile in many ways puts into question the linear arc of communication technologies from oral to writing to analog to digital. As we have seen, binary code was used with rope and knot memory systems, with extensive evidence of quipu use in the times of the Inca empire (Urton, 1998) and elsewhere in the world. As Barber argues, the probable first uses of fiber textile were for encoding information, not for keeping oneself warm. Therefore, many codes, including binary code, existed for a long time, only to be subsequently replaced by colonial technologies based on writing. The history of communication technologies thus tends to be more complex, cyclical, and layered in nature than was previously thought. And indeed, the study of such versatile sets of technologies such as the ones involved in textile-making opens up a world of communicative combinations that are still under-studied, particularly with regard to its affinities with analog and digital processes.

When we think about communication systems, we tend to think about the technical systems that allow for the transmission of information packaged into something that makes sense for us, and that therefore we can apply to our lives. Let's put aside for a moment the question of content and focus on its transmission. Typically, transmission involves the inscription of some kind of content (be it codified content or a sensory input) onto some kind of support. Such inscription is made possible through some kind of technical process that involves the use of a set of materials. Take for instance the written page: we use a technical tool and some material—the pen and ink—to inscribe information onto a piece of paper and through this, to engage with whoever is the intended recipient of a message, be it an individual or a group, people close to us, strangers or future generations. With analog technologies, more complex systems are in play. Analog photography, for instance, requires coating a support—most commonly film or paper—with a chemical mix that will react to light exposure. A technical device—the camera— allows for the light to hit the coated film, creating a set of reactions where the emanated light, depending on its intensity, will darken the film to various degrees. Another set of chemicals are then used to stop the coated support from reacting to light, thus creating a finished photograph. The process for digital technologies is even more complex and involves a series of software operations that are transmitted through some sort of hardware (e.g., computer cards, electronic networks) that often feature human-readable computer interfaces (e.g., a computer screen featuring recognizable information).

Given the attention paid to the overall complexity of more well-known communication technologies, it is somewhat puzzling to see that in the field of communication and media studies, textile is often only acknowledged when it is used just like paper or like a computer interface. Indeed, if we look at the existing literature on textile in communication studies, we can see two approaches. The classical approach is to notice textile when it is used as a support for words or images, when there are slogans or iconic images printed on, say, t-shirts. In the same vein, critical perspectives on textile and its role in social change tend to focus on the stories that can be carried through textile work. Textile is mainly recognized as a tool for carrying stories using universally recognizable visual representations. For instance, Chilean women during the Pinochet regime were encouraged by the Catholic church to do textile work both as a source of income and as a means expression. The resulting *arpilleras* (Agosin, 1987)—textile pieces featuring appliqués to create depictions of daily life—became a tool for Chilean women to express the daily struggles related to political oppression and the status of the *desaparecidos* (the disappeared) during the dictatorship. Smuggled out of the country, the *arpilleras* became testimonies to the world of the exactions of the dictatorship in Chile. A similar and more recent example is the history of contemporary Afghan rugs marketed in the United States, which evolved from depicting tanks and Kalashnikovs in the 1980s during Soviet occupation to representing the 9-11 attacks on the Twin Towers in NYC to now featuring U.S. drones (Bizzarri and Quartz, 2015). In this instance, textile becomes a tool for depicting the geopolitical forces that have shaped the sociopolitical situation in Afghanistan. Overall, there are many examples of textile being used to record and transmit stories of survival. Hmong refugees in Thailand in the 1960s used their embroidery skills to not only depict their ordeal fleeing the civil war in Laos, but also to remember their everyday lives before the war (Tanaka, 2013: 24). In all these examples, textile is used to create visual depictions of events and situations, and in that sense, they fit within a classic framework that sees communication as the exchange of meaningful stories.

The limitation of such an approach is that it focuses narrowly on a very specific type of textile and ignores many other ways in which visual elements are mobilized beyond explicit representation in the making of textile. More often than not, textile does not feature words or images but rather abstract or stylized patterns, that is, decorations rather than declarations. That most patterned textiles do not signify in the traditional linguistic sense of the term means that they perhaps best illuminate McLuhan's quip that the medium is the message. With patterns, there is no separate message: the entire piece is an expression of the medium itself. Because of our widespread cultural bias toward the printed page or the image as the traditional example of communication, when we look at how textile is ornamented in abstract or patterned ways, be it through specific weaves, dyes, prints, embroideries, or embossments and so on, we do not tend to ask about the kind of information such ornamentations carry. Rather, we often just decide whether we like it or not. And in many ways, ornaments do not carry the same sociocultural impact as a text or a representation: a paisley design does not say much apart from being a common design, and stripes, for instance, say even less. And yet, in bypassing traditional linguistic systems they can be mobilized to serve different sociocultural purposes. Patterns easily circulate across cultures, space and time: they are modes of inscriptions that work virally, by spreading a particular aesthetic and sensibility (Washburn and Crowe, 2004). And as we will see in subsequent chapters, patterns are about rhythms, that is, felt relations with a living world that do not detour through representation. Overall, most textile escapes classical analytical frameworks for understanding communication.

A second approach to the study of textile in the field of communication studies is related to digital technologies, as mentioned in the introduction. Artists have done work that highlight the similarities between knitting and binary code: it is possible, for instance, to knit computer viruses and other types of computer code

(Harlizius-Klück, 2017; Jefferies and Thompson, 2017; Griffiths and McLean, 2017). Another use of textile is as a network or conductor. Scientific and artistic innovation on what are called smart textiles, fabrics or wearables sees different types of computer networks and sensors embedded into fabric in order to create reactive, interactive textile that can both collect and broadcast some kind of information. For instance, Kasia Molga's *Human Sensor* project features garments that react to different levels of air pollution. Medical applications of smart textiles now enable new forms of monitoring health and protecting bodies against adverse conditions. Smart wearables promise to have significant and multiple impacts as well in sports and worker safety. In such contexts, textile does not feature representations, but becomes akin to a computer interface that features information. While these two uses of textile—as representation or as computer information—might seem utterly divergent, they both share in employing textile as visual support on which to transcribe some sort of information.

Toward a Third Aspect: Textile as Binding Worlds through Space and Time

So, how could we think otherwise about textile? One way, featured heavily in this book, is to see textile as the mobilization of worlds through the technological transformation of materials taken from the environment. We do not often think about textile in this way, mostly because of the mainstream use of human-made synthetic fabric (e.g., nylon, rayon and acrylic) and synthetic dyes today. Synthetic dyes and synthetic fabric date back from the mid- and late 1800s respectively, participating in the complete transformation of textile from small craft with substantial human intervention to industrialized mass-produced commodities. Up until the arrival of these synthetic replacements, only natural fibers (e.g., cotton, wool, silk), and natural dyes derived from various plants, soils, insects and small animals were used. Dyeing textile with natural dyes is incredibly complex: achieving even results requires skills and knowledge, some of which will be detailed in Chapter 7. Naturally dyed cloth is a form of recording of one's environment, that is, it involves the production of traces from the environment onto a piece of fabric. These traces are usually potent, and not just for their aesthetic value, but also because plants used for natural dyes almost always possess medicinal properties. Again, it is hard for us post-industrial consumers to imagine how the complexity of making natural animal or plant-based textile led to very rich and meaningful processes of communication and exchange with nature. As textile scholar Yuko Tanaka explains when describing the natural indigo dyeing process:

> For humans to vie with nature, in this case plants, is far from easy. In premodern times, the challenge must have seemed not unlike that of birthing a child and rearing it safely to adulthood. It stands to reason, then, that special ceremonial

textiles have been used throughout the world to mark children's stages of growth (such as three and five years) and their later attainment of adulthood. For elaborately worked textiles are the results of a successful communion with nature, a manifestation of nature in all its glory that humans have made their own in a sort of miracle.

Tanaka, 2013: 32

The meaningfulness of textile here lies in the making of it, in the process of exchanging with nature, of enabling environmental communication with the non-human as plants, chemical reactions and environmental factors. Of course, the finished pieces are some kind of crowning glory for the maker, but the lengthy and meticulous process of extracting from the natural world, of applying natural elements onto natural fibers is as yet an under-studied process of communication and composition between humans, non-humans, and environmental entities, a cosmotechnics, which will be explored in the rest of the book.

For now, let's focus on the fact that textile as material communication requires us to rethink the role and centrality of the visual as a category to analyze non-auditory communication systems. Part of the paradox of textile is that it is both something we look at and something we wear on our skins. Textile is not just like a piece of paper: when looking at a piece of textile, we immediately imagine how it would feel to touch it or to feel it on our skin. Textile scholar Mary Schoeser argues that "textiles are three-dimensional objects within which structure, texture, insertions, additions, manipulations and movement can interact. In fact, it is more accurate to describe textile not as a visual art, but as a sensory art, one that calls into play all of the senses: touch, sight, smell, sound and—for curious infants—taste" (2012: 463). And indeed, it is often hard to control our reflex to reach out and touch a piece of textile exhibited in a gallery. We access textile through both its visual presence and tactility, and this opens the door to multiple forms of expression through textile: not only through its visual elements, but also through its haptic characteristics. Haptic communication is usually considered essential for gathering information about an environment: whether something is hot or cold, for instance, is important information. It is also one of the most intimate modes of communication among humans: touching someone is no inconsequential gesture. There has been a growing interest in haptic communication more recently alongside the rise of wearable technologies and interfaces that react to touch. Much can be learned from textile as a visual and haptic interface with the world. As Tanaka recalls, the history of textile in Asia and in the west was partially shaped by a widely shared desire to access skin-like textile, and in particular fine cotton and silk. Hence the Silk Road—a vast Eurasian network of routes that spanned between 200 BCE and the middle of the fifteenth century to exchange originally exclusively Chinese-produced silk, along with other commodities. As Tanaka argues, the search for textile that would feel like skin also played a role in the global popularity of nylon, the first synthetic fiber that was commercialized and has been touted as a replacement for the much more expensive silk. However, Tanaka remarks:

One can tell the difference (...) if one touches nylon with the fingertips or strokes it with the palm of the hand. Despite the resemblance, this petroleum-based "skin" does not feel right. The skin of a living creature breathes, it is permeable, it perspires, it secretes (...). As a living, naturally moist layer, the skin is comfortable in contact with a limited range of fabrics, chiefly cotton, silk and wool, that is, materials of plant or animal origin (...). Silk comes particularly close to the sensation of skin on skin.

Tanaka, 2013: 58

But what kinds of skin-on-skin communication does textile such as silk produce? The feeling of cloth on one's skin is intimate, but as a haptic and visual interface with the world, it also provides for a range of communicative exchanges. One could refer to Erin Manning's insight that "when the skin becomes not a container but a multidimensioned topological surface that folds in, through, and across spacetimes of experience, what emerges is not a self but the dynamic form of a worlding that refuses categorization" (2013: 12). To understand this, we can turn to Tanaka's analysis of how the Japanese kimono embodies complex communicative layers between the self and itself, others and the environment. In *The Power of the Weave*, Tanaka explores the combination of haptic and visual processes in Edo-period landscape kimonos, kimonos made of silk, naturally dyed and featuring landscapes:

The artisans of the Edo period took the techniques of weaving, embroidery, and tie-dyeing to new heights. The result was the unique "landscape kimono." When spread out, each robe formed a seasonal vista like a painting (...). Plant-extract hues had long stood for nature, but in landscape kimono people could clothe themselves in nature in a very concrete way. As in other cultures, textiles were a medium between humans and the divine or natural world ...

Tanaka, 2013: 22

In such examples we find again the notion that textile weaves together different times, experiences and existences, from the innermost feeling of being in one's skin to the entire cosmos. Be it the high-end kimono of Edo Japan (Figure 1.4) or a *boro*-patched farmer's jacket, we see textile as a process of articulating together individuals, groups, and the environment through different times and spaces. Textile from this perspective should be described as a technology of transindividuation, that is, as a technology that allows for concurrent individual and collective transformation. Following Bernard Stiegler, transindividuation is a continuous unfolding process of figuring out who "I" was, am and want to be in relation to who "we" were, are and want to be. It involves the activation of psycho-social processes that both enable the past to continue in the present and to give shape to potential futures, to horizons of possibilities. To go back to previous examples, wrapping a newborn in cloth is both a necessity and a ritual performed by family members and helpers: textile transindividuates in that it first marks and inscribes something new—the birth of a human being and its recognition by

Figure 1.4 Unlined Summer Kimono (Hito-e) with landscape and poem, second half of the 18th century. Courtesy of the Metropolitan Museum.

others as an individual in accordance with a spiritual framework. In so doing, textile transforms and binds all the people participating in and witnessing this event in that it gives them a commonality that is not just the present moment, but the apprehension of an individual life unfolding, a new openness to the future. Such transformation is psycho-social: textile crosses through individuals; it creates communal bonding in the present, but also transcends the present by opening a window to a future in common.

Global Textile, or Communication as Expressive Power

Transindividuation through textile links the intimate of the person with the community, but also, and paradoxically, unsettles and revolutionizes modes of being when textile objects travel outside of the communities that make them. The unique characteristics of textile—its capacity to combine broad cultural encodings with the personal and the intimate—are key to understanding the impacts of its circulation across the globe. In that regard, it is important to take into account how textile has allowed for broad processes of transindividuation at the global level and how such expressive and transformative powers were subsequently harnessed and distorted through colonization and capitalism. While we have already seen that textile has long served to express cultural identities, what is also interesting, in turn, is the circulation of textile pieces outside of the cultures that produced them. Historically, this required a further transformation of textile from needs and means of cultural expression to valuable and desirable object. To become valuable, textile objects not only had to be rare or hard to find, they also had to demonstrate a level of aesthetic sophistication that could provoke desire and envy. Barber dates this shift in textile to the Neolithic and Bronze Age (around 4000 BCE), when technical specialization in general meant that there were "surplus commodities available to pay for things (…) not essential to daily life: items to indulge one's fancy, to make life easier (including slave labor as well as better tools), or to enhance one's prestige and position in society" (1994). As Barber further explained, while women in ancient Europe during the Bronze Age were "still busy with uncontrolled pregnancy and children," greater technical productivity in general meant more time for men to innovate and produce textile objects that featured aesthetic innovation through technical sophistication. While many women remained occupied with the domestic production of everyday textile, men were able to specialize as artisans and work outside of the home to produce luxury textile objects. Contact among different cultures meant that textiles from afar became objects of desire that spurred collective imagination and profoundly shaped cultures through weaving the global with the local. Economic empires that had a monopoly over a sought-after type of textile (for instance, China and its silk monopoly) came to have a profound influence on the other societies they came into contact with (Frankopan, 2017). Luxury fabrics, often featuring complex designs, became objects of desire, modes of cultural communication, and media for wielding economic and cultural power (Peck et al., 2013). Here the expressive power of textile lies in its capacities to foster new imaginaries. As opposed to Benedict Anderson's concept of "imagined communities" (2006) where citizens adopt practices and rituals that foster a sense of belonging to a nation, the kind of imaginaries that global textile creates are turned toward the foreign, the other, be it aesthetic, material or technical. Historically and from a Eurocentric perspective, these kinds of imaginaries mixed with a long history of colonialism and capitalism are inevitably tied up in Orientalism (Said, 1979), that is, the projection of an exotic and unreal otherness that serves to hide actual conditions of exploitation. But textile has, again, a longer and more complex history than the trajectory of orientalism to present-day cultural and technical appropriation, and one that, in Europe at least, takes us to moments when the aesthetic and technical superiority of non-European cultures in relation to European ones, particularly China and India, could not be denied.

A theoretical detour is required before delving into some of the key aspects of textile as a global object of exchange and medium of cultural, political and economic influence. How do we understand the processes by which the material qualities of a given communication system enable sweeping political, economic and cultural effects? Typically, as we have seen, when we think about communication and communication systems, we refer to a specific category of technologies used to store and transmit information, from writing to computer networks. Within such a framework, the study of communication is inseparable from the study of the rise and fall of communities and societies at all levels: cultural, of course, but also economic, political and psychosocial. This we see in the work of Harold Innis in *Empire and Communications* (2007), which analyzed both the history and affordances of communication systems to track the formation of geopolitical empires. For Innis, acquiring and harnessing the potentials of communication systems has historically been essential to the development of geopolitical empires, from the Roman empire to the twentieth-century US empire. According to Innis, the affordances of different communication systems shape the rise of specific ways of life, from culture to administration. Communication systems allow for the rise of specific monopolies of knowledge, by which Innis meant not just repositories of information, but modes of selecting which information is deemed useful enough to be stored and used, as well as processes for mobilizing such information for governing purposes, from dispensing education, to establishing spiritual institutions and practices and law enforcement. Innis argues that communication systems typically favor either the storing of information through time or the mobility of information through space, and that therefore different communication systems will tend to be biased toward preservation in time or circulation in space. One of Innis's famous examples is that of the co-existence of papyrus and parchment during the Roman empire. Papyrus being light and portable allowed for extension through space, and thus for responsive centralized governance and bureaucracy over vast territories. While papyrus was fragile and deteriorated fast, the parchment codex on the other hand was durable, and proved to be the communication technology of choice for the temporal safeguarding of Christianity into a stable institution partially reliant on guarded access to key texts in monastic libraries.

The problem with Innis's work is that it is organized around broad historical transitions from oral societies to writing societies, and from writing societies to analog and electric ones. As we have seen, the history of textile challenges such organization. Still, Innis presents us with a way of further understanding broad processes of transindividuation that emerge and circulate from specific communication systems, and how they not only give rise to specific cultures, but also how they enable intercultural contacts and the rise of global flows of communication. It is worthwhile in that regard to think about how textile helps us understand the complexity of changes at the global and local levels. It might seem difficult at first to see how valuable textiles that spurred early global flows of exchange might fit with Innis's analysis of communication systems: after all, their primary purpose was not to transmit what we usually think of information, that is, some useful set of facts. But valuable textiles carry other kinds of information: ones that are more about cultural aesthetics, often meant to evoke prestige and refinement and the extraordinary, and ones that are affective, in the haptic sense of textile described in the previous section. Altogether, these two types of cultural and haptic information open up new imaginaries about contact with faraway lands, refined techniques and new sensations.

Furthermore, the kind of communicative uses of textile seen above fit broadly within the category of non-durable and portable communication technologies that deteriorate fast, and that need to be constantly remade. While this characteristic might give the impression that non-durable technologies are somewhat less worthwhile than durable ones, having to constantly remake textile enables very specific forms of continuity through time. Textile requires passing down craft and technical knowledge through apprenticeship, spurring continuous technical and creative inventions. At the same time, textiles circulating across continents via trade and exchange routes spurred envy not only from the buyer side, but also from the making side: the history of textile is filled with efforts to copy and reinvent new techniques from far away. How the copying takes place, under which conditions and through the use of which techniques raise important political questions about the relationship between technical and cultural appropriation and intercultural exchanges.

Textile enables new processes of intercultural exchange as it is being copied in different contexts. This can include the export of technologies and technical processes for making textile, the invention of new technologies and fabric to mimic a sought-after textile and copying ornamentations. In short, the circulation of textile involved both technical, practical and aesthetic levels that each evolved in their own way, depending on the historical context. This recalls in many ways Innis's complex historical analysis of circulation of communication technologies alongside and in relation to many other technical, social, spiritual, ideological and political processes. This goes against the commonly shared, mistaken impression that a hard kind of technological determinism is at work in Innis's thought. However, the inherent biases of communication technologies do not dictate sociopolitical and cultural change, but rather articulate themselves with other processes to create limits and potentials. These limits and potentials can in turn be harnessed and used by an existing system of power rather than destabilize it.

Textile has long embodied and materialized global political and economic relations of production and consumption. Because historically different parts of the world had access to different materials and techniques to make different kinds of textile, there was, until nineteenth-century industrialization, global flows of textile that allowed sustained intercultural exchanges. Before mass industrialization, the global networks of textile that involved Europe can be divided into two broad periods, the first being the Silk Road, which spanned from the first century BCE with the introduction of Chinese silk into the Roman Empire and continued up until the late fifteenth century. The Silk Road comprised a vast network of mostly overland trade routes that stretched from Japan to China, the Indian subcontinent, the Arabic Peninsula, the horn of Africa and the Mediterranean. It allowed for intercultural exchange of goods, ideas, technologies and crafts, Chinese silk among them. As opposed to the everyday textile described above, Chinese silk was a *valuable* commodity, a rare luxury product, especially when its production was under Chinese monopoly. As Morris Rossabi recalls:

> To foreigners, the silk conveyed along the Silk Road became as valuable as gold. Similarly, the Chinese prized silk for the astonishing variety of uses it served—as a gift, in rituals, as a demarcation of social status, and as payment of taxes. Like the foreigners, the Chinese virtually converted silk into gold by using it also as currency.
>
> Rossabi, 1997: 7

Further along, Rossabi notes that:

> Chinese silk was so highly prized that foreigners refrained from belligerent or provocative acts in order to obtain it, and silk became a weapon in China's foreign relations arsenal. Repeatedly, silk was offered to foreign rulers as a means of averting attack.
>
> Rossabi, 1997: 10

The commerce of silk circulated not only cloth, but also designs and patterns, as well as materials, techniques and artisans. Rossabi (ibid.: 8) explains that Chinese silk workers in the seventh and eighth century not only relocated outside of China where their skills were in high demands, they were also protected and gained special status. Highly ornate, luxurious silks circulated, spurring constant aesthetic exchanges. Focusing on examples of two Central Asian luxury silk artefacts in the time of the Mongol empire in the tenth and eleventh century, Rossabi adds that what makes these silks characteristically Central Asian is not only unique design elements, but the combination of eastern and western design motifs:

> The primary motifs (animals and birds) in the two silks derive from the models that were current in the eastern Iranian world, while the secondary motifs (e.g., the cloudlike background ornament and the decorative details) were inspired by

Chinese sources. The latter, however, are so far removed from their original context that the result is neither Chinese nor Eastern Iranian but essentially Central Asian.

Rossabi, 1997: 127

The Silk Road and the circulation of luxury silks thus enabled what we can now understand as forms of remixing—of copying and borrowing while innovating—to give rise to new forms of cultural expression.

But there is more to textile than silk, of course, and the kind of global exchange and intercultural dialogue seen above can also be found in the global trade of cloth from the fifteenth century up until industrialization. At that time, India indeed was a key global center of textile arts and crafts, renowned for its cotton production that involved many kinds of fabric, from heavy cotton to sheer muslin, as well mastery of steadfast natural colors and rich designs (Crill, 2015). As Peck explains:

> . . . textile had been traded between Asia, the Middle East, Africa and Europe for hundreds of years, along lengthy routes that were traversed primarily over land until the mid-fifteenth century, when the fragmentation of the Mongol Empire signaled the end of the vast Silk Road. (. . .) at the end of the fifteenth century, the Europeans set sail in search of an ocean route to the Spice Islands of Southeast Asia and found exotic [e.g., Indian] textiles to trade along the way. The newly discovered sea routes that directly connected Europe to the rest of the world enabled the creation of the first truly global trading community, and as the Europeans found that textiles were welcome currency for other goods (including human cargo in appalling numbers), the scope of the textile trade expanded significantly.

Peck, 2013b: 3

The kind of skills that produced Indian textile—be they fine weaving, mastery of natural dyes or skills in ornamentations such as embroidery—were sought after and copied all over Europe and as far east as Japan (Kamada, 2012). Similar to silk, Indian textile was used to barter—it served as a form of proto-currency for exchange with other goods. Indian cotton fabrics were sought after not only for the quality of their fabrics, but also for their designs. Furthermore, being relatively inexpensive, Indian cotton fabrics in the 1600s were:

> worn by all classes and, indeed, created something of a social revolution, since previously it had been easy to distinguish between the gentry, dressed in patterned silks, and the common folk, in plain wools and linens. When everyone could afford and preferred the fashionable, highly decorative patterned cottons, class lines blurred.

Peck, 2013a: 105

Chintz (Figure 1.5)—Indian hand-printed cotton fabrics featuring motifs from the natural world (flowers, leaves, birds and so on)—became so popular in the late

Figure 1.5 Chintz panel (India), 18th century. Author unknown. Courtesy of Cooper Hewitt, Smithsonian Design Museum and Wikimedia Commons.

seventeenth century in Europe that its import was banned in the UK and France because local textile producers could not compete (Crill, 2008). The patterns were so popular that they were in turn copied by French and British artisans, giving rise to motifs that we would now consider as quintessentially "Old Europe" aesthetics, such as the Toile de Jouy (Figure 1.6). Despite disputes over importation of Indian

Figure 1.6 Example of Toile de Jouy, 18th century. Courtesy of the Metropolitan Museum and Wikimedia Commons.

cloth, Britain, through the English East India Company, nevertheless exported chintz and other Indian cotton all over the world and to the new colonies in North America up until the establishment of American cotton production in the late eighteenth century. The global trade of textile both as fabric and aesthetic was of such intensity until then that it created a global aesthetics. As Peck argues:

> Because the scope of the textile trade was so widespread by the mid-seventeenth century, the constant interchange of exotic motifs, fibers, and dyes between these now interconnected markets brought in to being, for the first time, a common visual language of design that was recognized throughout the world.
>
> Peck, 2013b: 3

Such common visual language and the development of common aesthetic proclivities was not only reliant on the circulation of fabric, but also of materials to be used for textile-making and in particular, dyestuff to obtain bright yellows, deep blues and brilliant reds as well as dye-processes to render these colors lightfast. In the same catalog, Elena Phipps adds:

> More than just commodities to be traded on an economic front, colorants were sources of cultural knowledge and identity as well as inspiration for creativity and ingenuity. The quests for these precious raw materials in turn spurred long-distance interactions, social transformations, scientific development, and artistic

achievements whose profound implications are still being unraveled and understood today.

Phipps, 2013: 135

The circulation of textile globally thus encompasses many different aspects: technical, practical, material and aesthetic. All of these aspects in turn circulated in different ways to produce new forms of cultural expression and new ways to yield economic and political power. While today textile seems to be entirely in the hands of the global capitalist enterprise, it is, as we will see in the remainder of the book, a way to untangle and contest global inequalities and formulate new socioeconomic relations.

Textile, a Medium of Struggle

It should come as no surprise that the capacity for textile to be a global object of desire would place it at the core of colonial and capitalist logics. Not only was the trade of textile goods—from materials to finished cloth—a promising profitable enterprise, but the appropriation and development of techniques and materials was key to socioeconomic expansion the world over. Textile was key to the transatlantic slave trade: European-produced textiles were exchanged for slaves in Africa, slaves were then sent to America to work in cotton fields, and American-produced commodities such as raw cotton and indigo were then shipped back to Europe. During the industrial revolution, textile continued to be a major player for political and economic domination as well: the United Kingdom was the first exporter of woven cotton in the nineteenth century thanks to its mechanized looms (Beckert, 2015). Cotton served first and foremost to assert British economic and colonial power all over the world, a power that was built on the subversion of other, non-European textile centers. Indeed, the industrialization of textile in the UK was not a simple story of a machinic production replacing forms of human labor: it demanded the opening of new markets, which meant eliminating domestic textile production in other places. It required in particular the quasi-complete destruction of both India's global economic role through the textile trade and the Indian cultural traditions that were expressed through textile arts and crafts. India was forced to grow cotton to be shipped at a low price to England, where it would be processed and woven, and sold back on the Indian market at a much higher price (Marx, 1853). Exploitation—both of workers and consumers—was central to making cotton a profitable and key commodity up to the present day.

The qualities of textile objects—tactility, visual appeal and so on—came to play a paradoxical role in this period: as objects of desires, textile commodities served to hide and erase the actual conditions of production and the many kinds of violence that they entailed, promoting a certain kind of blindness and amnesia for consumers of textile. Today, textile materializes the worst in both environmental destruction and global systemic exploitation and inequalities. It is the most polluting industry in the world after oil, relying on constant exploitation of labor forces in the Global South, and massive use of chemicals for dyeing that are highly toxic to humans, all to create cheap commodities (O'Connor, 2017). Fast fashion cycles have meant that textiles are meant to be quickly discarded, generating immense volumes of waste, with only a small percentage being recycled. It also requires cheap labor to drive prices down, which means unsafe and exploitative labor conditions that target especially women and children (Moulds, 2020). Environmentally, conventional textile production is catastrophic: cotton uses high amounts of pesticides and water, a main factor, for instance, in the drainage and pollution of the Aral Sea throughout the 1980s and 1990s (Environmental Justice Foundation. n.d.). Finished textiles are coated with chemicals such as phthalates, which have been found to be endocrine disruptors and linked to developmental disorders, birth defects and cancer (Li et al., 2019). Overall, the global state of textile today epitomizes the Anthropocene: the capacity for the capitalist system to forfeit the very possibility of life—both human and non-human—in the pursuit of ever-expanding profits. The function and meaning of textile today reach far beyond whatever personal satisfaction and pleasure we derive from possessing it: textile now not only expresses but reinforces a global capitalist system of economic, political and social relationships, and in that sense, it functions today as part of the capitalist communicative system. Beyond whatever signs are inscribed on it—images, slogans and so on—it serves as a tool of *existentialization* for the global capitalist machine, that is, the deeply cruel process by which the vast majority of our needs for both material subsistence and meaning can only be fulfilled by participating in the destruction of everything else. In that sense, to follow the reflections of Bernard Stiegler, textile today is more a tool of de-individuation than transindividuation. It both is the product of, and further intensifies, geopolitical divides and the exploitations of some groups and their environment to produce soon-to-be obsolete commodities for others. And the sheer scale and force of industrial textile today seems to preclude the possibility of composing other potential futures and ways of being together.

Yet, also unsurprisingly, textile has been a site of key political struggles since the nineteenth century. The original Luddites—workers who dismantled, sabotaged and destroyed machinery in the UK in the nineteenth century—were textile workers. It is a common misconception that Luddites were against technology: rather, they were against technology that enabled worker exploitation by factory owners through the replacement of skilled artisanship with machinic repetition of gestures (Hobsbawm, 1952). The fear of de-skilling was not simply about loss of social and economic status, it was also about a loss of meaning in one's very existence. That some textile workers found weaving meaningful should not be seen as individual perception alone; it expressed a way of being and relating to the world. One of the key case studies for this is the textile work of nineteenth-century artist and socialist William Morris (Thompson and Linebaugh, 2013). Morris's textiles and patterns are still famous today the world over, and Morris combined artistic pursuit and political advocacy at a time when the industrial revolution was proceeding at full speed. He advocated for workers' rights and the meaningfulness of skilled work (Brantlinger, 1996). This led Morris to reconsider how textile was produced. He advocated for the rediscovery and use of traditional techniques, especially block-printing, which originated in India. In addition, he refused to use synthetic dyes and rediscovered how to use natural dyes extracted from plants, insects and minerals. As we will see in Chapter 7, natural dyes are much more difficult to master and apply than synthetic dyes, which offer fairly simple processes with almost immediate results. But Morris was convinced that natural dyes were important for their capacity to directly express, and therefore link to, nature. Against intensive and polluting production cycles involving de-skilled labor, Morris made use of traditional skills and crafts to create aesthetic textile products that reasserted the importance of the natural world. In that regard, he was influential for his avant garde understanding of the need for deep relationships with natural environments in the production of objects, advocating for craft-based ways of expression based on natural materials. Morris's push for another mode of more mindful and careful consumption of high quality crafted products, rather than mass-produced cheap ones, finds a clear echo today in fair-trade and conscious consumption movements.

Another key historical instance of textile-making as a key political site of intervention, struggle and reinvention is India's independence and self-reliance (Swadeshi) movement (Gandhi, 1997; Gandhi and Vassanji, 2011). Symbolically, it makes sense that textile would play a key role in India's independent movement as it epitomized both the long history of India's cultural aesthetics and technical prowess worldwide, and the political, economic and psychosocial violence unleashed by colonial capitalism. The famous picture of Gandhi spinning cotton with a Charkha is emblematic of the importance of material practice for political transformation. Hand spinning cotton was an act of defiance against British rule. It meant not having to import overpriced industrially produced British cloth and signaled economic independence and environmental sustainability (Gandhi, 1997; Gandhi and Vassanji, 2011). Done by all, hand spinning transcended language and literacy barriers and thus was seen as a way to dismantle the social and cultural inequalities of the Indian caste system. Last but not least, hand spinning cotton led to both individual and collective healing: it quietly yet powerfully addressed the enormous wounds left by British colonialism in the nineteenth century (Marx, 1853), that is, the spiritual, economic, social and cultural destruction of the textile skills and crafts that had made Indian textiles some of the most admired and sought-after textiles in the world since Roman times. Further, the weaving of cotton cloth (khadi) was meant to reinvent social practices as well through technological development. It is a common misconception again that making khadi cloth meant a refusal of technology. Rather, as Swati Venkat argues, the development of khadi involved "the novel and visionary use of technologies in pursuit of an alternative modernity grounded in the core precepts of non-violence and self-reliance" (Venkat, 2014: 1). Again, there are parallels here with William Morris and the British Arts and Craft movement: it was not about refusing technology but rather seeking technologies that were meaningful and empowering for the makers. Further, these ideas around meaningful technologies at the service of material cultural production are found in the American Arts and Craft movement and in the Folk Craft (Mingei) movement in Japan in 1920s. The question of creating technological alternatives to mass industrial technologies keep resurging over the course of the long-in-development environmental crises we are so familiar with today.

Both William Morris's textile work and the development of khadi in India met with limited success. Morris's fabrics are still famous and there is a global market for khadi, but both are comparatively expensive. It is important nevertheless to acknowledge that textile-making has long been a site of political struggle parallel to its rise as a vector of colonial capitalism and industrial capitalism. Inspirations and impulses for the kinds of rebellions found in Morris and the Swadeshi movement and beyond (Bryan-Wilson, 2017) abound; they are at play in the case studies I present here in this book. Rethinking processes of making, translating social and environmental values onto a product, forging new relations with consumers of cloth—these are key forms of working with technologies as mediators among human actors and between human and non-human actors and their environment. Let me now turn to one such key instance of non-industrial and non-western textile, and how it intervenes in neocolonial politics: the case of Quechua weavers in the region around Cusco, Peru.

References

Agosin, Marjorie. (1987). *Scraps of Life: Chilean Arpilleras: Chilean Women and the Pinochet Dictatorship*. Translated by Cola Franzen. Trenton, NJ: Red Sea Press.

Anderson, Benedict. (2006). *Imagined Communities: Reflections on the Origin and Spread of Nationalism*. Verso Books.

Barber, Elizabeth Wayland. (1994). *Women's Work: The First 20,000 Years Women, Cloth, and Society in Early Times*. New York: WW Norton.

Beckert, Sven. (2015). *Empire of Cotton: A Global History*. Reprint edn. New York: Vintage.

Bizzarri, Cosimo, and Quartz. (2015). "Drones Are Now Appearing on Afghan Rugs" *The Atlantic*. January 30, 2015. (Accessed July 20, 2017). https://www.theatlantic.com/technology/archive/2015/01/drones-are-appearing-on-afghan-rugs/385025/.

Brantlinger, Patrick. (1996). "A Postindustrial Prelude to Postcolonialism: John Ruskin, William Morris, and Gandhism." *Critical Inquiry* 22 (3): 466–85. https://doi.org/10.1086/448802.

Bryan-Wilson, Julia. (2017). *Fray: Art and Textile Politics*. Chicago: University of Chicago Press.

Carey, Margret. (1986). *Beads and Beadwork of East and South Africa*. Aylesbury: Shire Publications.

Crill, Rosemary. (2008). *Chintz: Indian Textiles for the West*. London: V & A Publishing.

Crill, Rosemary, ed. (2015). *The Fabric of India*. London: V & A Publishing.

Environmental Justice Foundation. (n.d.). "The True Costs of Cotton: Eradicating the Human and Environmental Abuses Associated with White Gold." https://ejfoundation.org/what-we-do/cotton/the-true-costs-of-cotton?gclid=CjwKCAjw_LL2BR AkEiwAv2Y3Sc715qarNmo7c_n7Wr8Wht6WDU2nxi16jC9KWgxmEzTCS VQq3h1XkRoCyo0QAvD_BwE (accessed May 26, 2020).

Frankopan, Peter. (2017). *The Silk Roads: A New History of the World*. Reprint edn. New York: Vintage.

Fuller, Matthew, and Andrew Goffey. (2009). "Towards Evil Media Studies." In *The Spam Book: On Viruses, Porn and Other Anomalies from the Dark Side of Digital Culture*. Edited by Jussi Parikka and Tony D. Sampson, 141–159. Cresskill, NJ: Hampton Press.

Gandhi, Mohandas. (1997). *Gandhi: "Hind Swaraj" and Other Writings*. Edited by Anthony J. Parel. Cambridge: Cambridge University Press.

Gandhi, Mohandas K., and M. G. Vassanji. (2011). *Gandhi: An Autobiography, The Story of My Experiments with Truth*. Markham, Ont.: Fitzhenry and Whiteside.

Graham, Richard. (2014). "A 'History' of Search Engines: Mapping Technologies of Memory, Learning and Discovery." In *Society of the Query Reader*. Edited by René König and Miriam Rasch, 105–20. Amsterdam: Institute of Network Cultures.

Griffiths, Dave and Alex McLean. (2017). "Textility of Code: A Catalogue of Errors." *TEXTILE* 15: 198–214.

Harlizius-Klück, Ellen. (2017). "Weaving as Binary Art and the Algebra of Patterns." *TEXTILE* 15 (2): 176–97. https://doi.org/10.1080/14759756.2017.1298239.

Hobsbawm, E. J. (1952). "The Machine Breakers." *Past & Present*, 1 (1): 57–70. https://doi. org/10.1093/past/1.1.57.

Hyland, Sabine. (2017). "Writing with Twisted Cords: The Inscriptive Capacity of Andean Khipus." *Current Anthropology* 58 (3): 412–19.

Innis, Harold A. (2007). *Empire and Communications*. Toronto: Dundurn Press.

Innis, Harold A. (2008). *The Bias of Communication*. 2nd edn. Toronto: University of Toronto Press.

Jefferies, Janis, and Kelly Thompson. (2017). "Material Codes: Ephemeral Traces." *TEXTILE* 15 (2): 158–75. https://doi.org/10.1080/14759756.2017.1298327.

Li, Hai-Ling, Wan-Li Ma, Li-Yan Liu, Zhi Zhang, Ed Sverko, Zi-Feng Zhang, Wei-Wei Song, Yu Sun, and Yi-Fan Li. (2019). "Phthalates in Infant Cotton Clothing: Occurrence and Implications for Human Exposure." *The Science of the Total Environment* 683 (September): 109–15. https://doi.org/10.1016/j.scitotenv.2019.05.132.

Manning, Erin. (2013). *Always More Than One: Individuation's Dance*. Durham, NC: Duke University Press.

Marx, Karl. (1853). "The British Rule in India." *New York Daily Tribune*, 1853. https://www. marxists.org/archive/marx/works/1853/06/25.htm.

Moulds, Josephine. (2020). "Child Labour in the Fashion Supply Chain." *The Guardian*. https://labs.theguardian.com/unicef-child-labour/ (accessed May 26, 2020).

O'Connor, Morgan. (2017). "The Monster in Our Closet: Fast Fashion & Textile Waste on the Rise." *Center for EcoTechnology* (blog). October 11, 2017. https://www. centerforecotechnology.org/fast-fashion-textile-waste/.

Ong, Walter J. (2012). *Orality and Literacy: 30th Anniversary Edition*. 3rd edn. London: Routledge.

Peck, Amelia. (2013a). "'Indian Chints' and 'China Taffaty': East India Company Textiles for the North American Market." In *Interwoven Globe: The Worldwide Textile Trade, 1500–1800*. Edited by Amelia Peck. 104–119. New York: Metropolitan Museum of Art.

Peck, Amelia. (2013b). "Trade Textiles at the Metropolitan Museum: A History." In *Interwoven Globe: The Worldwide Textile Trade, 1500–1800*. Edited by Amelia Peck. 2–11. New York: Metropolitan Museum of Art.

Peck, Amelia, Amy Bogansky, Joyce Denney, John Guy, Maria Joao Ferreira, Elena Phipps, Marika Sardar, Cynthia V. A. Schaffner, Kristen Stewart, and Melinda Watt. (2013). *Interwoven Globe: The Worldwide Textile Trade, 1500–1800*. New York: Metropolitan Museum of Art.

Phipps, Elena. (2013). "Global Colors: Dyes and the Dye Trade." In *Interwoven Globe: The Worldwide Textile Trade, 1500–1800*. Edited by Amelia Peck. 120–135. New York: Metropolitan Museum of Art.

Postrel, Virginia I. (2020). *The Fabric of Civilization: How Textiles Made the World*. New York: Basic Books.

Rossabi, Morris. (1997). "The Silk Trade in China and Central Asia." In *When Silk Was Gold: Central Asian and Chinese Textiles*. Edited by James C. Y. Watt and Anne E. Wardwell [catalog]. New York: Metropolitan Museum of Art in cooperation with the Cleveland Museum of Art.

Said, Edward W. (1979). *Orientalism*. New York: Vintage.

Schoeser, Mary. (2012). *Textiles: The Art Of Mankind*. Illustrated edn. New York: Thames and Hudson.

Siegert, Bernhard. (2015). *Cultural Techniques: Grids, Filters, Doors, and Other Articulations of the Real*. Translated by Geoffrey Winthrop-Young. New York: Fordham University Press.

Tanaka, Yuko. (2013). *The Power of the Weave: The Hidden Meanings of Cloth*. Tokyo: International House of Japan.

Thompson, E. P., and Peter Linebaugh. (2013). *William Morris: Romantic to Revolutionary*. Oakland, CA: PM Press.

Torimaru, Tomoko. (2018). "Considerations on the Origin of Textiles + Uzbek Tablet Weaving." In Slow Fiber Studio, San Francisco, CA.

Urton, Gary. (1998). "From Knots to Narratives: Reconstructing the Art of Historical Record Keeping in the Andes from Spanish Transcriptions of Inka Khipus." *Ethnohistory* 45 (3): 409–38.

Venkat, Swati. (2014). "Reinventing the Wheel: Technologies in Gandhi's Khadi Movement 1919-1935." [MA Work]. London: Royal College of Art. https://www.rca.ac.uk/students/swati-venkat/ (accessed July 19, 2023).

Washburn, Dorothy K., and Donald W. Crowe, eds. (2004). *Symmetry Comes of Age: The Role of Pattern in Culture*. Seattle: University of Washington Press.

Weiner, Annette B., and Jane Schneider, eds. (2013). *Cloth and Human Experience*. Reprint edn. Washington, DC: Smithsonian Books.

Chapter 2

QUECHUA TEXTILITY

Archeological digs in Peru have led to the discovery of troves of ritual textiles and ceramics revealing a rich cultural legacy of pre-Columbian Peruvian cultures and civilizations. Apart from its Amazonian region, Peru has a dry desert climate which preserved textiles that have disappeared elsewhere. Archeological work has so far revealed diverse histories of textile going back 10,000 years and spanning many civilizations both in the Andes and along the desert coast (Dransart, 1999; Universidad Ricardo Palma et al., 2007; Harcourt, 1987). Visiting the Amano textile museum in Lima is a deeply moving experience: the array of sophisticated pre-Columbian textiles there, spanning successive and contiguous civilizations up to the times of the Incas boggles the mind, especially as their colors and many intricate ornamentations have remained steadfast across millennia. And even more touching are the remnants of everyday textiles, which are much rarer than the ritual textiles found in burial sites as they were not meant for preservation: there is nothing quite like discovering that the common check pattern was already in fashion some 2,000 years ago. Pre-Columbian textiles link together incommensurable worlds: cultures that existed without any external contact with other continents now address us across thousands of years, and the multisensorial qualities of textile mentioned in the first chapter play a unique role in creating such a phatic presence that bridges time and space. In Peru, we enter a pluriverse (de la Cadena and Blaser, 2018; Escobar, 2018): this newly shared presence of other worlds from past and the present does not mean that eventually otherness disappears into some kind of a global village; on the contrary, the richness of pre-Columbian textiles points in directions that are unknown to us, to other modes of being and existence. Importantly, pre-Columbian textiles are not like antique texts that depict a past long gone—they are live presences that currently play, in Peru, a fundamental role in allowing for new modes of existence to emerge (Berlo, 1992). This is due to the long history of Indigenous textile practices in Peru, which continue to the present day (Arnold and Dransart, 2014) and which are currently undergoing a revival as fair-trade textile production is being developed within the framework of neoliberal multiculturalism (Hale, 2005)—a set of policies that encourages and celebrates cultural differences in order to foster new economic markets (Figure 2.1). Within the neoliberal multiculturalist framework, locally

Figure 2.1 Textile market in Pisac, Peru. Courtesy of the author.

made commodities, especially the arts and crafts variety, gain monetary value by showcasing their otherness, their exoticism, and their association with simpler, more authentic ways of life. The question then arises about what happens when traditional textiles transition from the domestic and intracultural sphere to the sphere of global commodity capitalism, when Indigenous textile media encounter the dominant matrix of power.

In the previous chapter, I highlighted how textile functioned as a medium of communication until its appropriation by the dominant matrix of modernism, capitalism (at the time, industrial capitalism) and colonialism, and how such appropriation was not without intense political struggles, both in Europe (as we will further see in Chapter 3) and the rest of the world. Such struggles continue today as non-industrialized textiles, especially Indigenous craft textiles are being rediscovered and hailed in the search for alternatives to the dominant matrix and its relentless consumerism and exploitation. This chapter first looks at the long history of Indigenous textiles in Peru and their continuous encounter with the dominant matrix of power, in the past through colonialism, and today through mass tourism. I look specifically at Quechua textiles in the most visited region of Peru: Cusco and its neighboring towns, villages and Inca ruins, among which the world famous Macchu-Picchu. Beyond exploring the troubled context of neoliberal globalization for such rediscovery by the western world of Quechua textiles, I want to show how the question of making comes to the fore in the strategies developed by Quechua weavers to assert the mediating value of their textiles to non-Indigenous audiences. Making takes many guises, from questions about the quality of materials and the meaning of techniques to the display of the makers themselves as visible Indigenous interlocutors. I argue the following: that Quechua textiles are Indigenous media objects, but in order to be recognized as such in a context of mass tourism, this requires strategies for rendering visible the network of Indigenous textile-making. And I further argue in this chapter that the complex and paradoxical encounters and entanglements between Indigenous textile makers and mass tourism illustrate the capacity for textile to allow for plays of power, as mentioned in the introduction: to continue to escape and challenge the dominant matrix of power while at the same time being constantly subject to its dynamics of appropriation and exploitation.

Peru is a welcome shock to the western ideological system. The diversity of pre-Columbian Andean societies, their cultural and spiritual richness, their deep cosmovisions and complex rituals, their sophisticated technical and artistic knowledge, which they exchanged and circulated across the Andean mountains, along the desert coast and through the Amazonian jungle—all of this negates and puts to shame any colonial ideologies based on a supposed supremacy of European civilization. Despite centuries of brutal colonization that saw the systematic dismantlement and destruction of pre-Columbian techniques, knowledge and art, Peruvian Indigenous cultures and the continuation of textile practices from pre-Columbian times stand as a reminder of other possibilities, other ways of being, and of endurance. This chapter delves into the role textiles have played and continue playing in such history and in nurturing a broad reflection on crafting modes of existence, values and identities that work within (and yet at the same time against and outside of) the colonial and postcolonial power structures, including ones linked to capitalist exploitation. In Peru, indeed, we find at least 10,000 continuous years of textile making. While industrialization in Europe and North America has meant that making textile by hand almost disappeared until a recent revival through craft, everyday domestic weaving, knitting, crocheting and embroidery is still very much a norm in many regions of Peru. Many cultural and Indigenous groups in Peru have textile traditions that act both as a main identity marker against the legacy of colonialism and racism, and increasingly in tourist regions as an economic means of survival. In this new context, handmade traditional textile is invented as a vector of power—not of power over, but power to create other conditions of existence in the face of dominant systems of economic exploitation and cultural subjugation. What I am particularly interested in is this clash of power—the legacies of colonialism and the pressure of mass consumption and capitalism against the work of sustaining Indigenous existences. This creates a complex situation of power play, where, to borrow from Deleuze and Guattari, lines of flight emerge and create new existential terrains that are then at risk for appropriation and reterritorialization by neo-colonial and capitalist power formations.

Pre-Columbian Textiles: Media and Power

From a communication and media perspective, pre-Columbian Peru provides a unique site of analysis as its rich civilizations and complex societies operated with media systems that were vastly different from those of Europeans. These civilizations operated without written language and without paper (Boone and Mignolo, 1994), but they had codes and sign-systems based on textiles and ceramics, and a great number of such artefacts have been recently found and preserved. In addition, production of Indigenous textile never quite ceased despite relentless efforts to erase it throughout centuries of colonization.

Pre-Columbian textiles have been of particular interest to anthropologists, as "they provide a mirror in which the economic, social, political and religious development of every culture of ancient Peru is reflected, as well as defining the rank and status of the individual for whom they were made, possessing as they do a great mythical-sacred content through the incorporation of iconic elements" (Gheller Doig, 2017: 16). The oldest weavings found in Peru in the form of strings, baskets and matting date back to 8000 BCE (38), with wearable woven cloth made of cotton or wool appearing in 2500 BCE. While it would not be possible here to explore the many Pre-Columbian cultures that existed before Inca unification throughout the fifteenth and sixteenth century, one can nevertheless point out the immense cultural legacy of pre-Columbian textiles and the aesthetic and technical refinement they demanded. Pre-Columbian textiles displayed political and ideological power, both through garments and through large-scale decorative and functional pieces. The capacity to produce textile in that context is proof of the sophistication of pre-Columbian cultures in terms of agricultural skills for cultivating different kinds of plant (mostly cotton) and animal (especially camelids such as llamas, alpacas, guanacos and vicuñas) sources of fibers, technical ability in processing fibers into fine threads and dyeing them with natural dyes extracted from plants, insects, clay and minerals, and craftmanship and aesthetic sensibility in terms of weaving, embroidering or drawing onto cloth iconographic figures, symbols and patterns. The Nasca culture (100 BCE–800 CE) for instance represented the epitome of textile craftsmanship (Frame, 2004; Silverman, 2002; Martin, 2006), with knowledge about how to create 200 colors from natural materials and twenty textile techniques, many of which have been lost today (personal conversation). High-end textile production for the elite and for spiritual purposes was highly specialized and time-consuming. Many types of cloth were developed, from heavy alpaca (Trelles, 2005) to the lightest cotton gauze (Corcuera, 2015), with a wide array of textile techniques, including different kinds of complex weave structures, embroidering, lace work, tapestry and knitting. As demonstrated by pictorial illustrations on ceramics, for instance from the Moche (200–800 CE), weaving became a specialized craft early on (Quilter, 2011).

Throughout the different cultures of Peru, weaving was not simply a necessary practice for producing usable goods, but a medium that asserted continuity and power through time and space. Pre-Columbian textiles represented political and ideological power with garments for the elite featuring intricate design and time-consuming embellishments. There are several indications that clothing was closely associated with power, including mystical power. Moche ceramics for instance depict vanquished warriors being stripped of their clothes, and the Incas believed in burning the clothes of the enemy as a way to weaken them during military conflict (Murra, 1962: 718). Clothing indeed displayed physical and spiritual power. The Huari (600–900 CE) culture for instance is famous for embellishing garments dedicated to their elites with colorful feather embroidery (King, 2012: 3). The Incas (1200–1532 CE) embellished ritual garments with metalwork that could thus reflect light-rays and transformed the wearer into a sun-god (Dransart, 1999). Textile in those instances mediated supernatural and non-human powers onto the ruling elite, transforming the wearer into a broadcaster, a mediator and embodiment of those powers. The vast array of intricate pre-Columbian textiles demonstrated aesthetic sophistication, as well as a deep understanding of how the multisensorial qualities of textile could be mobilized to foster social hierarchies and differences: visual of course with the use of many color combinations, some tonal, others working with contrasting hues, but also haptic in the use of different techniques to play with varying degrees of thickness and weight. The contrast between a thick, colorful brocade tunic and one of fine, loosely woven white gauze, for instance, demonstrates the range of qualities that textile can evoke—sturdiness, longevity, embodied presence as opposed to lightness, weightlessness and ethereality. The majority of pre-Columbian textiles that have been found were the product of highly specialized labor at the service of ideological propagation that was not only political (Phipps, 2018; Hughes, 2010), but also spiritual. Indeed, a large part of the textiles that have been preserved to the resent day were meant for ritual purposes around death (Heckman, 2003). Pre-Columbian cultures overall saw a continuity between life and death and the burial process was meant to ensure that the newly departed could transition and travel to the realm of the dead. Special burial textiles were used, both as objects to accompany the departed and as mantles to protect and indicate special status, especially in the Paracas culture (700–100 BCE). The mantles and shrouds for burial were large pieces of textile. Murra, for instance, gives the example of 300 square yards (roughly 250 square meters) for one shroud, concluding: "how many woman-hours of weaving and spinning time involved is incalculable" (1962: 713).

By the time of the Spanish invasion of the Inca empire, cloth was used as currency and as an object of exchange and political negotiation. Instances of giving cloth to conclude military and diplomatic negotiations, as well as the mass distribution of cloth as a way to gain popular consent and assert power over conquered territories were common practices (Murra, 1962: 721). Also prevalent in the Inca empire was the use of textile to record and store information and therefore to administer all kinds of resources in a territory. *Quipus*—systems for recording information by using strings of ropes and knots—were widely used, and it has been noted that they acted in the same way as our contemporary databases (Urton and Llanos, 1997; Hoffman, 2014). They required a code in order to be deciphered, which was memorized and held by specific officials known as *quipucamayocs*. Another less understood mode of recording information was through *tocapus*, rectangular designs featured on textiles and ceramics, which have been found in different pre-Columbian cultures. *Tocapus* are in turn described as signs, symbols or graphs. In Inca culture, they are abstract geometric designs, and it is surmised that they indicated important information about the status of the wearer, including place and role in the hierarchy, group of origin and so on. Often, *tocapus* are described as pictorial designs that might have evolved into written language systems, with debates as to whether they are, for instance, akin to Egyptian hieroglyphs.

Overall, we see in pre-Columbian cultures an ongoing preoccupation with textile production especially for ideological, spiritual and political purposes that demonstrates the centrality of textile as a way to assert power, engage in intercultural exchanges, and reflect on one's places in complex cosmologies. Textile was a medium of communication that circulated throughout an immense territory by the time of the Inca empire: it displayed symbols and information, had a crucial role as a gift object that fostered new social relationships of obligations and acknowledgement, and its multisensorial qualities were used to display and broadcast superhuman and non-human qualities and power. Spanish colonization led to a complete destruction of textile systems and the imposition of both new aesthetics, new economic relations such as mercantilism and a change in techniques for textile production (Assadourian, 1992; Graubart, 2000). The arrival of smallpox along with the colonizers wiped out the majority of the Indigenous population, "from an estimated nine million people in the 1520s to only 600,000 a century later,"[1] leading to profound upheaval and the collapse of the socio-political system within which pre-Columbian textiles operated. The imposition of new systems and new technologies meant a complete destruction of traditional textile practices and structures. High-end textile production ceased and instead the colonial powers progressively imposed a new structure of *obrajes* (Assadourian, 1992: 64–65) or small factories devoted to the weaving of lower quality textiles for the general population, while higher quality textiles were imported. Sheep were introduced to produce wool cloth, and consequently, cotton production collapsed in most areas (ibid.). High-end textile techniques and skills were lost while a new aesthetics based on representation was imposed to replace the previous Inca aesthetic of abstract figures and use of geometric shapes (Allen, 1998). At the same time, a few traditional textile techniques and skills survived, especially for the making of Indigenous garments and objects. While the Spanish tried to force Indigenous populations to adopt western dress, Indigenous garments became a factor of resistance against colonialism and preservation of identity.[2]

Indigenous Identities in Contemporary Peru

Traditional textile in contemporary Peru is at a crossroads. Peru itself is now a mosaic of different identities and cultures: mestizos—people of mixed Amerindian and European heritage—represent 60 percent of the population, Indigenous people constitute a little over 25 percent of the population, including Highlands groups such as the Quechua (22.7%) and the Aymara (2.7%), as well as Amazonian groups (1.8%), some of them still uncontacted. Descendants of African slaves and of Asian immigration (China and Japan)[3] have had an important cultural presence and legacy, with white people representing a little less than 5 percent of the population. The question of Peruvian national identity and the space left for Indigenous people is a complex one, and while I cannot aim to explore all its intricacies here, I would like to offer a few pointers that are relevant for understanding contemporary traditional textiles in Peru. Overall, the question of Peruvian identity and Indigenous identity are contested and in flux, located at the crossroads of nationalist policies and ideologies (Callirgos, 2018), struggles for equality and access to civil rights (Garcia, 2003; 2005), cultural and land protection (McDonell, 2015), neoliberalist policies, and the rise of Indigenous activism as "eco-politics" (Greene, 2006: 353). The aftermath of the independence of Peru in 1821 saw the beginning of an ongoing political debate around defining a uniquely Peruvian identity. Political efforts to develop a Peruvian identity led to the creation of what Marisol de la Cadena calls *indigenismo*—a "modern intellectual, moral and political nationalist movement... which sought to root the image of Peru in its pre-Hispanic Inca tradition" (de la Cadena, 2001: 67) at the beginning of the twentieth century. Indigenismo was supposed to "produce a countrywide spiritual transformation that would, in turn, result in a unified and renovated culture-race purged of colonialism and rooted in national sentiment" (de la Cadena, 1998: 147). As de la Cadena explains, such a movement celebrated and idealized pre-Hispanic Inca traditions and defined a strong polarization between the educated urban elites in charge of directing the indigenismo project; poor, uneducated rural "Indians"; and mestizos defined as former Indians who had abandoned their traditional ways of life to move to cities and were accused of all sorts of degeneracy. Paradoxically, such a movement served to further other and racialize Indigenous people in multiple ways. First, Indigenous people from the Highlands were deemed uneducated and therefore unworthy of civic rights, and second, the purist view of what constituted "Indianness" pushed many Indigenous people who did not fit with the rural "Indian" traditional image to the margins. For this reason, Indigenous activists from the Highlands have reclaimed the identity of the *mestizo*:

> They use it to identify literate and economically successful people who share Indigenous cultural practices yet do not perceive themselves as miserable, a condition that they consider "Indian." Far from equating "Indigenous culture" with "being Indian"—a colonial label that carries an historical stigma of inferiority—they perceive Indianness as a social condition that reflects an individual's failure to achieve educational improvement. As a result of this redefinition, "Indigenous Andean culture" exceeds the scope of Indianness; it broadly includes Cuzqueno commoners who claim Indigenous cultural heritage, yet refuse to be labeled Indians. They proudly call themselves "mestizo," without, however, agreeing to disappear in the cultural national homogeneity that the current dominant definition of mestizo conveys.
>
> de la Cadena, 2001: 21–22

Third, the focus on an Inca heritage and efforts from governments to define Indigenous identity negated the specificities of other Indigenous groups in Peru, particularly Amazonians. As Greene (2006) explains, the early 2000s were marked by the rise of an alliance of Amazonian and Andean Indigenous groups against state-led efforts to define an Indigenous rights framework. Environmental advocacy in response to land exploitation and resource extraction by national and foreign companies as well as protection of Indigenous ways of life including scientific knowledge, cultural symbols and practices are all part of this new-wave activism, which not only has local or national but also important international repercussions with regard to the reality of human-produced climate change.

The question of Indigenous cultures and ways of life, which provide the context for traditional textile, has therefore long been a contentious one in Peru, not only for political reasons, but also for economic reasons. The more recent turn to neoliberal economic policies in Peru has meant refocusing the question of Indigenous culture as a market opportunity. The term "neoliberal multiculturalism" usefully encapsulates the state's promotion of "cultural-ethnic recognition, backed by the very global institutions of neoliberal development" (Greene, 2006: 330). This has typically given rise to forms of defense and promotion of Indigenous cultures, but only of these aspects of Indigenous cultures that could potentially fit into the development of economic opportunities. In Peru, this often takes the form of tourism, particularly cultural tourism and ecotourism, where the development of a tourist market is seen to be the way to ensure cultural survival and protection of environments. In addition, international trade partnerships, such as the one between Peru and Canada (2008) see the paradoxical development of the opening of lands to the foreign resource-extraction industries (which typically leads to destruction of habitat and eco-systems), foreign support for access to educational and health resources for Indigenous people, and foreign grants to develop and market Indigenous crafts on the global market. The question of contemporary traditional textiles in Peru has therefore to be seen in the context of these often-paradoxical claims of valorization and exploitation of Indigenous cultures, and the work on the ground by Indigenous groups and NGOs has to be located within this uneasy space where some aspects of Indigenous cultures are valorized, while Indigenous ways of life, including environmental rights and claims for civil rights are undermined. In response, traditional Indigenous textiles are invested with a wide array of potentials: protection and expression of cultural identity, social mobility, women's rights, economic opportunities. Also, as Marisol de la Cadena indicates (2015) Indigenous politics—as they engage with non-Indigenous worlds—struggle with neocolonial attempts to assign some fixed Indigenous identities belonging to the past, which erases the real and continuous fight to define what it means to be Indigenous in the present through constant encounters with the dominant matrix of power. Traditional textile, I argue, stands as a medium that carries these competing claims, existing in the tense space between power-over and power-against, between control and escape, between neoliberal territorialization and lines of flights towards other modes of existence.

The rediscovery of pre-Columbian symbols and abstract forms, particularly those of the Inca, played a key role in crafting a contemporary Peruvian aesthetic that could assert a link with Peru's past before the Spanish invasion, and this link, as I explore below, is the site of competing cultural claims. Furthermore, the discovery throughout the twentieth century and up to the present day of important archeological sites containing ceramics and textiles also played a central role in the promotion of pre-Columbian art and international appreciation of the richness of the varied modes of expression it carried, from exquisite representational ceramics (for instance, in the Moche culture) to stylized symbols and abstract geometric patterns. The growing knowledge of cultures predating the Incas has also provided a broader lens to look at a wide array of cultural references. Against indigenismo, standing as a specific form of racism based on cultural purity (de la Cadena, 2015), alternative cultures, subcultures and popular culture movements have claimed and embraced mixity and hybridity, particularly in the rise of Chicha culture (Cánepa, 2017).

The Revival of Quechua Textiles

Traditional Indigenous textile techniques were not officially valorized as an important cultural heritage in Peru until recently, when both international and national institutional support networks for traditional textiles started appearing. The case of traditional textiles in the Peruvian highlands around the Cusco region offers an illustration of this process of revival. In Cusco, this took place in the late 1970s. Historically in Cusco, traditional textiles were part of the struggle between claiming an Indigenous identity or, on the other hand, favoring industrially produced western-style clothing as a sign of progress, as a way to express social and economic aspirations for getting an education and stable job, of getting out of poverty and out of the margins of society (Femenias, 1994). This competition between pressures of assimilation to mainstream society and defense of Indigenous identity, along with the importance of traditional textiles for important ritual purposes echo some of the broader cultural conflicts in postcolonial Peru. The revival of textile traditions around Cusco started with informal gatherings of Quechua weavers within a context of growing international tourism and eventually resulted in organized and formalized weaving groups, the first and most famous of which are gathered under the umbrella of the Centro de Textiles Tradicionales del Cusco (CTTC). Nilda Alvarez, the founder of CTTC recalls training herself in traditional techniques as a child and teenager, selling her wares to tourists and realizing "that there was value in creating the more intricate, traditional styles rather than the usual simple pieces made of bright synthetic yarn that most people were weaving for the tourist trade" (Alvarez, 2007: 17). As a university student in Cusco supporting herself through weaving, she further noticed that "good traditional weaving was highly valued by collectors (ibid.)." The idea of providing economic income through the making and selling of traditional textiles was central for CTTC, whose mission statement is that it "enables the weavers to maintain their identity and textile traditions while improving their quality of life."[4] Interestingly, the revival of traditional textiles was always based on a link between inside and outside, between members of Indigenous communities and the external world of collectors, researchers and tourists. This dynamic alliance was particularly central to the birth and continuing success of CTTC. As Alvarez further recalls, informal gatherings of young weavers in the 1990s (Alvarez et al., 2017: 3–4) to learn weaving techniques and patterns that could be used as a source of revenue was financially sponsored and personally supported by a couple of American researchers (Elizabeth and David VanBuskirk) who were fascinated by Quechua culture. The group grew in size and scope and now comprises around 200 young weavers, organized in different local groups, who go on to subsequently join adult weaving groups. The organization of weavers into groups gained popularity beyond CTTC, enabling weavers to pool resources, establish support networks and engage in advocacy and development of the traditional textile tourist market.

The success of CTTC and of the revival of traditional textiles in the Cusco regions did not simply involve producing traditional textiles to sell to the external tourist market; it has also required a set of strategies to highlight for tourists the uniqueness of traditional textiles beyond their aesthetic aspects. That is to say, while the meanings of traditional textiles include their undeniably high aesthetic qualities and exquisite craftmanship, a large part of their effort has been focused on promoting textile as a carrier, a medium for Indigenous identity and ways of life in contrast to the dominant, fast-paced, consumption-based way of life that most tourists experience. This involves casting traditional textiles not so much as objects, but as mediators through which specific sets of relationships between tourists and Indigenous interlocutors can be established. Today, 3.1 million people visit Machu Picchu every year, and almost all these visitors will have to spend at least two to three days in Cusco and around in order to acclimatize to the altitude. This has allowed for the development of tourist infrastructures in the region, including a "discourse network" around traditional textiles. I use the term discourse networks in reference to Friedrich Kittler's book (1992), which describes the networks of institutional, technical and human relays that create a communication infrastructure through which specific discourses can reach an audience, in this case, international tourists. This kind of network has an educational purpose: it aims to educate tourists about the importance and aesthetic value of traditional textiles, and about their cultural significance and crucial importance to maintain, support and develop Indigenous ways of life. CTTC, for instance, has a museum, organizes events with local and international participants, offers weaving classes and weaving tours to tourists, sells publications as well as textiles. The educational focus is partly on traditional textiles as a link to a pre-Columbian past and therefore as a mode of resistance against colonialism. In addition, educational texts focus on the meaning of the patterns—how they derive from the natural world (e.g., landscapes, rivers, animals), but also from important gestures of communion with an environment. For instance, one of the simplest patterns taught to foreigners at CTTC is called *Kuti* and mimics the gesture of using a hoe for digging up potatoes—one of the prized Indigenous crops of the Andes, which boast over 3,800 potato varietals that have been cultivated since the Neolithic period. The handout to foreign tourists taking a weaving class at CTTC insists on the link between the habitual and ancestral manual gesture of harvesting and its spiritual dimension: "...some weavers say that this design represents the beginning and returning of time, or the continuous run of time in a cyclical pattern." Such messages that link traditional textile objects and patterns with a deep Andean cosmovision that celebrates a profound relationship with the environment are repeated in all textile and cultural institutions in the region, from large museums to weavers' cooperatives, and that echoes contemporary discourses about forging Indigenous, non-capitalist, decolonial relationships under the umbrella concepts of *sumak kawsay* (Quechua for "good living") and *buen vivir* (Spanish version). And indeed, while the term discourse network might conjure up a certain abstraction of information as it circulates in immaterial forms through networks and cables, the discourse network around traditional textiles in the Cusco region is about materializing complex spiritual ideas and values: it is about making tangible Indigenous Andean cosmovision.

Such making tangible also takes place through offering textile classes to foreigners. It is interesting to note that even though an institution at the forefront of the promotion of traditional textile such as CTTC offers spinning, weaving and knitting classes, those are limited to teaching the basics over a maximum of three days. CTTC states on its website that it:

> ...does not offer more than three days of classes in any given course out of respect for the weavers. This knowledge is their cultural patrimony and heritage. They choose to share it with you out of a desire that more people should come to respect Cusqueñan textiles, and a belief that one of the best ways to foster this respect is to teach the very basics of techniques and designs. If you would like to learn more about the intellectual rights of Indigenous peoples, we suggest the book *Who Owns Native Culture?* by Michael F. Brown.
>
> Centro de Textiles Tradicionales del Cusco: n.p.

Such a statement echoes many instances of Indigenous textile makers protecting their traditional textiles from cultural and commercial appropriation by pushing back against the fashion industry for using and copying traditional designs without permission and arguing for better protection of their intellectual property. CTTC therefore sets a framework for the relationships between external actors and Indigenous weaver: knowledge can be exchanged for as long as it promotes an appreciation of traditional textiles and their makers, but making has to remain in the hands of the Indigenous weavers. The classes thus serve a dual function: they make it possible for foreigners to directly experience how complex traditional textiles are and to gain a new respect for the weavers. Further, by setting a limit on how much can be learnt through making, weavers themselves are appropriately promoted as guardians of cultural tradition and the only enduring makers of traditional textiles. Again, a set of material practices enables setting up the parameters of the relationships between foreigners and textile, and in so doing, makes visible the labor, skills and crucial importance of the weavers.

Such discourse around traditional textile circulates not only through educational texts and actors—pamphlets, guide books, tourist guides and so on—as well as educational practices, but also involves providing foreigners experiences with Indigenous interlocutors along the tourist circuits: weaving demonstrations by artisans wearing traditional clothing, opportunities to feed and pet alpacas and lamas, visiting textile markets in traditional villages and towns such as Pisac and Chinchero and talking to women weavers there, and taking pictures (in exchange for a tip) of women and children with their pet alpacas dressed in festive outfits in the historical downtown center of Cusco and around textile markets. This network is based on constructing an experience of cultural authenticity for tourists (Hill, 2008). How Indigenous interlocutors, principally women in the case of textile, present themselves and construct an Indigenous identity for tourists is crucial. Such transformation of cultural capital (indigeneity) as economic capital is mediated through traditional clothing. And such performance of identity for a specific audience raises critical questions, particularly whether the commodification of Indigenous identity might actually lead to a hollowing out of Indigenous identity as pure spectacle. Furthermore, it is recognized that for some, engaging in performance of Indigenous identity opens up new forms of marginalization, racism, sexism and exploitation. This is particularly the case with the *Sacamefotos*—women dressed in traditional festive clothing posing for tourists in exchange for a tip—who are often subject to "social condemnation from within and outside of their communities" because they are perceived as little more than beggars who distort the purpose of traditional festive clothing to attract the tourist's gaze (Ypeij, 2012: 32). In the Cusco region, however, women weavers wearing traditional clothes tend to have more positive experiences of exchange with tourists. The work of promoting traditional textiles for women weavers still involves "Indigenous femininity, female bodies, clothing, and weaving art as they mirror tourists' desire for romantic images" (Ypeij, 2012: 31). However, women weavers are particularly successful in benefiting from this translation of cultural capital into economic capital as some have become important income generators for their families, enabling a new form of "social mobility," especially as their "economic success challenges the linkage between ethnicity and class and the related association between femininity, indigenousness, and poverty" (ibid.). Such displays of Indigenous identity through dress are also accompanied by a set of strategies to foster personal, one-on-one relationships between tourists and women weavers. This aspect of the traditional textile discourse network is based on fostering affective bonds that further deepen tourists' experiences and is expressed in multiple ways. In stores selling high-quality traditional textiles, there is an extra tag for each piece stating the name of the weaver, along with a short bio that explains to the potential buyer who the weaver is and the specific community she is part of, what her intentions were in creating this particular piece using specific patterns, and which human values she hopes to communicate through her craft. As such, buying provides a degree of intercultural and interpersonal connection, rather than self-centered commodity consumption. In textile centers, women weavers not only talk to tourists directly to explain traditional textile processes, but they also do so in domestic, intimate settings, transforming domestic space into spaces to further display Indigenous bodies, identities and practices (Garcia, 2018). In Chinchero, for instance, where the revival of traditional textiles for tourist markets started, women's textile groups and cooperatives are located in traditional houses, with low benches and a traditional wood-fired kitchen, complete with guinea pigs under the hearth, and used to demonstrate the traditional natural dye processes. Visiting these places is completely different from instructional museum visits—they are based on demonstrating skills as much as having interpersonal communication and exchanges that establish appreciation of traditional crafts and skills, and rely on a level of trust (Figures 2.2, 2.3, 2.4 and 2.5).

Figure 2.2 Demonstration of cochineal dyeing, Cinchero. Courtesy of the author.

Figure 2.3 Backstrap weaving demonstration, Cinchero. Courtesy of the author.

Figure 2.4 Explanation of weaving pattern. Courtesy of the author.

Confronting Appropriation

Ultimately, the point of this discourse network around textiles is to convince tourists to purchase textile, or at least gain an appreciation that they can then propagate back home, when they talk to others about their experiences with Indigenous pre-Columbian cultures of the Andes. While traditional textiles in the Cusco regions are hailed as a success story, there are however a set of deep tensions around textile that reveal a more complex struggle between traditional textiles and how they are embedded within competing economic models. While the model put forward by places like CTTC is about making it possible for weavers to transform traditional textiles into sources of income that allow for social mobility, ongoing expression and exploration of cultural identity, and communicating such identities internationally, other models are based on constant competition to lower prices to capture a bigger share of the tourist market as well as commodity fetishism based on the otherness of Quechua culture. Quechua textiles exist in a state of ambiguity: the efforts from women weavers to educate and reach out to tourists, to foster genuine connections, even for a moment, are often part of a strategy to counter a broader set of commodification and economic and cultural appropriation of traditional textiles. At the same time, there is sometimes real competition among textile groups, leading to questions of renewed exploitation (Garcia, 2018) and the shortcutting of traditional production processes. The core of the issue lies in how the value of traditional textiles is defined and perceived. In the Cusco region,

Figure 2.5 Finished textile wares. Courtesy of the author.

traditional textiles involve alpaca wool that is hand spun, naturally dyed and woven using a backstrap loom. All three processes are time-consuming and require expert knowledge. Typically, tourists are completely unaware of the time and effort spent on producing traditional textiles, which is why demonstrations are so crucial to the strategy of local weaving groups: it is only through demonstrating each step of the process that tourists can gain an appreciation of at least the human labor time involved in the making of traditional textiles, and it is through the development of moments of interpersonal connection with weavers that tourists can start understanding how traditional textile practices confer a sense of dignity and are a crucial medium of cultural expression. These strategies might in turn have an influence on the perception of the monetary value of such textiles. Handmade traditional textile using traditional techniques are quite expensive compared to other textiles found in Cusco. For instance, a poncho might sell for 40 USD in one store, but a traditionally made poncho will sell for over 600 USD. The differences between the two items are quickly obvious: knock-offs and imitations are not as sophisticated and intricate as the original, and do not feature the complex and time-consuming back-strap weaving techniques. In the competition between these two items, we experience the current struggle over textile as a low-value commodity for personal consumption, and textile as a carrier of important cultural values and ways of life that are opposed to capitalist exploitation. Materially and technically, the difference between the knock-off and the traditionally made textile object also involves the use of synthetic materials as opposed to alpaca; machine-spinning and use of synthetic dyes as opposed to hand-spinning and natural dyes; automated power loom as opposed to backstrap loom; and cheap labor, including prison labor at times, from China or Bolivia. Economically, the knock-offs that are found everywhere in Cusco and the region feed into the stereotypical neocolonial belief, reinforced throughout the tourist literature (guidebooks, blogs and online reviews) that developing countries should amply provide for the budget traveler and that tourists should seek the lowest bargain possible. The market for antique traditional textiles is also not exempt from ruthless economic exploitation, albeit one that usually takes the form of buying personally meaningful textiles from impoverished families that are far from urban centers and selling these antiques to the collector market at a high price.

Economic and cultural appropriation of traditional textiles takes on multiple forms and reveals some of the complex tensions in the constant competition between traditionally made textiles and textiles that imitate or are derived from them. For instance, high-end companies such as KUNA and Sol Alpaca have established successful businesses developing alpaca and vicuña clothing lines that are inspired loosely by Quechua culture. Their stores can be found in the downtown of major cities such as Lima, as well as at many shopping malls in Peruvian airports. These lines include vague references to Andean cultures, claiming a synthesis between millennia of craftmanship on the one hand and high-end technical innovation and innovative, contemporary design on the other. While they use locally produced wools, these lines of clothing are made using automated machines and processes that are not traditional. Moreover, their designs are loosely inspired by pre-Columbian and Quechua ones, but reinterpreted to appeal to the global consumer market. In other words, closeness by geographic proximity (the Andes) and use of materials (alpacas and vicuñas) results in a claim of legitimate cultural affiliation. This interesting rhetorical exercise in the marketing of high-end alpaca products reveals an uneasy dynamic for textile companies that obey the dual logic of the global fashion market of crafting an authentic identity while producing industrial goods at a large scale. It is interesting to note that the references to Andean cultures, including magic, mysticism, wisdom and mystery are key to this kind of commodity fetishism whereby the actual conditions of production—automated machinery for large market, as opposed to small-scale manual production by Indigenous people—can get hidden away.

The competition between different types of textile, from traditionally made to knock-offs, also means that individual weavers and weaving groups themselves have to deal with market pressures and consequently have developed a range of responses and tactics. Places like CTTC and their affiliated groups do not deviate from the traditional techniques and processes for making traditional textile and acknowledge that in consequence, the price point for their textile means that it will not appeal to most tourists. CTTC is aware that its wares appeal to a niche clientele that is not necessarily a luxury crowd, but one that appreciates traditional textile techniques and is open to directly supporting Indigenous weavers. Other actors focus on lowering production costs by using machine-spun wool, synthetic dyes that mimic natural colors, and floor-looms, thus being able to claim that they are still selling hand-woven textiles, albeit ones that are not made using the original traditional processes. Many weavers and knitters, particularly those working by themselves, also rely on synthetic wools, producing wares whose quality is lower than the traditional ones, but still have a handmade feel to them and can be sold as part of an interpersonal connection with tourists. Weaving groups also deal with the pressures to offer lower prices by widening the range of textiles at their centers, from machine knit scarves to traditionally made textiles, thus appealing to the collectors, the textile enthusiast, the tourist in search of nice presents and the one in search of cheap trinkets. There are, however, real concerns that the demand for lower prices might lead some to cut too many corners, and in so doing devalue the reputation of what is labelled "traditional" textiles from the Cusco region.

Overall, it is important to note that traditionally made textiles and traditional weavers in the Cusco region occupy a central and yet complex and uneasy space: they constitute an unavoidable reference point despite being subject to all kinds of exploitation. The dominant framework under which they have been forced to evolve—that of indigeneity defined through the lens of mass tourism—further highlights some of the profound contradictions and limitations of the neoliberal approach to indigeneity: one that as Greg Coulthard (2014) shows seemingly accepts indigeneity, but only if it fits into the dominant capitalist worldview. And yet, the knock-off market as well as the luxury market still rely on the presence of rich and intricate textiles made and worn by Quechua people in order to create a desire for commodity purchase. However, these markets establish Indigenous textiles as an abstract sign and a blurry and unclear one as well, but one that encompasses values such as authenticity, simplicity, tradition and otherness—a grab bag of commodity fetishism. On the other hand, local weavers materialize Indigenous textiles not only through making them, but through making visible and tangible the human labor and ways of life associated with them. Traditional textile in this particular configuration are not vague abstract signs, but key levers to enact and make visible modes of existence that are not based on capitalist logics, but on social equity. Traditional textile embodies and materializes a specific Indigenous discourse network that materializes through gestures, encounters and relays key values about what it means to be Indigenous. This discourse network is about the materialization and actualization of such values through relational encounters, between tourists and weavers, between weavers and their materials, between makers and those who, by and large, have rarely engaged in making as a form of expression, between capitalist subjects and non-western, non-capitalist, Indigenous cosmovisions. There is therefore a competition and uneasy coexistence between capitalist models based on economic exploitation and commodity fetishism and the model put forward by Indigenous weaving groups of promoting traditional textile outside of their communities in order to attain social equity.

We thus see tremendous efforts on the part of Indigenous makers to establishing traditional Quechua textile techniques as the key cultural focal point for a space like the Cusco region, which articulates together Pre-Columbian and postcolonial local and national identities and political struggles with global tourist flows. In that regard, Quechua textile like the ones developed in the Cusco region by organized groups such as CTTC work to create bridges between Indigenous and non-Indigenous world. As Marisol de la Cadena (2015) explores, this kind of struggle to establish the relations between Indigenous and non-Indigenous worlds that are fundamentally divergent is a difficult exercise in resisting the folding of Indigenous worlds into the dominant world. With Indigenous textiles, this is made all the more complicated as the very infrastructure that links Indigenous and non-Indigenous worlds is one that actualizes the specific interests of the dominant matrix of power. The careful delineation of what foreigners can experience and how they get to learn about Indigenous textiles showcase the struggle to establish links between worlds that have nothing in common. If anything, this gestures towards de la Cadena's proposal for cosmovivir: "a politics that, rather than requiring sameness, would be underpinned by divergence" (de la Cadena, 2015: 285–86). It is key to note that this struggle takes place at the level of everyday encounter, in seemingly small gestures of encounter, trade and exchange. And for this reason as well, Quechua textiles still exist in precarious positions within multiple dynamics of cultural and technical appropriation and exploitation. The biggest trouble, perhaps, is the lack of recognition outside of the Quechua artisan community and archeology groups of textile as a medium of communication. More often than not, Quechua textiles are still seen by tourists as quaint cultural forms of expression for a small community of women, rather than sophisticated forms of engagement with Quechua cosmovision, ways of life and philosophy. This is not just a contemporary phenomenon, but one that has been taking place since colonization. The response from Quechua weavers has been to invest in and shape the space of Cusco tourism: to inhabit it both physically and symbolically through objects, demonstrations, and wearing Quechua clothing which then become nodes in an emerging educational discourse network. Overall, the main dynamic used has been to make makers visible as interlocutors that can talk about traditional textiles and establish their meaningfulness and to explain why and how they matter. Such discourse network establishes boundaries that attempt to contain forms of appropriation as much as it establishes a relational framework whereby the textile makers stand as interlocutor from the Quechua world, not just as silent or invisible worker. Such troubling of the space of commodity exchange (i.e., tourism) is not the only tactic employed by Indigenous weavers in Peru, as we shall see in Chapters 4 and 6, where we will see self-reflection from a decolonial trajectory, and a radical challenging of consumer perceptions, respectively. But before we can get there, let me continue in the following chapter with the question of making as a political act of mediation and engagement with power and how this, in turn, raises questions around technique and creativity. Let's go closer geographically and historically to the center of the dominant matrix of power and examine weaving technologies in France in the nineteenth century—particularly the Jacquard mechanism—and its less understood history, and the imagining of textile as a digital medium.

Notes

1 http://worldpopulationreview.com/countries/peru-population/.
2 http://www.textilescusco.org/andean-textiles.
3 http://worldpopulationreview.com/countries/peru-population/.
4 CTTC "Meet the Weavers" page. https://www.textilescusco.org/our-communities/.

References

Allen, Catherine J. (1998). "When Utensils Revolt: Mind, Matter, and Modes of Being in the Pre-Columbian Andes." *RES: Anthropology and Aesthetics*, no. 33: 18–27. http://www.jstor.org/stable/20166999.

Alvarez, Nina Callanaupa. (2007). *Weaving in the Peruvian Highlands: Dreaming Patterns, Weaving Memories.* Cusco: Centro de Textiles Tradicionales del Cusco.

Alvarez, Nina Callanaupa, and The Weavers of the Center for Traditional Textiles of Cusco. (2017). *Secrets of Spinning, Weaving and Knitting in the Peruvian Highlands.* Cusco: Centro de Textiles Tradicionales del Cusco.

Arnold, Denise Y., and Penny Dransart, eds. (2014). *Textiles, Technical Practice and Power in the Andes.* London: Archetype Books.

Assadourian, Carlos Sempat. (1992). "The Colonial Economy: The Transfer of the European System of Production to New Spain and Peru." *Journal of Latin American Studies* 24 (S1): 55–68. https://doi.org/10.1017/S0022216X00023774.

Berlo, Janet Catherine. (1992). "Beyond Bricolage: Women and Aesthetic Strategies in Latin American Textiles." *RES: Anthropology and Aesthetics*, no. 22 (October): 115–34. http://www.jstor.org/stable/20166857.

Boone, Elizabeth Hill, and Walter D. Mignolo, eds. (1994). *Writing Without Words: Alternative Literacies in Mesoamerica and the Andes*. 2nd edn. Durham, NC: Duke University Press Books.

Brown, Michael F. (2003). *Who Owns Native Culture?* Cambridge, MA: Harvard University Press.

Callirgos, Juan Carlos. (2018). "Neoliberal Discourses and Ethnonormative Regime in Post-Recognition Peru: Redefining Hierarchies and Identities." *Cultural Studies* 32 (3): 477–96. https://doi.org/10.1080/09502386.2017.1420088.

Cánepa, Gisela. (2017). "Chicha and Huayno: Andean Music and Culture in Lima." In *The Lima Reader: History, Culture, Politics*. Edited by Carlos Aguirre and Charles F. Walker, 232–35. New York: Duke University Press.

Corcuera, Ruth. (2015). *Gasas prehispánicas*. Buenos Aires: CIAFIC.

de la Cadena, Marisol. (1998). "Silent Racism and Intellectual Superiority in Peru." *Bulletin of Latin American Research* 17 (2): 143–64. http://www.jstor.org/stable/3339226.

de la Cadena, Marisol. (2001). "Reconstructing Race: Racism, Culture and Mestizaje in Latin America." *NACLA Report on the Americas* 34 (6): 16–23. https://doi.org/10.1080/10714839.2001.11722585.

de la Cadena, Marisol. (2015). *Earth Beings: Ecologies of Practice across Andean Worlds*. Illustrated edn. Durham, NC: Duke University Press.

de la Cadena, Marisol, and Mario Blaser, eds. (2018). *A World of Many Worlds*. Illustrated edn. Durham, NC: Duke University Press.

Dransart, Penny. (1999). "Clothed Metal and the Iconography of Human Form among the Incas." In *Precolumbian Gold: Technology, Style and Iconography*. Edited by Colin McEwan, 76–91. London: British Museum Press.

Escobar, Arturo. (2018). *Designs for the Pluriverse: Radical Interdependence, Autonomy, and the Making of Worlds*. Illustrated edn. Durham, NC: Duke University Press.

Femenías, Blenda. (1994). "Ethnic Artists and the Appropriation of Fashion: Embroidery and Identity in the Colca Valley, Peru." *Textile Society of America Symposium Proceedings*, January. http://digitalcommons.unl.edu/tsaconf/1058.

Frame, Mary. (2004). "Motion Pictures: Symmetry as Animator, Classifier, and Syntax in the Nasca Embroideries of Peru." In *Symmetry Comes of Age: The Role of Pattern in Culture*. Edited by Dorothy K. Washburn. Seattle: University of Washington Press.

García, María Elena. (2003). "The Politics of Community: Education, Indigenous Rights, and Ethnic Mobilization in Peru." *Latin American Perspectives* 30 (1): 70–95. https://doi.org/10.1177/0094582X02239145.

García, María Elena. (2005). *Making Indigenous Citizens: Identities, Education, and Multicultural Development in Peru*. Stanford University Press.

Garcia, Pablo. (2018). "Weaving for Tourists in Chinchero, Peru." *Journal of Material Culture* 23 (1): 3–19. https://doi.org/10.1177/1359183517725098.

Gheller Doig, Roberto. (2017). *Textiles of Ancient Peru – Tejidos Del Peru Antiguo*. Lima.

Graubart, Karen B. (2000). "Weaving and the Construction of a Gender Division of Labor in Early Colonial Peru." *American Indian Quarterly* 24 (4): 537–61. http://www.jstor.org/stable/1185889.

Greene, Shane. (2006). "Getting over the Andes: The Geo-Eco-Politics of Indigenous Movements in Peru's Twenty-First Century Inca Empire." *Journal of Latin American Studies* 38 (2): 327–54. http://www.jstor.org/stable/3875502.

Hale, Charles R. (2005). "Neoliberal Multiculturalism." *PoLAR: Political and Legal Anthropology Review* 28 (1): 10–19. https://doi.org/10.1525/pol.2005.28.1.10.

Harcourt, Raoul D'. (1987). *Textiles of Ancient Peru and Their Techniques.* Seattle: University of Washington Press.

Heckman, Andrea M. (2003). *Woven Stories: Andean Textiles and Rituals.* Albuquerque NM: University of New Mexico Press.

Hill, M. (2008). "Inca of the Blood, Inca of the Soul: Embodiment, Emotion, and Racialization in the Peruvian Mystical Tourist Industry." *Journal of the American Academy of Religion* 76 (2): 251–79. https://doi.org/10.1093/jaarel/lfn007.

Hoffmann, Carmen Arellano. (2014). *Sistemas de notación inca: Quipu y Tocapu : actas del simposio internacional, Lima 15-17 de enero de 2009.* Ministerio de Cultura, Museo Nacional de Arqueología, Antropología e Historia del Perú.

Hughes, Lauren Finley. (2010). "Weaving Imperial Ideas: Iconography and Ideology of the Inca Coca Bag." *TEXTILE* 8 (2): 148–78. https://doi.org/10.2752/17518351 0X12791896965538.

King, Heidi. (2012). *Peruvian Featherworks: Art of the Precolumbian Era.* New York: Metropolitan Museum of Art.

Kittler, Friedrich. (1992). *Discourse Networks 1800/1900.* Translated by Michael Metteer. Stanford, CA: Stanford University Press.

Martin, Lois. (2006). "Nasca: Woven Cosmos and Cross-Looped Time." *Textile: The Journal of Cloth & Culture* 4 (3): 312–38. https://doi.org/10.2752/147597506778691530.

McDonell, Emma. (2015). "The Co-Constitution of Neoliberalism, Extractive Industries, and Indigeneity: Anti-Mining Protests in Puno, Peru." *The Extractive Industries and Society* 2 (1): 112–23. https://doi.org/10.1016/j.exis.2014.10.002.

Murra, John V. (1962). "Cloth and Its Functions in the Inca State." *American Anthropologist* 64 (4): 710–28. http://www.jstor.org/stable/667788.

Phipps, Elena. (2018). "Garments, Tocapu, Status, and Identity." In *The Oxford Handbook of the Incas.* Edited by Sonia Alconini and P. Alan Covey. New York: Oxford University Press.

Quilter, Jeffrey. (2011). *The Moche of Ancient Peru: Media and Messages.* Cambridge, MA: Peabody Museum Press.

Silverman, Helaine. (2002). "Differentiating Paracas Necropolis and Early Nasca Textiles." In *Andean Archaeology II: Art, Landscape, and Society.* Edited by Helaine Silverman and William H. Isbell, 71–105. Boston, MA: Springer.

Trelles, Lucila Castro de. (2005). *Los Tejedores de Santiago de Chuco y Huamachuco, de Cumbicus a Mitayos, Obrajeros y Mineros.* Lima: Minera Barrick.

Universidad Ricardo Palma and Instituto Cultural Peruano Norteamericano. 2007. *La trama y la urdimbre: textiles tradicionales del Perú.* Lima: Universidad Ricardo Palma and ICPNA.

Urton, Gary, and Primitivo Nina Llanos. (1997). *The Social Life of Numbers: A Quechua Ontology of Numbers and Philosophy of Arithmetic.* Austin: University of Texas Press.

Ypeij, Annelou. (2012). "The Intersection of Gender and Ethnic Identities in the Cuzco–Machu Picchu Tourism Industry: Sácamefotos, Tour Guides, and Women Weavers." *Latin American Perspectives* 39 (6): 17–35. https://doi.org/10.1177/0094582X12454591.

Part II

TECHNOLOGY AND IMAGINATION

Chapter 3

JACQUARD AND THE CREATIVITY OF EXTENSIONS

Textile weavers in Europe were among the first to see their entire livelihoods fall apart through automation of the workplace and subjection to industrial capitalist logics. Combined with an already long-established global colonial textile trade network of raw fibers, dye products, and finished cloths alongside the millions of enslaved people forced to work the cotton fields in the Americas, a technological device—the power loom—propelled the United Kingdom to the status of global superpower in the nineteenth century. This "Empire of Cotton" (Beckert, 2015) saw the articulation of scientific and technical innovations with new ideas around labor management and the rationalization of work productivity to answer to the constant demand for new markets and ever-increasing profits. And ever-increasing profits required lowering wages and the price of raw materials by all means possible, from violent repression to enslavement to the replacement of human workers by machines. Textile weavers were the first to suffer from and rebel against this new state of affairs, which we now describe as the great industrial revolution of the nineteenth century. In that regard, they were a key instance of an early attempt to delink from a new articulation at the time of the dominant matrix of power: the leveraging of scientific and technical innovation for capitalist expansionist logics. In the UK, the Luddites were first composed of textile weavers who saw the introduction of new technologies as threat to their survival. Automation meant de-skilling, job loss, lower wages, as well as loss of meaning. Similarly in nineteenth-century Lyon—then the center of silk-weaving in France— the silk-weavers organized the first ever labor-driven social movement in history, with the motto: "*Vivre en travaillant ou mourir en combatant*" (my translation: "Live working or die fighting"). Notice here that the meaningfulness of work—not only living wages, but also pride in one's craft and one's sense of identity as skilled maker—were equally threatened with the arrival of the new industrial machines combined with attempts to increase productivity and lower wages. In subsequent mainstream accounts, the Luddites are often described as anti-technology, and their refusal of automated technology has since been equated with a refusal against progress. But the Luddites and the Lyon silk-weavers, better-known as the *Canuts*, were not against technology per se. Rather, they were against a certain type of technological development that would alienate them from the product of their labor, not only economically in the classical Marxist sense, but also existentially.

To be a weaver is to engage daily, repeatedly and profoundly with technical tools and machines in order to produce woven cloth. The meaning of such cloth was varied: obviously it was a necessity carrying a price, but also a mode of cultural expression.

In this chapter, I am particularly interested in the production of highly intricate woven silk cloth including brocade, damask, matelassé (whose techniques originally came from China during the Silk Roads), which required professional skills and complex and high-end technical set-up and innovations, including the world-renowned *Jacquard mechanism*. The pride taken by highly skilled artisans in producing these exquisite and intricate woven silks and to see it become a source of desire and admiration the world over needs to be acknowledged in order to understand what was erased by mass industrialization. Indeed, and this is one of the core arguments of this chapter, mass industrialization of textile weaving took place at the very moment when the potential of textile as a modern medium was being formulated. In particular, the high-end silk cloth produced in Lyon, France at the time, made possible by technical innovations culminating with the Jacquard mechanism (Figure 3.1), reflected multiple and new understandings of textile as a *digital* medium: not only as a rich mode of cultural expression or object of desire and admiration, but also as a way for using digital technologies to create intricate visual representations and patterns capable of surpassing the existing old and new visual media of the time—painting, engraving and photography. The Jacquard mechanism is the key invention epitomizes this moment of bifurcations in nineteenth-century Lyon silk-weaving away from the logic of ever-increasing capitalist productivity towards exploring the creative potentials in augmenting bodies and mind via technology. In this chapter, I argue that there is a profound misunderstanding of the Jacquard mechanism and its place within the intertwined histories of industrial capitalism and digital computing: before it was further assembled into the capitalist machine, the Jacquard mechanism spurred a flurry of creativity that had nothing to do with the capitalist production of commodities, and everything to do with a kind of cyborg creativity.

The Jacquard Mechanism, Automation, and Digital Media

While media theory has long posited media as distinct and separate from other technologies because of their specific focus on the broadcasting of immaterial information, signs and discourses, the present situation offers quite a different scene, which offers a useful parallel with the invention of the Jacquard mechanism and the power loom in the context of eighteenth- and nineteenth-century industrial capitalism. With the rise of digital, networked media in an intensively capitalist-oriented environment, there is a reconceptualization of media away from the production and broadcasting of content alone, to the capacity to connect information to different targets in order to control, organize and modulate all aspects of individual and collective life, in both local and global contexts (Bucher, 2018). While media has always been a key part of industrial production and diverse

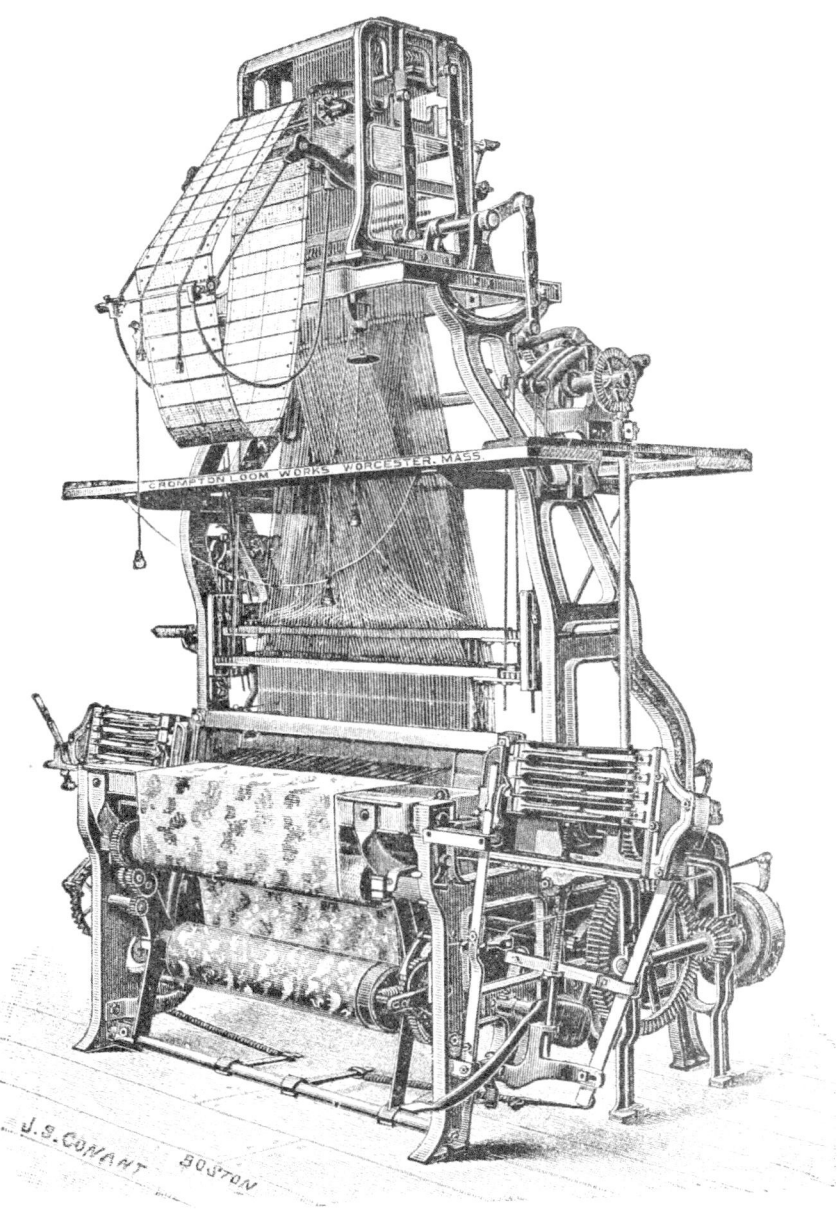

Figure 3.1 Carpet loom with Jacquard attachment, 1891, author unknown. Courtesy of Wikimedia Commons.

forms of governance, they have now risen to prominence in new ways: software, algorithms, big data and augmented intelligence have taken on the automated responsibility of management of all aspects of human life, embedding them within diverse infrastructures, from supermarket to cities, from transportation to health and fitness. In such a context, there is a greater autonomy for "intelligent" media systems to make decisions and enact specific courses of action, with little human oversight (Parisi, 2019). Hence, the current worries and intense discussion around AI and ethics, around the biases that can be embedded into automated systems, around data justice and the generalized risk of humans ceding autonomy to intelligent machines (Eubanks, 2018; Noble, 2018; O'Neil, 2017). In many ways, whereas the nineteenth century was the age of the industrial revolution, where the relationships with our environments were reconfigured in terms of the constant mining of resources for the large-scale production of commodities, the current age is about the industrialization of the psychosocial, where consciousness, knowledge and memory work are performed through and by non-human machines and mobilized to achieve a wide variety of goals. However, the key aspect of the Jacquard mechanism was not automated production, but indeed embedding the psychosocial world of the maker into the broader technical system of weaving. The Jacquard mechanism, in other words—even in the nineteenth century— formulated very contemporary concerns around the distribution of not only physical, but also intellectual and creative abilities onto machines that could surpass human capacities. But the *Canuts* had a very different approach to the question of the more-than-human machine, embracing it indeed in ways that might seem counterintuitive to the contemporary reader.

Indeed, while media has always been central in organizing, managing and running larger technosocial systems, it is only now that this particular logistics aspect of media is garnering public interest, because the kinds of technosocial systems that are now being developed are taking over levels of knowledge acquisition, decision making and even creativity that used to be entirely in human hands. It is useful to understand that this logic is not radically new, and actually has a complex history to it. Here, I want to delve further into the question of automated media systems that engage with thought and creative processes within technosocial networks through the Jacquard mechanism. The Jacquard mechanism is famous for two things: it is often praised as a prototype for modern day computing, and it is also regarded as playing an important role in the industrial revolution and in the automation of textile production (Essinger, 2007). The history and function of the Jacquard mechanism, however, is more complex than such a teleological account would have it, and I argue that it provided a unique moment when the question of what media could be in relation to technosocial systems came to the fore: it ushered in a set of unique experiences that interrogated the many potentials in the relationship between digital media, semi-autonomous machines and human agency in order to enhance complex thinking and creativity.

Let's start with the myth surrounding the Jacquard mechanism, a myth that has been turned into common history. According to this myth, the Jacquard mechanism, invented by Joseph-Marie Jacquard (1752–1834) in 1804, marked a turning point in textile industry both locally in Lyon, France, where it was first introduced, and soon after all over the world. It allowed for productivity gain by decreasing the length of time that it took to weave fabric. To understand the Jacquard mechanism, it is necessary to go back to the basics of weaving. Weaving requires that vertical threads (warp) intertwine with horizontal threads (weft). The simplest weave is the plain weave, which involves lifting up every other warp thread, laying a weft thread in between, and then repeating the operation by reversing which warp threads are lifted. There are different techniques to create patterns on woven fabric, and typically they involve lifting different combination of warp threads, along with using different colored warp or weft threads. Through an ingenious punch card system, the Jacquard mechanism enacted a series of actions: each punch indicated which set of warp threads to lift, thus automating this key process of weaving.

The perceived impact of the Jacquard mechanism, however, was not limited to productivity gains in making woven fabric. It also provided an inspiration for the design of a device capable of conducting complex mathematical calculation in an autonomous manner: Charles Babbage and Ada Lovelace's analytical engine (1837), which is also known as a precursor to our modern-day computer (Essinger, 2007, Fernaus et al., 2012; Koetsier, 2001). Babbage and Lovelace were fascinated by the use of punch cards that recorded a program of actions. In that regard, the Jacquard mechanism can be considered as a precursor to today's software: it enacted a set of commands that transformed data (in the case of the Jacquard mechanism, warp and weft threads) into actual useful materialized information (i.e., a piece of patterned fabric). Ada Lovelace described the parallel between the Jacquard mechanism and the Analytical Engine as such: "...the Analytical Engine *weaves algebraical patterns* just as the Jacquard-loom weaves flowers and leaves" (Essinger, 2007). Beyond Lovelace and Babbage's work, the Jacquard mechanism influenced the history of computing up to the present day, especially with the use of punch cards to record and process information, a system most famously used by the Hollerith tabulator which subsequently evolved to be one of the core technical assets of the International Business Machines Corporations, or IBM (Essinger, 2007). With the Jacquard mechanism, we see the unfolding of two parallel stories of progress: first, technological progress with the industrialization and the automation of material production; and second, the story of the birth of new digital media when eventually computers would be connected with each other through networks such as the internet, and be deployed to automatically manage and control broader technical systems. All stories of progress are not without discontent however, and accordingly there is a famous illustration of Jacquard being thrown in the Rhone River by disgruntled silk weavers in Lyon. This illustration of the silk-weavers' hatred of Jacquard echoes actual historical upheavals in Lyon. As mentioned above, the silk-weavers in Lyon—the *Canuts*— led the first worker insurrections in history, rebelling against the degradation of their working conditions throughout the 1830s and 1840s (Rude, 2007).

Such a story is, however, a fabrication. Jacquard was never thrown in a river, nor was he ever targeted personally by disgruntled workers (Jarrige, 2009). The story was invented after Jacquard's death, in an effort to cement his legend as one of the French fathers of the great industrial revolution, martyred for the cause of scientific and technical progress. And the device that came to be known as the Jacquard mechanism has a more complex history and required years of amelioration before it became widely used, after 1817: the mechanism is best understood as part of a long series of technical innovations throughout the seventeenth, eighteenth and nineteenth centuries. Further, the *Canuts'* insurrections were not about refusal of newly automated industrial technology and were not about de-skilling and loss of identity as craft-making was replaced by the assembly line. They were primarily about wages and the brutal exploitation of weavers by intermediaries that set the price for woven fabrics. While the Jacquard mechanism was indeed first met with deep suspicion, it eventually became a welcome addition because it transformed the technosocial system of weaving in Lyon in positive ways for the local silk-workers, leading to the development of new horizons for textile as a mode of cultural expression.

It is misleading to lump in the Jacquard loom with other inventions from a similar period which, taken together, paved the way for the industrial revolution and the rise of industrial capitalism. The Jacquard mechanism cannot be compared with the power loom that could automatically weave fabric. Although both the power loom and the Jacquard mechanism were invented a few years apart (1784 for the power loom and 1804 for the Jacquard mechanism), they were developed in very different contexts—the cotton industry in the UK; the silk industry in Lyon—and for different purposes. Whereas the power loom found its place in a new industrial capitalist logic of mass commodity production (Beckert, 2015), the Jacquard mechanism was introduced to the high-end silk-weaving industry in Lyon (Charlin, 2003). While in both cases the arrival of new weaving machines is usually described as enabling a gain in productivity, it is important to recognize that the concept of productivity means different things in different contexts. In the context of mass production of textile, in order to submerge both local and overseas markets with cheap fabric, productivity gains involved lowered production costs through getting rid of expensive specialized human labor (the weaver) and increasing the speed of production with an automated machine capable of weaving faster than any human beings. In the context of silk-weaving in Lyon and the arrival of the Jacquard mechanism, however, productivity gains were about lowering the errors that were made during the weaving process and enhancing the capacity to develop more complex and intricate patterns. While there was an increase in the speed of weaving with the Jacquard mechanism, it was nowhere near that of the power loom: it could still take up to a full day of work for a silk-weaver to weave up to three centimeters of intricately patterned multi-colored brocade with the Jacquard mechanism. Finally, while the power loom de facto got rid of the weaver and the labor cost associated with paying a skilled worker, the Jacquard loom required highly skilled human labor for setup and operation. The fully automated loom with the Jacquard mechanism attached to it would come at a much later date, and as will be explained later, could never attain the level of complexity that the hand-operated Jacquard mechanism could help achieve.

What should be remembered about the Jacquard mechanism, however, is that it enabled dealing with a kind of complexity that could not be attained through human capacities—both physical and intellectual—alone. In that regards, Babbage and Lovelace's well-documented admiration reminds us that the Jacquard mechanism was unique in that it could be programmed to undertake a complex set of actions which in turn allowed for the development of a new expressive possibilities. Indeed, what Babbage and Lovelace admired in the mechanism was its capacity for greater flexibility and therefore for new potentials for undertaking all kinds of complex operations that would not be otherwise possible. Again, dealing with increased complexity rather than speed of productivity was a key aspect of the Jacquard mechanism. It is telling in that regard that when Babbage visited Lyon, he purchased a woven portrait of Jacquard (Figure 3.2)—a made-to-order and time-consuming piece of woven fabric that required 24,000 punch cards and took over eight hours of straight work to be woven (Essinger, 2007). Such a choice is curious, because Babbage, if he had been interested in the qualities of the Jacquard mechanism that dealt with repetition and automation, could have easily chosen a patterned fabric, which offers a great illustration of how the mechanism functioned as a reliable piece of software that could go through repeating its program with no errors. The woven portrait, on the other hand, is a long stand-alone sequence that is not repeated, and it is admirable for what we would now call its image resolution (Tomlinson, 1852: 959). At first view indeed, the woven Jacquard portrait looks like a very fine engraving.

Weaving Digital Images

So rather than machinic automated reliability through repetition, it is more useful at this point to look at the Jacquard mechanism with regard to the production of intricate designs. We should consider how the Jacquard mechanism intervened in the weaving process as a digital technology. I am not referencing here how the intersection of warp and thread can be read as binary coding (Harlizius-Klück, 2017), which is another discussion. Rather, I would like to examine weaving as the material production of digital images. As Schneider recalls: "Ever since the invention of the loom, weavers have produced structurally rastered patterns and pictures" (Schneider, 2015: 142). This is particularly visible with fabric woven with thick wool or cotton threads: the qualities of the designs are reminiscent, to the contemporary eye, of magnified pixels. Similar to the availability of different screen resolutions, the smaller the thread, the smaller the woven "pixel," to the extent that the whole composition can be perceived by the human eye as similar to a smooth drawing, painting, or even photograph, rather than made up of tiny little crosses of color. Silk was particularly appreciated in that regard, because on top of its aesthetic qualities—soft, shiny, and incredibly comfortable for the human skin—it is one of the thinnest and sturdiest threads available, with a diameter of 0.01 mm for a silk fiber. For the Lyon silk-weavers, silk enabled woven textile to develop qualities that could make it compete with both fine arts—painting and engraving, in particular—

Figure 3.2 Woven portrait of Joseph-Marie Jacquard, 1839. Courtesy of Bonhams and Wikimedia Commons.

and with the new media technology of photography ("La Fabrique des grands hommes," 2011). The Jacquard mechanism spurred intense development with regard to the quality of the images produced through weaving, and it was able to do so by enabling a very unique and specific type of collaboration between machines and weavers.

The Jacquard mechanism was among the first in a special category of media technology that could mobilize automated machinic actions to support processes of creativity and imagination. In order to do so, it relied on another invention—the detachable *semple*—by Philippe de Lasalle in 1776 (Hafter, 1977: 146), which involved the capacity to externalize designs onto a material memory system. What the Jacquard mechanism did in turn was to automate a program of action onto this memory system. In that regard, it is important to note that the punch cards in the Jacquard loom were not meant to store data—this particular use of punch card came much later with the Hollerith tabulator (Essinger, 2007). Rather, the punch card in the Jacquard mechanism recorded a set of actions: which warp threads should be lifted in sequence in order to realize intricate designs.

To further understand the articulation between automated action and the production of digital textile images, let us step back and examine the entire organization of the weaving process. First, a design is created. Second, this design has to be mapped and blown out onto a grid paper. The grid represents the intersection of warp and weft, and this step is crucial to see if the design is technically feasible. The smaller the thread and the more complex the design, the more time-consuming it is to draw the grid design. In contemporary parlance, this is the step where the design is rendered digitally as pixels on paper. The grid should be understood as a system of notation, and is, following Simon Yuill, akin to programming—"a form of mark-making that encodes and guides processes of production—marks which precedes the realization of an entity" (Yuill, 2005: 87). Weaver Anni Albers further explains that notation systems such as the grid "give an accurate account of the construction of the weave" (Albers et al., 2017: 20), and in nineteenth-century Lyon silk-weaving shops, it is the starting point by which other forms of programming can take place. Third, the grid design is used to set up the warp section of the weaving machine (Vauchey, 1945). For complex designs such as the ones created in Lyon, a special weaving loom was used: the drawloom, a type of floor loom with a system of drawcords connected to heddles that can be set up to lift sets of warp threads. The system allows for multiple combinations of warp and weft threads, and therefore for more complex designs. Setting up this system—which drawcord connects to which set of warp threads—is a process of externalization and translation of an abstract design onto a material support. Once the heddles system was set up and connected to another system to lift them (the *semple* mentioned above)—a process that usually took between three and eight weeks—the weaving itself could begin. When Philippe de la Salle invented the removable *semple* system, specific setups could be removed from the loom and stored—before that, the setup would have to be destroyed every time a new pattern was to be woven. This detachable *semple* system is a memory card of sorts: it contains the entire warp dataset that needs to be processed in order to produce fabric. It is important to thus note that the Jacquard mechanism operates within a long chain of processes of material externalization (onto paper and cord systems such as the *semple*) of abstract translation of information (as codes mapped onto a visual grid and punched into cards). Before the arrival of the Jacquard mechanism, the *semple* was operated by human agent—the drawboy or drawgirl—working in tandem with the weaver. In Lyon, it was usually women who took up the position. The work was demanding, both mentally and physically, and was usually where productivity stalled as it was prone to errors (Huchard, 2014). Weavers had systematic troubles finding workers to operate the *semple* mechanism, so difficult, physically taxing and unpleasant was the task.

The arrival of the Jacquard mechanism automated the work of the drawboy or drawgirl. The punch cards connected to levers that lifted the drawcords. The punching itself was done by reading the grid pattern and translating the sequence of drawcords that needed to be lifted as a series of holes on each of the cards. To use Actor-network theory, the Jacquard mechanism is a technical actant that replaced a human actant (Latour, 2007), but in so doing, transformed the weaving networks in ways that do not fit with the mass industrialization framework it is often associated with. The Jacquard mechanism took over a set of actions that were difficult for human actants to do, both mentally and physically, and it is partly for this reason that it eventually received a warm welcome and was hailed by the silk-workers as crucial to their identity as high-skill workers. Furthermore, the Jacquard mechanism, even though it cancelled one (demanding and difficult) job in the weaving system, created two new jobs: one for punching cards—a key position that demanded careful reading of the grid design; and two, the more manual job of tying together the sequence of punch cards (Huchard, 2014). Further, the Jacquard mechanism was a semi-autonomous system that still required activation by the weaver, and in that way involved a specific kind of collaboration between machine and human in the weaving process that enabled for the creation of further intricate and complex designs. In that regard, it is necessary to remember that the Jacquard mechanism was a specialized machine in charge of lifting warp threads. The weaver was still in charge of the overall weaving process and had to memorize the entire design, which included the sequence of punch cards as well as when to add supplementary color weft thread, if and when necessary: it required great memory both abstract and embodied in the series of gesture with hands and feet that operated the different components of the drawloom. The weaver's job did not get any simpler with the arrival of the Jacquard mechanism, but the mechanism enabled a form of technical assistance that made it possible for the weaver to better control the materialization of the design. Which brings us to the final product that emerged out of this complex techno-human assemblage: the exquisite and intricate woven silks, brocades, matelassés and damask that gave Lyon silk-weaving an international reputation. As Anni Albers explains, the Jacquard mechanism and removable *semple* allowed for an explosion of creativity:

> Whereas previously, a loom was rigged up cumbersomely for one pattern and was repeatedly used for just the one, a shift from one to another was so easy now

that the market became flooded with designs of all kinds. In the struggle for the attention of the buying public, the manufacturers outdid each other with constant changes of design—a situation we are still witnessing today.

Albers, 2017: 17

The dialogue between machine and human, between the loom fitted with an extension such as the Jacquard mechanism and the human imagination gave way to new types of creativity ("La Fabrique des grands hommes," 2011), which translated in turn, into a spurt of inventive exploration of textile as a mode of expression on a par with the dominant visual media of the time. Here, it is key to focus on the highest selection of the already high-end product that were produced in Lyon. These silks were incredibly expensive to produce, destined for royalty and the immensely rich, but were also meant to showcase Lyon's craftsmanship the world over through participation in world exhibitions. A selection of these high-end textiles was exhibited at the Génie de la Fabrique exhibition at the Musée des Tissus in Lyon (2015–2018). *Les papillons de fleurs* (*Flower Butterflies*) from Maison Schultz et Béraud is one such instance of a piece of woven cloth that won a prize medal at the London World Fair in 1862. The pattern is composed of butterflies and dragonflies against a white background, with each insect made up of tiny colorful flowers. Some 299 different colored silks were used to create these intricate, delicate, fairy-tale butterflies. The amount of work that must have been required to plot each tiny flower as part of the composition for only one insect is almost impossible to imagine. Another masterpiece of woven silk Jacquard which received the Grand Prix at the Universal and Colonial World Fair in Lyon in 1894 is *Les Hirondelles* (*Swallows*) by Maison Les Petits-Fils de C.-J. Bonnet et Cie. The piece depicts swallows flying over waves in monochromatic black against a white background. This piece is particularly striking for its borrowing from Japanese and Chinese ink painting, both in the subjects depicted (swallows and the waves of the sea) and the garment made with the cloth, which was largely inspired by the Japanese kimono. The piece is strikingly dynamic, with a swarm of swallows emerging from the waves, and each of the birds going generally in the same overall direction but at the same time diverging a little as they battle the wind, giving us a real sensation of the struggle to maintain group cohesion in flight. To refer to the notion of imaginaries, these two instances (among many) of the kinds of craftsmanship—drawing, composition, weaving—that emerged around the Jacquard mechanism were not about cloth as a common commodity. They expressed something about how a mechanical, highly technical process could start competing with the high art of painting and how weaving could indeed remediate painting and perhaps even surpass it in its capacity for reproduction. In these pieces, then, we see the exploration of the expressive capacity and cultural value of a new kind of media: digital visual media.

Indeed, a series of innovations prior, during and after the arrival of the Jacquard mechanism enabled exploring how capacities for reproducing high-end resolution woven images could compete with reproduction techniques of the time: namely intaglio, lithography, and letterpress printing, as well as the newly discovered process of analog photography. The woven portrait is an illustration of this. While the popularity of woven portrait disappeared at the turn of the twentieth century, they were the site of numerous experiments by several Lyon silk artisans and workers. One key figure is Philippe de Lasalle (1723–1804) mentioned above, who was also a skilled drawer, painter, and innovator specializing in the *mise en carte*— of translating drawings into the gridded maps that plotted warp and weft. Lasalle was famous not only for his artistic talent, but also for his technical innovations, and his woven portraits translate a vision where technical innovation enables artistic and creative revolution. Lasalle's woven portraits are trompe l'oeil: his famous portrait of Catherine the Great represents the empress in profile mimicking camaïeu monochromatic technique, while surrounded by intricate colorful flower garlands. In the same period, Gaspard Grégoire (1751–1846) realized a series of woven velvet portraits of other important figures such as Napoleon. His work looks like fine oil painting, and the secrets of his technique died with him. In 1827, another Lyonnais textile artist and innovator Étienne Maisiat turned his attention to typography and engraving with woven texts, such as a woven *Testament of Louis XVI* (1827). Here, we can see a shift from the competition with fine art such as painting to technologies of reproduction such as typography and engraving. In other words, textile started to think about itself on par with the dominant medium of the time: print. In the second half of the eighteenth century, woven portraits, especially those made by Carquillat (1804–1884) turned towards one of the new media of the time: analog photography. Today, we could say that the resolution of Carquillat portraits equals and surpasses analog photographic techniques in the mid-nineteenth century. But they also surpassed photography at the time by offering the option of color. And indeed, it is eerie looking at the back of Carquillat's portrait: they do look like photographic negatives rather than textile. The woven portraits of the nineteenth century were celebrated the world over as technical innovations and new forms of art. They played a key role in establishing the international renown of Lyon woven textiles.

The reasons for the subsequent decline of the silk-weaving industry in the late 1800s are complex. The successive revolutions of the nineteenth century in France and Europe operated a shift in fashion tastes, where less ostentatious textiles such as cotton and more muted color palettes rose in popularity (Charvet, 1870: 4–5). Many of the fine Jacquard textiles were destined for the nobility, which also progressively disappeared and, or shrank significantly. Many Lyon textile weavers continued to work individually, which led to a refusal of trade unionism and other forms of worker associations that could have helped valorize their work and organize training, especially training to develop new designs and aesthetics (Association des Typographes Lyonnais, 1890; Charvet, 1870). The Jacquard mechanism is still in use today, mostly on automated looms, and the setup is much simpler thanks to computer software that translates designs into grids and tests out sample fabric. The fully automated and computerized Jacquard loom, however, cannot compete with the semi-autonomous system of the 1800s in terms of complexity: the automated loom can only accommodate a limited number (ten to twelve) different color threads on the weft, whereas the original system onto which the Jacquard mechanism was added allowed for many more as it was controlled by the weaver.

Weaving as Extension

To weave has always been thoroughly technical and technological, and the sheer volume and pace of technical innovations from the first backstrap loom to the Jacquard mechanism sitting atop the massive drawlooms that filled entire rooms in nineteenth-century Lyon is quite staggering, marked by the desire to not only improve productivity and quality control, but also to achieve aesthetic prowess in the form of complex weaving techniques on a large scale. To be a weaver is therefore to be technological, starting from the very fact that one's body and mind have to work in tandem with technical tools. The oldest form of weaving—backstrap weaving—after all requires turning one's body into part of a machinic assemblage. Assemblages, to use Deleuze and Guattari's vocabulary (1987), coordinate bodies (including senses, gestures and movements), minds (including affective, attentional and intellectual capacities), and information and knowledge by distributing them through connected humans and non-humans. In particular, the human body becomes a component of the weaving machine: gestures with hands and feet not only activate the weaving process, but also adapt to the specificity of the loom, producing a rhythm that enables continuous production, rather than stop and go. This close association between the bodies of weavers, non-human technical extensions and the production of visual mathematical objects in the form of woven cloth never disappeared in all the weaving innovations up until the invention of the power loom, which did away with human bodies and minds altogether. To be a professional weaver in France and in the UK in the nineteenth century meant being surrounded by complex technologies that not only processed materials but encoded such materials. The nineteenth-century *Canut* was surrounded by technology both big and small along with a team of professionals, which served to mediate, transcribe and translate complex abstract visual patterns as woven cloths. The professional weavers in Europe had developed technologies that extended, supported and transformed mathematical capacities: the professional weaving shop, in that regard, combined proto-computing of information and technical production of textile objects, with the Jacquard mechanism being the epitome of such development.

The Jacquard mechanism reveals something particular and often forgotten about the relationship between human and technologies in the production of objects. Often there is a separation in scale and impact between two types of technologies: pre-industrial technologies that are commonly described as craft and operate on a small scale, and industrial technologies that intervene at a large scale, transforming the entire context of production. Pre-industrial technologies are often seen as small, and deceptively simple while industrial technologies are complex and massive. In his work, Lewis Mumford (1964) developed a theoretical framework that opposed two kinds of techniques: democratic ones vs. authoritarian techniques. While democratic techniques tend to be small-scale, controllable, meant for sustainable processes of transformation, authoritarian techniques on the other hand are deployed at a massive scale, radically transforming and destabilizing environments to assert specific forms of power, and usually requiring an immense amount of human and environmental exploitation. Authoritarian techniques existed long before industrialization—think of large-scale works such as the Egyptian pyramids—but the arrival of automated machinery during the industrial revolution elevated them to the dominant mode of technological development worldwide. In Mumford's work we find a focus on scale and complexity as differentiating factors between technologies that are meaningful and those that assert massive and unequal forms of power and control, while Ursula Franklin's work establishes an opposition between two types of technologies and ways of making based on the relationship between process and makers. Franklin puts forward a first model of craft-oriented technologies, where the maker controls and manages the entire process of production, from extraction of materials to their transformation into objects. By contrast the other kind of technology is based on loss of control by makers as making processes are broken down into small units and distributed. The assembly line epitomizes this model, which results in alienating makers from the objects they are producing. Heidegger famously provides another dividing line between two forms of techne: the first—based on craft—that reveals the essence of something, with the maker able to coax out of a raw material an exquisite finished product, and the other enframes the world through the lens of instrumentalization: rather than the poetic revealing of the essence of things hidden in raw materials, we witness the reduction of everything to standing reserves for instrumental planning aiming for absolute control over humans and their environments.

While any summary of the works of such important and complex thinkers of technology in one paragraph is most definitely incomplete and full of sweeping generalizations, I simply wish to highlight this shared effort to find the dividing line between technosocial models that transcribe radically different sets of ethics (or lack thereof), purpose, meaning and value by centering on the relationship between human makers and their machines. Often the work of the craft maker, seen as involving controllable tools, is opposed to that of the complex technological system that transform human makers into extensions of machinic processes. But the notion of extension, and the dynamics through which humans extend themselves through technological tools and in turn become extensions of the machine, throws this neat duality askance. Indeed, the question of extension troubles binary thinking about technologies and requires us to turn to the concept of the creative assemblage where the relationships between machines and humans become so entangled and complex that they foster new possibilities of expression rather than control, a dynamic epitomized in the adoption of the Jacquard mechanism in the textile world.

McLuhan posited that media extend human capacities, be they physical, psychological or intellectual. With the question of extension, McLuhan did not differentiate between symbolic technologies (e.g., media technologies) and technologies that worked directly on the real. Nor did his original formulation start with the human at the center of the extension rather than the human being extended in turn. Indeed, the question of extension is also one of transformation, which today we relate to through the concept of the cyborg. The cyborg is an uneasy figure: rather than simply having their power extended, humans who become cyborg internalize radically non-human processes: they put themselves at the mercy of non-human technological processes. And while the question of the cyborg raises the specter of becoming an extension of an artificially intelligent machine in mainstream entertainment, Donna Haraway (1996) suggests that the cyborg is a site of new relationships, new agencies coming together, new ways of thinking and creating as a well as new ways of acting and transforming the world. But the question is also how cyborgs work together with other machines in a technological context. The silk-weaver extends himself and is extended through different machines that allow for the management of relationships between the material and the immaterial: making, thinking, imagining, producing and knowing are not separate processes, but rather are components of assemblages.

Which aspects of these elements and capacities are mobilized and how they are linked with and transform each other has effects as disparate and far-reaching as rewiring brains, transforming identities, ushering in new social formations, enabling new economic relations and transforming collective life, from politics to everyday habits. Technological assemblages can permeate our lives at a scale and pervasiveness that is impossible to control individually, but that does not mean that they necessarily serve dominant power formations. Indeed, the silk weaving shops of nineteenth-century Lyon saw the unleashing of creative potential of media through the assemblage of extended and hybridized humans, media processes that encode and render information, and technological processes that transform raw materials into objects. What lessons then can we draw from high-end luxury Jacquard fabrics from the nineteenth century? Overall, it is best to think about the Jacquard mechanism as a media component in the technosocial system of silk-weaving in Lyon, a system that required translating information (a design) and action upon this information (the weaving of the design) onto different material supports (grid paper, drawcords, punch cards), using a complex apparatus of weaving techniques and machinery that worked in tandem with human actants. Weaving in that period emerged as a form of hybrid circuitry based on the constant interaction and dialogue between machines and humans. It therefore presents us with a model that is a far cry from the contemporary, black box models of technical machines operating autonomously and engaging in cognition process with little human intervention (Hayles, 2017). The weaving shop was, for all purposes, an open box where information circulated in multiple forms, was translated both as abstract grid design and punch holes and as material setup.

The Jacquard mechanism therefore opens up a new perspective on the question of dominance with regards to digital media. The problem, as I have said earlier, is not so much one of media technological determinism: media extend by intervening and taking over very human processes of attention and memory and in that sense they determine. That is to say, they both delineate and enable new capacities of expression and interventions in the world. Rather, the key problem is one of power and dominance, that is, of the deployment of specific media technologies within broader systems of subsumption to a (dystopian) vision of a world where all aspects of life can be controlled, managed and marketed. If the field of communication and media studies is to participate in the formulation of new directions and alternatives to the increasingly dystopian deployment of new communication technologies, it becomes important to question our teleological understanding of the history of media solely as the history of dominant media, or rather, the history of media technologies as already captured by and fully folded into dominant power formations. Media archeology can in that way be political. The example of the Jacquard mechanism as a technology for enabling complexity through human–machine collaboration is an instance of a not-yet-dominant digital media system, one that fostered immense creativity while it was not integrated into a mass-industrialization, mass-production and mass-commodification system.

One could rightfully argue that while high-end silk-work with the Jacquard mechanism did not fit into the nascent capitalist matrix of the time, it nevertheless articulated itself around two centers of power: the old monarchical system, which required high-end textile to display its power, and the newer modernist imaginary that saw the establishment of the western colonial power as the center of techno-scientific and cultural innovation. I would like the reader to keep the question of articulation with different centers of power in mind and to understand how these centers of power can be linked and delinked from the dominant matrix of power. As we have seen in the previous chapter on Peru, the articulation between high-end textile and power was prevalent as well in pre-Columbian times, not only with regards to political centers of power, but also spiritual ones as demonstrated, for instance, with funeral textiles. It is key to pay attention to how textile perhaps not only articulates itself within a node of power, but can also be mobilized to reshape and delink that very node of power from the dominant matrix. While the *Canuts* ultimately could not achieve such a goal, their textile legacy profoundly disrupts teleological understandings of media technology and capitalism.

The disappearance of highly skilled textile work was but part of the sweeping transformation that transformed textile from involving human attention, care and creativity to relying on automation, machines and mass production. Let me now operate a bridging of sort by continuing with the question of making, extension and creativity, and the assemblages they produce, assemblages that hardly fit within the dominant matrix of power. As opposed to skilled male artisans in nineteenth century France, let me now turn to skilled Indigenous female artisans located in Northern Peru, who use technical tools that at first seem much simpler than the Jacquard loom: the backstrap loom and the crochet needle. Behind this seeming simplicity is a complex set of human-technical extensions and other ways of engaging with digital mediations, that in turn, fosters specific creative lines of flights. These very lines of flight engage more directly with the dominant matrix of power by formulating, in turn existential and decolonial practices that cross spatial and temporal abysses.

References

Albers, Anni, Nicholas Fox Weber, Manuel Cirauqui, and T'ai Smith. (2017). *On Weaving*. New expanded edn. Princeton, NJ: Princeton University Press.

Association des Typographes Lyonnais. (1890). *Délégations ouvrières et administratives à l'Exposition Universelle de Paris en 1889*. Lyon.

Beckert, Sven. (2015). *Empire of Cotton: A Global History*. Reprint edn. New York: Vintage.

Bucher, Taina. (2018). *If. . .Then: Algorithmic Power and Politics*. New York: Oxford University Press.

Charlin, Jean-Claude. (2003). *Histoire de La Machine Jacquard*. Pfaffikon, Switzerland: Staubli.

Charvet, L. (1870). *Étude sur les Beaux-Arts. De l'enseignement des beaux-arts au point de vue de leur application à l'industrie lyonnaise*. Lyon: Aimé Vingtrinier.

Deleuze, Gilles, and Felix Guattari. (1987). *A Thousand Plateaus: Capitalism and Schizophrenia*. University of Minnesota Press.

Essinger, James. (2007). *Jacquard's Web: How a Hand-Loom Led to the Birth of the Information Age*. Oxford: Oxford University Press.

Eubanks, Virginia. (2018). *Automating Inequality: How High-Tech Tools Profile, Police, and Punish the Poor*. New York: St. Martin's Press.

Fernaeus, Ylva, Martin Jonsson, and Jakob Tholander. (2012). "Revisiting the Jacquard Loom: Threads of History and Current Patterns in HCI." In Proceedings of the SIGCHI Conference on Human Factors in Computing Systems, 1593–1602. Austin, TX, May 5–10, 2012. New York: ACM Press.

Hafter, Daryl M. (1977). "Philippe de Lasalle: From Mise-en-carte to Industrial Design." *Winterthur Portfolio* 12: 139–64. https://www.jstor.org/stable/1180584.

Harlizius-Klück, Ellen. (2017). "Weaving as Binary Art and the Algebra of Patterns." *TEXTILE* 15 (2): 176–97. https://doi.org/10.1080/14759756.2017.1298239.

Haraway, Donna Jeanne. (1996). *Simians, Cyborgs and Women: The Reinvention of Nature*. 2nd edn. London: Free Association Books.

Hayles, N. Katherine. (2017). *Unthought: The Power of the Cognitive Nonconscious*. Illustrated edn. Chicago: University of Chicago Press.

Huchard, Jean. (2014). "Regards sur la soierie lyonnaise: l'histoire méconnue du lisage de dessin: 1ère partie." *Bulleting Municipal Official de La Ville de Lyon*, November 3, 2014.

Jarrige, François. (2009). "Le martyre de Jacquard ou le mythe de l'inventeur héroïque (France, XIXᵉ siècle)." *Tracés. Revue de Sciences humaines*, no. 16 (May): 99–117. https://doi.org/10.4000/traces.2543.

Koetsier, Teun. (2001). "On the Prehistory of Programmable Machines: Musical Automata, Looms, Calculators." *Mechanism and Machine Theory* 36 (5): 589–603. https://doi.org/10.1016/S0094-114X(01)00005-2.

"La Fabrique des grands hommes." (n.d.). Accessed January 30, 2019. https://www.museedestissus.fr/pages/exposition/19:exposition-la-fabrique-des-grands-hommes.

Latour, Bruno. (2007). *Reassembling the Social: An Introduction to Actor-Network-Theory*. New York: Oxford University Press.

"Le Génie de la Fabrique." (n.d.). Accessed January 30, 2019. https://www.museedestissus.fr/pages/exposition/9:exposition-le-genie-de-la-fabrique.

Mumford, Lewis. (1964). "Authoritarian and Democratic Technics." *Technology and Culture* 5 (1): 1–8. http://www.jstor.org/stable/3101118.

Noble, Safiya Umoja. (2018). *Algorithms of Oppression: How Search Engines Reinforce Racism*. New York: New York University Press.

O'Neil, Cathy. (2017). *Weapons of Math Destruction: How Big Data Increases Inequality and Threatens Democracy*. Reprint edn. New York: Broadway Books.

Parisi, Luciana. (2019). "Critical Computation: Digital Automata and General Artificial Thinking." *Theory, Culture & Society*, 36 (2): 89–121. https://doi.org/10.1177/0263276418818889.

Rude, Fernand. (2007). *Les révoltes des canuts – N° 260:* Paris: La Découverte.

Schneider, Birgit. (2015). *The Technical Image: A History of Styles in Scientific Imagery*. Edited by Horst Bredekamp and Vera Dünkel. Chicago: The University of Chicago Press.

Tomlinson, Charles. (1852). *Cyclopædia of Useful Arts & Manufactures*. Vol. 1. London: James S. Virtue.

Vauchey, Eugène. (1945). "Le Lisage." In *Mémorial de La Soierie. Suite de Propos et Rapports. États Généraux.*, 81–82. Lyon: Imprimerie commerciale.

Yuill, Simon. (2005). "Programming as Practice." In *Hothaus Papers: Perspectives and Paradigms in Media Arts*. Edited by J. Gibbons and K. Winwood. Birmingham: ARTicle Press.

Chapter 4

COMMUNICATING ACROSS THE ABYSS

Bordered by the Andes, the desert coast of Peru features a unique climate and environment that has provided for human life for millennia, and for the preservation of its traces to the present day (Figure 4.1). The earliest traces of human activity in this region date from 3000 BCE, with the development of sedentary societies reliant on fishing. Some of the first textile objects used there after ropes were fishing nets—tools that not only allowed for subsistence, but also cultural techniques that enabled a constant exchange with the sea, a communication repeated daily, a rhythm, a refrain. The fishing net connects and delineates the boundaries between the human and the non-human entity that is the sea, what can be caught (fish) and what is uncontrollable—the environment. Fishing nets are already both means of existence and means of communication with the environment. And for humans along the coast of Northern Peru, trying to understand the environment was a central concern, as they faced what we now call El Niño: every five years or so, their worlds would be turned upside down (Allen, 1998); torrential rains would flood houses and fields and turn the desert into a garden, and the fish would disappear. The inability to make sense of the

Figure 4.1 Huacas del Sol y la Luna (Moche), Trujillo, Peru. Courtesy of the author.

phenomenon, both in terms of being able to manage food for survival and coming to terms with the seemingly nonsensical upheaval of the cosmos led a few pre-Columbian civilizations, including the Moche, to collapse. I was repeatedly told in Peru through guided archeological site visits that Peruvian Pre-Columbian civilizations, in order to survive, had to rely on a tripartite system: a political system to administer resources, a knowledge system to understand, work with and predict life conditions, and a spiritual-ideological system to make sense of it all. All three systems rely on each other: without the appropriate knowledge, resources cannot be administered and the spiritual and ideological context will soon collapse. If there are no spiritual or ideological ways of making sense of life and one's experience in the world, then the political and knowledge systems cannot sustain themselves for long. Cultural techniques enable communication between these three aspects, and textile, alongside ceramics and metal work, was key in that regard. Thus, I follow Denise Arnold's argument about southern Andean weaving that:

> ... the theory that underlies ritual technique is a "science of life," whereas ritual technique itself constitutes an "applied science of life," the actions and instruments of ritual practice being effectively "techniques" to secure life. I argue that weaving, too, in theory and practice, through its attention to life-giving processes, is directed towards coordinating the productive interrelations of a common way of life and that weaving techniques assure the continuity of these interrelations.
>
> Arnold, 2018: 239

In addition to Arnold, however, I show in this chapter how weaving techniques, under their seeming repetitive gestures, "assure continuity" through invention and reinvention.

I focus in this chapter on the mobilization of traditional textile techniques to create non-traditional items, including ones developed for different kinds of global and local markets, and how this establishes Indigenous textile as a decolonizing medium. This is not a simple transition by any means, but one that requires, much like the Pre-Columbian civilizations of the past, struggling and defining the political, economic, cultural and spiritual role of traditional textile-making today. Whereas Chapter 2 delved into the preservation of traditional Indigenous techniques, patterns and symbols in Peru, this chapter focuses on the experience of diaspora for Peruvian Indigenous textile makers and how they reinvent their craft, and in so doing forge new economic and cultural contexts for themselves, which in this case, means the bridging of a new past as much as efforts to innovate in the present. Specifically, I argue that the kind of profound existential reinvention of makers as individuals, as members of collectives, as women, as part of a continuous textile culture since pre-Columbian times is often hidden away by most discourses that see locally made craft as means to maintain cultural identities while providing socioeconomic benefits for the makers. While this is undeniably the case, I want to argue that the refashioning of existence, both individual and collective, in the present but also through the refashioning of pre-Columbian histories and through projection into unknown futures reveals a key function of Indigenous textile as medium today: that it highlights the divergences (Stengers, 2001) between dominant colonial epistemologies and ontologies and the Indigenous epistemologies and ontologies it constantly works to make invisible.

Behind the handmade textile object, in other words, lies countless efforts on the part of the textile makers and designers to figure out ways of refashioning existence that ultimately engage with the question of decoloniality, of the possibility for delinking with the "matrix" of capitalism, colonialism and modernity (Mignolo and Walsh, 2018). In paying attention to these processes and struggles that are usually glossed over, I aim to bring to the fore how something seemingly so minor as textile craft practiced by groups of women along the northern coast of Peru is actually decolonial praxis through making. Further, decolonial practices can only take place in the reconfigurations of the connections that usually serve dominant power: decolonial praxis through textile-making is again ambiguous, in that it rubs against the workings of power, both bringing to the fore radical differences as much as it attempts to bridge and cross these differences.

I examine this decolonial refashioning of existence by bringing to the fore three incommensurabilities of textile as a medium that both delineate the abyssal line (Santos, 2018) between makers and textile markets and that are usually completely glossed over by western perspectives. The first concerns the mobilization of pre-Columbian signs-as-patterns as a way of reinventing new directions and meanings through signification processes that do not fit into traditional western frameworks for understanding how signs function. The materialization of signs-as-patterns fosters not fixity of meaning, but the channeling of transformative fluidity. The second is the embodied techno-human mathematics required to make textile, which mobilizes and coordinates minds and bodies in complex ways to create digital textile objects, but which is again, typically glossed over. The third is the meaning of making as work, and the subsequent difficulties of attributing values to textile work that would propel new understandings of textile craft, from conditions of production to its valuation on local and global markets. All three incommensurabilities point to this: that to understand textile-making as mediation, it is necessary to understand how it links the material with the abstract, local practices with the cosmos, the moment of making with existence, bodies with minds. It should be clear at this point why I am moving away from traditional western analytical frameworks centered on signification and narrative analysis. As I mentioned before, I am interested in examining how textile-making as mediation involves the articulation of the abstract (symbols and codes) and the material (actual materials and practices). This articulation allows for the formulation of new modes of existence, which are themselves abstract (felt, imagined, thought, invented) and material (practiced, ritualized, embodied). I am moving away from traditional understandings of "content," which typically ignore the material in favor of the abstract: of the ideas that are carried and expressed. Such an approach does not grasp at materialization as a particular moment of making as mediation, one that most directly engages with the question of what Karen Barad calls "mattering" (2007). Textile is culturally meaningful because it materializes the abstract into an object that (should) matter. The carefulness and sophistication that goes into non-industrialized textile-making is often disregarded, as I will recount in more specific details in this chapter. But in turn, making becomes a challenge, a question that asks: what should matter?—and that engages in mattering that which has been rendered meaningless and invisible by the dominant matrix of power. This chapter is as much an exploration of incommensurabilities that have historically and structurally relegated Indigenous textile as anything but communication and mediation, as it is an attempt to start formulating, through following textile makers, new frameworks for understanding non-western modes of mattering, of the specific alliance of expression and existence.

Of the Meanings, Symbols, and Patterns in Diasporic Textile

The northern coast of Peru in the region north of Trujillo is renowned for its surfing and archeological sites. In the area between the towns of Chocope and Pacasmayo, the landscape is dotted with small monticules and hills for kilometers on end—all architectural remnants of the Moche civilization (Bourget and Jones, 2009). Near the city of Trujillo, the Chan Chan archeological complex spreads over twenty square kilometers, offering a unique glimpse into the Chimu civilization. The economy of the region, especially compared to the Sacred Valley near Cusco that includes world-famous sites such as Machu-Picchu, is quite modest. While in Cusco the presence of Indigenous Quechua population and their weaving practices has been continuous ever since the times of the Incas, along the coast of northern Peru, Quechua-speaking textile artisans, always women, are all recent immigrants from the mountains, and have moved to the coast as jobs are more readily available there. The ethnographic work I conducted involved following two textile designers, one from Peru, the other from Canada, both based in the seaside town of Pacasmayo, and visiting and interviewing three of the weaving communities of women they work with. The designers have many years of experience working with local textile communities all across Peru. The focus on the Northern region of Peru was fairly recent, around four years old at the time of writing. At the time, there were very few organized textile groups in the region in existence, and the designers were very busy building textile groups in different cities and villages from the ground up. As new economic opportunities for men appeared, many Quechua-speaking families from the northern Andes have moved to the coast, settling and building houses, often in unclaimed lands bordering the town of Pacasmayo and nearby towns with minimal to non-existent city infrastructure: some clean water via a small pipe and often no sewers; some electricity, usually through small solar panels. Households typically have a vegetable patch and fruit trees, along with chickens and guinea pigs for subsistence. There have been several waves of migration over the years and some of the weaving groups that I visited were older, more established and prosperous than others. The oldest group I visited was eleven years old, the more recent less than a year old. These women continue

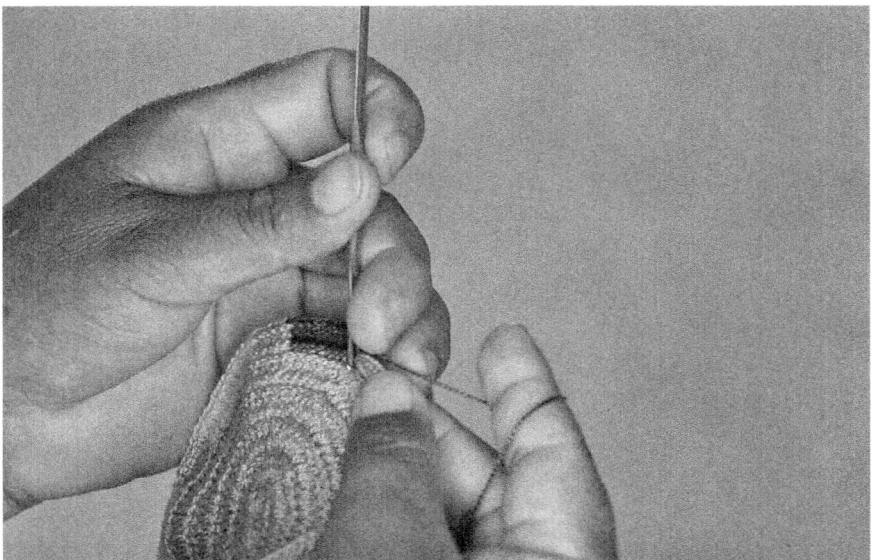

Figure 4.2 Weft crochet weaving. Courtesy of the author.

to hold weaving traditions that have existed since pre-Columbian times but have also adopted a hybrid technique that resulted from the encounter between pre-Columbian weaving and the Spanish introduction of crochet needles. Call it weft-crochet, as the technique does not involve knots like traditional crochet, but rather using one set of threads as weft coils that are attached together with another interlacing set of threads (Figure 4.2). The origins of weft-crochet are pretty much unknown, but it has by now definitely been adopted as a cultural and Indigenous technique. It is practiced in northern Peru but also by other Indigenous groups, notably the Wayuu group in Columbia and Venezuela. One can surmise that weft-crochet gained in popularity as it is a very portable technique: one only needs a crochet needle, thread and two hands to realize all kinds of textile objects. The women I interviewed said that traditionally, weft-crochet fulfills domestic needs for carpets, rugs and bags.

The effort to develop and reinvent handmade textile for local and foreign markets in order to provide women with some income is relatively new here and has led to an important set of encounters between the women coming from the mountains and the existing environment, which are both *historical*, with the many remains of the Moche civilization, and *environmental*, with the sea, new landscapes and therefore new colors. And indeed, two key aspects of the textile objects developed were the incorporation of Moche symbols and patterns (Figures 4.3 and 4.4) which are culturally completely foreign to the women makers, and the development of new color schemes and combinations that reflected the daily landscape they were

Figure 4.3 Moche symbol, Huaca de la Luna, Trujillo. Courtesy of the author.

surrounded with: soft pastels, neutrals and desert and sea colors (Figures 4.5 and 4.6), rather than bright colors that they would traditionally use.

The history of the oldest group was telling with regard to how the diasporic experience provided new creative opportunities. The group was composed of twenty women, most of them now in their forties, who started meeting in the evenings, and as interests converged, more regularly. The group focused primarily on weaving, which all women had learned in childhood, following a millennial transmission of backstrap weaving techniques. Back in their home villages, their weaving work was not much valued, and was mostly focused on the production of domestic wares such as rugs. The move to the coast changed traditional division of household labor, and the women started developing the idea that their woven wares could be sold. The auspicious coincidence for this group was the nearby archeological site El Brujo. The El Brujo complex was built during the Moche era, between 200 BCE and 600 CE and is composed of three *huacas*, or buildings that played an important sociopolitical and spiritual role in Moche culture. El Brujo is a unique archeological site because it contains the tomb and remnants of an important figure nicknamed "La Senora de Cao" discovered in 2005. La Senora de Cao was between 25 and 30 years old when she died due to complications in childbirth, and it is supposed that she was an important spiritual figure. Typically examples of Moche culture (wall paintings and carvings, ceramics) tend to represent male figures engaged in combat or being ritually sacrificed, giving the impression that the Moche culture was intensely male dominated. La Senora de Cao showed for the first time that women played an important role in Moche

Figure 4.4 Moche symbols on sample weft-crochet bags. Courtesy of the author.

culture (Villavicencio, 2017: 98), as testified by the careful embalming and the vast array of treasures—jewelry, ceramics and textiles that she was buried with.

For the weaving group, the proximity of the El Brujo complex first meant tourist traffic and the potential to sell textile craft. The group started by doing demonstrations of backstrap weaving at the El Brujo site. Eventually, they incorporated Moche patterns and symbols in their woven products to sell to visitors, mostly bags and small objects. At some point, the group met with one of the designers, which led to the development of more experimental designs, in particular woven jewelry and the use of natural dyes, which continues to the present day. When I met with them, the group was busy weaving handles for bags and developing prototypes for grass-woven objects. At this point, the group is well established with a production studio and a shop near El Brujo. They have a coordinator and the work for new projects is shared among the group members. Each group member

Figure 4.5 Fishing port, Pacasmayo. Courtesy of the author.

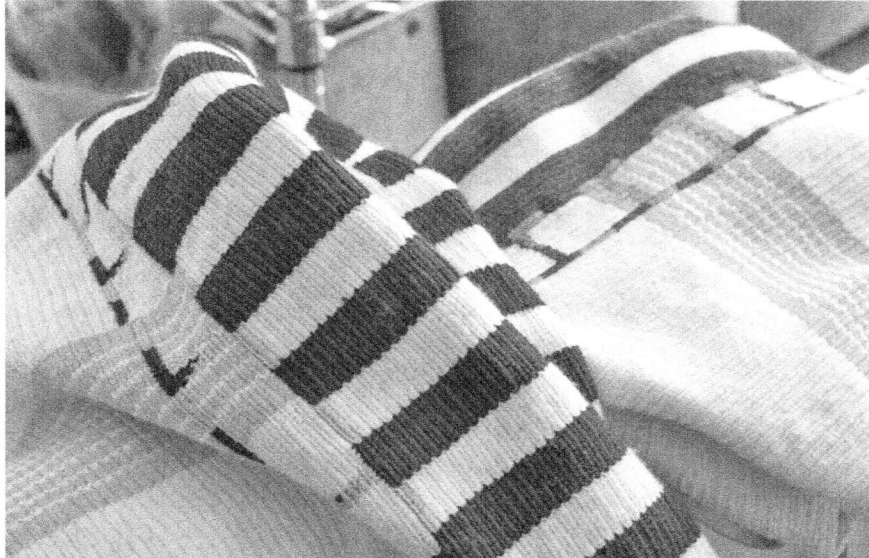

Figure 4.6 Weft-crochet samples with Pacasmayo color combination. Courtesy of the author.

does the bulk of the work in her home, and then they gather together, mostly to get more materials and do quality checks and plan new projects. The group continues to collaborate with the designers alongside their own production lines for their store. They continually experiment with new designs that can attract customers, recognizing that different groups have different preferences: they jokingly recalled that their preferences are for bright color combinations, but that they also developed more neutral color designs specifically geared towards Japanese tourists. The group has been successful: its members earn enough money to have socioeconomic agency and participation in their household life, thus showing how traditional craft can be reinvested and reinvented as a way for women's empowerment and emancipation.

But this description is too simplistic and does not do justice to the deep communication taking place between the artisans and their changing conditions of existence as it is mediated through textile work. It would be an unfortunate mistake to see the incorporation of Moche patterns and symbols as simply an opportunity for economic development: the status of pre-Columbian iconographies in Peru is much more important, and complex. Pre-Columbian iconographies have always been central to the definition of an independent anti-colonial Peruvian identity and today in urban centers such as Lima, are constantly present in popular culture and aesthetics (Leon and Caroline, 2018; Salmón, 2009). At the same time, pre-Columbian iconographies cannot be treated like western signs—they function more like indicators of worlds, paths and movement, which has enabled them to circulate across pre-Columbian civilizations separated by time and space (Washburn and Crowe, 2004). Take for instance the figures of the serpent (Trever, 2005), the feline (Saunders, 2013) and the bird: these are found both as realistic depictions and as stylized patterns in all pre-Columbian civilizations of Peru. They represent respectively the world of the dead, the world of the humans and the world of the gods. It is important to note that pre-Columbian civilizations were organized around possibilities of communication between the three worlds, and on maintaining these channels of communication through practices and rituals, for instance through burial practices, and rituals around opening tombs to communicate with the dead. In that sense, these symbols also mean transformation as opposed to the western notions of categorization and fixity of meaning. They are meant to circulate and do not belong to one culture or civilizations; and the cultural history of Peru up to the present day is marked by the reinvention and resurgence of these symbols in very different political, spiritual and ideological systems. Take for instance, the urban Chicha movement in Peru (Salmón, 2009), which, through music and street art mixing the different cultures of Peru gives a voice and aesthetic language to marginalized groups, including migrant workers newly arrived in big cities and youth living in the slums. Chicha visuals use brash and flashy colors and reinvent the serpent and the feline as stylized Asian dragons and tigers respectively, borrowing from kung-fu and carnival aesthetics to articulate contemporary political demands. The inclusion of Moche patterns and symbols for the textile group near El Brujo, should be understood as part of a long and multifaceted tradition of thinking and materializing cultural and political change. Further, other Moche patterns and symbols, such as the three steps—again representing the three worlds, but also waves, sun, moon and fish—indicate the importance of non-human elements in both daily and spiritual life: they ask about relationships to one's environment and do not function like western texts or discourses that would explain and justify. Rather, they open up fields of relations between humans, non-humans and the cosmos. The incorporation of these symbols into textile-making is not therefore pure economic opportunity, but a way to further entrench the potential for change and transformation of conditions of existence, a way to engage with the diasporic experience. And indeed, the discovery of the Senora de Cao as well was not simply a welcome coincidence, but rather spurred deep communication through time: the discovery of La Senora de Cao for the group was about communication with the dead, and communication with a powerful female spiritual figure that reinforced a vision for contemporary forms of female empowerment.

As such, if we were to try to find an echo in western critical theory to the process of working with pre-Columbian signs, I would suggest that it is akin to *anasemia*, which, as Derrida defines it, is "a process of problematizing the meaning of signs in an undetermined way" (1977: 66). *Anasemia* refers to a process wherein signs and symbols are approached not with the idea of assigning fixed meanings to them, but as indeterminate and at times conflicted, that is to say, indicative of change, of multiple directions, of untapped and dormant potentials. I would argue that it is in that fashion that those of us too aligned with western conceptions of signification as fixity of meaning could try to approach the question of pattern. Typically, communication and media studies tend to ignore patterns—because the repetition of the same—sometimes a recognizable sign, but often an abstract figure—does not lend itself to the kind of rich narrative that the field has traditionally favored. However, as Washburn and Crowe show in *Symmetry Comes of Age: The Role of Pattern in Culture* (2004), patterns are both universal and specific, and tie individuals, communities and intercultural exchange in ways that have not fully been understood, because we need to understand them as establishing relationships between symmetry and rhythm in non-verbal ways. Indeed, patterns are geometrical manipulation and play on symmetry: a pattern unit can be in turn repeated, mirrored, expanded, scaled down, inverted. It can use the same color combination throughout or undergo multiple color changes. So, for instance, the inclusion of new color schemes that are reflective of the seaside landscape—something that was not done consciously but rather developed over time as the women and the designers continued experimenting—marked a diasporic journey as well, and the explorations of new surroundings and environments. All of these manipulations create rhythm effects, which play an important cultural role. Washburn and Crowe for instance talk about how mourning rituals involve specific kinds of rhythms, which can be acoustic, but also visual. Again, through the notion of patterns as rhythm, we have both a kind of positionality with the environment—certain patterns might be appropriate for specific settings and situations only—but they overall establish a resonance among people and with the environment. The textile objects thus created express different modalities of communication between makers and their environment—explorations into different modes of being, empowerment and existence.

Textile communicates, but it cannot be analyzed through traditional western semiotics, which see language as made up of interlinked units of signification, each with a somewhat precise definition (Saussure, 1999). This is not to say that there is no semiosis in textile: patterns (Bier, 2004; Paternosto, 1996) and symbols have values and meanings, some of which are highly cherished and protected by their communities. But what is meant by meaning here is not a set of dictionary definitions, but rather paths to navigate the complexity and plurality of the cosmos, a way to combine with different forces. In other words, meaning in textile is not fixed, but rather is about the opening of pathways through combinations of materials, gestures and designs. The question, in turn, is about the materialization of such a journey via textile-making.

Mathematics, Rhythms, and Signs

Textile-making practices mediate in complex ways: they do not just represent, nor do they simply record or transcribe. Rather, they compose with and combine different elements and processes: material and mathematical, abstract and symbolic, rhythmic, haptic, and visual. It is for this very reason that it is difficult to see them as media practices from a western perspective. For the women of the weaving and crochet communities, the incorporation of new symbols and patterns is a work of sociocultural construction and imagination. But such work is not abstract—the incorporation of signs—but also material and physical: the production of textile objects. Typically, little attention is paid to the work of making textile from thread, but another key incommensurability lies in the fact that to weave or weft-crochet textile is to practice mathematics. The makers here become mathematical beings—and this is something that we tend to forget in the west as the weaving and making of cloth has been taken over by machines. Textile-making processes of this sort are a unique kind of digital media practice, and one that does not fit into western conceptions of what constitutes the digital. By digital here, I mean not only numbers, but also fingers, and the kind of textile techniques used by the groups are exemplary in that they are about materializing mathematical processes by hand.

Textile-making often suffers from a negative reputation of being repetitive, tedious, physically taxing and better left to machines. And indeed, textile weaving and crochet is physically taxing—the back and eyes get tired, which is why it is also best as a time-limited activity. Anyone doing full-time, intensive, repeated weaving or crochet work would end up with a broken body and poor eyesight. But the kind of textile-making the women do—backstrap loom weaving and weft-crochet—also requires both mathematical minds and deft and skillful hands and eyes. Weaving and weft-crochet (along with knitting) are digital in that, in the words of T'ai Smith (2018), they reproduce a "binary logic": "the alternate interlacing of warp and weft threads" for weaving, and similarly the looping of warp thread around the weft thread for the weft-crochet technique. As Smith further explains:

...woven patterns and structures are essentially manipulations of algebraic equations. This was clearly demonstrated by an American weaver and mathematician, Ada Dietz, who exploited this principle in the 1940s and published a short treatise on it in 1949 (...). It is not so difficult to imagine, then, that the rule and the change in rule could become a code, a method for communicating through the manipulation and deciphering of slight changes in the pattern.

Smith, 2018: n.p.

The similarities between textile techniques that follow a binary logic and contemporary digital media have long been recognized: computer code can be knitted, or woven. Artist Vincent Vulsma for instance realized a series of woven Jacquard textiles for the *Cultural Threads* exhibit at the TexteilMuseum in Tilberg (2018) where he used data from the log books of the Dutch Middelburgse Commercie Compagnie (MCC), which in the eighteenth century engaged in the trade of "guinea textiles, gunpowder, indigo, but also slaves" (Hemmings, n.d.). Vulsma's woven pieces are all white, with subtle patterns variations that indicate the presence of data to address the infrastructure of colonial power. In so doing, as exhibition curator Jessica Hemmings explains, Vulsma "seeks to 'bypass the visual' and instead focuses on the nature of weaving to (...) potentially carry information on a structural level" (Hemmings, n.d.). Such carrying of information at the structural level is key to understanding the techniques of weaving and crocheting analyzed here. Weaving and crocheting are digital practices in that they rely on mathematical operations to embed information in their very structures. Compare this, for instance, with painting on a piece of textile: the textile here becomes a support to carry visual information. In the case of weaving and crocheting, by contrast, the piece of textile is the information. As T'ai Smith explains, the mathematicity of textile requires specific algorithmic processes:

...the rule-pattern logic (the algorithm) that is *necessary* to follow to produce a textile (...) is less important to other media. For instance, in pottery, stone carving, or painting, there is more room to depart from shape-defining rules. Though those media often *depict patterns*, they do not, in and of themselves, require adhering to a discrete pattern of practice.

Smith, 2018: n.p.

In other words, to weave requires mathematics and we should realize that woven, knitted and crocheted textile pieces are based on a principle of rendering information as data points on a grid to obtain visual, spatial and multidimensional forms. Anthropologist Gary Urton (1998; 2003; Urton and Llanos, 1997), whose research focuses on the practice of mathematics in pre-Columbian Peru, from the Quechua's use of weaving to the Inca *Quipus*, further explains this in detail. In the case of weaving, mathematical (and in particular arithmetic) operations are first of all central to setting up the warp—the vertical threads—on a backstrap loom. If one is to produce woven patterns using different colors, then one needs to carefully count the warp color threads and map how they will intersect with the weft thread. Consider, for instance, that a finished woven piece will have an edge, then be composed of different sections with different designs and color combinations, such as panels with figures separated by narrow bands featuring geometric designs (Urton and Llanos, 1997: 120): the weaver has to figure out the set of colored warps to realize such intricate compositions. Urton explains that the warpers:

> ...are working with fairly large numbers, combining and recombining various groupings of decimal values in sophisticated and generally symmetrical arrangements. (...) warping is very much concerned with the art of counting, but it is not *just* about counting: clearly there is a complex interplay of attention to, and knowledge about, both numerical information and spatial arrangements and organization involved.
>
> Urton and Llanos, 1997: 124

Weaving as a practice itself further translates mathematical processes into aesthetic shapes. As Urton further explains, the weaving process itself, in the case of Quechua weaving, requires following a specific series of steps, or picking sequences. The weaver passes the weft thread through the warp, and carefully places the weft thread underneath or over specific warp threads in order to realize a pattern. This involves learning picking sequences that then have to be repeated in order to create a pattern. As Urton further explains when describing Quechua children learning to weave, weaving is about counting but not just counting warp threads to be picked:

> In the long term—over the course of performing and repeating several full sets of picking sequences—the production of these designs instills and reinforces an awareness of, and a sensibility to, "reciprocal" relations between larger sets of numbers through the various rotational and reflection symmetry that are used in producing the different designs.
>
> Urton and Llanos, 1997: 128

Weaving is, then, art based on counting and geometry, and it is interesting to note that to become an expert weaver, one not only has to master mathematical skills, but also master them to the level that they become non-conscious, kinesthetically felt as a weaving rhythm. In my own very limited experience in weaving a *watu*—the narrow bands that Quechua children first start learning weaving with—at the Traditional Textile Centre in Cusco, it became apparent that the challenge of such a weaving process is not only to learn the picking sequences so that one can focus on the weaving itself rather than constantly checking up the instructions. The subsequent challenge is to develop a kind of feeling for the design, a non-conscious prehension of what threads need to be picked, so that one's mind is not only focused on materializing an actual sequence, but can feel its relation to the overall design. Only then can the actual weaving become more regular. In my experience, the constant back and forth of checking in on picking sequences and counting threads resulted in a piece that was poorly woven—some lines too tight, others too loose, accompanied by a very sore back, and a headache from eye strain. This kind of weaving experience—that one needs to gain a *feeling* for the overall design in order to have one's body relate to the materials in such way as to produce a good weave—is not limited to the backstrap loom techniques traditionally used in Peru, but is common for many other forms of weaving, and for the weft-crochet techniques employed by the women from the textile groups I followed. As Urton states, it was easier for him to learn weaving from younger weavers as:

> Older women—the master weavers—have routinized and incorporated the rhythms of weaving so deeply into their bodily movements that it is difficult for them to articulate clearly the step-by-step movements, especially the regimes of counting, that are required to weave a particular design.
>
> Urton and Llanos, 1997: 115

The weft-crochet technique that is used by the women in the textile groups I followed requires similar kinds of embodied mathematics, which is why the women described the overall process as calming and meditative: once they have a rhythm, to the outsider the crocheted piece seems to appear almost seamlessly, like a perfect choreography, because the counting of stitches is completely incorporated and embodied. The added challenge for the groups I met with was a change in the kind of shapes the women were crocheting. Traditionally, these kinds of crochet techniques were used to produce flat objects such as rugs. Traditional weft-crochet bags, even, are constructed out of two flat sides with the sides stitched to each other. The designers, however, introduced more spherical shapes, such as bags with a circular base that would then go up in an oblong shape, planters and other spherical forms. This transition to these new three-dimensional shapes does require an adaptation of the patterns to a spherical, rather than a plane surface, something which again, requires mathematical operations.

The skills required to weave and weft-crochet encompass mathematical and geometrical processes to follow the logical sequence of thread combinations in order to create three-dimensional shapes. At the same time, it would be a mistake to consider only the purely abstract aspects of such mathematical processes. Indeed, the act of making textile requires a coordination between abstraction and materialization, between the mathematical models in the mind of the textile maker and the actual encounter between the mind and bodies of the makers and the agencies of materials. However, this key characteristic is often ignored, as western epistemologies that prioritize minds over bodies continue to dominate and relegate to the margins, at best, epistemologies of the South, where such separation does not happen. How have digital technologies that have existed long before our contemporary digital technologies and media forms been rendered invisible and assigned mostly a negative value, or at best viewed as romantic remnants of a past unsullied by modern technologies? Here is an illustration to explore this crucial juncture of mathematical abstraction and textile materialization and the kind of problems of translation it poses: the designers I followed in Northern Peru have been exploring the relationship between textile digitality and the contemporary digital landscape. There has been wide interest in exploring how ancient digital technologies such as textile weaving and knitting could be linked to contemporary digital technologies. In particular, the designers were very interested in QR codes—labels made of black squares arranged in grid-like patterns on a white background—because they share a visual affinity with some traditional pre-Columbian aesthetics, some of which make intensive use of visual elements as squares or rectangles on a diagram. As an exercise, the designers had asked one of the weavers to weave a large-scale QR code, providing her with a full-size model printed on transparent paper. But the weaver struggled: to be machine readable, the black squares of a QR code have to be perfectly straight. And in order to achieve perfectly straight black squares on the inside of the woven piece, the weaver had to keep adjusting thread tensions, resulting in a piece with very uneven edges. In other words, the materials—the threads—prevented a perfect translation from the image on transparent paper to its three-dimensional rendering. Such tension between abstract model and its materialization are actually quite common in textile-making, and the reality is that there is always a need for a back and forth recursive process between design and production in order to make a textile object that is satisfactory. This is the reason why, in my interviews with designers working globally with non-western textile craft, it often transpired that many projects involving Indigenous or traditional textile practices encountered difficulties. Often, the designers would come in with prepared designs meant to adapt Indigenous or non-western aesthetics and skills to western markets and audiences. The designers would often expect these designs to be seamlessly rendered as textile objects, only to find that this eventually was not the case and be disappointed. One could blame the artisans' lack of skills, but this would not make sense when one sees the craftsmanship involved in making traditional textile objects. Rather, the error is that some designers expect perfect *translation* of their ideas and ignore how textile materials and techniques react and sometimes resist the imposition of abstract models. This is what Ingold highlighted is a quality of textile-making: it resists the "hylomorphic" model, whereby one can impose form onto material. This echoes Bruno Latour's key insight in developing Actor-network theory (1999): materials have agencies of their own and can resist and subvert the plans of action that mobilize them in the first place.

But translation is not only about getting technical actants to materialize a plan of action: it is also, as Warren Sack (2019) reminds us, about the power to establish equivalences between processes that are radically different. In other words, whoever can make equivalencies and have them accepted yields tremendous power: whoever can say that a data-based matching app is the same as finding love and be taken seriously is able to bridge two radically different processes and therefore has the power to reshape perceptions and experience of love and relationships. In the vignette that I just presented, it first seemed that the equivalencies should have already been there: textile weaving is mathematical and involves diagrammatic visual renderings. QR codes are diagrams that communicate digitally encoded information. Therefore, weaving and QR encoding should be equivalent. The reality, however, is that we are dealing with two worlds that are incommensurable: the world of textile-based digital technologies as they have been practiced from pre-Columbian, pre-colonial times onward, and the world of western-centric dominant digital technologies. How is it, then, that processes that might seem similar—such as the use of digital processes to create objects can be in the end so dissimilar as to exist on completely different planes? Here, we need to move away from the question of actualization and production of objects to look at the dynamics through which only certain kinds of mathematical processes can gain some form of legitimacy. Here is another vignette to illustrate this incommensurability: one weaver recounted that her son, who was under the age of ten, had been interested enough in the weaving process to inquire about learning it. His father, however, discouraged the idea: weaving is for girls, and is not a useful skill to learn—better focus on doing well at school. But weaving is arithmetic, geometry and logical sequencing, demanding highly sophisticated mathematical skills that would be useful for anyone to learn and cultivate, especially in our STEM-oriented societies. This is not to say that the father in the story is a stereotypical patriarchal figure, but rather that he expressed the immense divide that exists between mathematics as they are envisioned in dominant neocolonial culture—abstract, with paper and numbers as a starting point, to evolve towards complex computing models that enable large-scale control—and mathematics as they are practiced through textile—unseen, mostly taking place silently between threads, hands and minds, and as they are traditionally practiced in Peru, without any kind of paper support, let alone computers and dealing with uncertainty and ambiguity rather than clarity. There is thus an incommensurability between the mathematician and the textile weaver: these two worlds are kept separate, and one is glorified over the other, even though they both require mathematical skills.

This is something that the designers working with Peruvian artisans kept highlighting for me: a large part of the production work included trying to find ways to translate worlds that are made incommensurable by the very dominant structures of translation and equivalencies used both locally and globally. The divide between the mathematical world of the textile makers and the mathematical underpinning of the dominant culture and the dominant textile industry kept resurging. In one of the meetings I observed, the designers asked one of the weft-crochet artisans to demonstrate her skills for me. The latter was first given beige and green threads and asked to work on a cylindrical shape—a round base that would then curve up into a straight edge—and to incorporate a green pattern. As the artisan started the work, the designer came back to give orange and pink threads, asking the artisan to incorporate them as well in the pattern. It was quite astounding to see how seamless and effortless this whole process was for the artisan, who was able on the fly to modify the pattern to incorporate the new colors. Working from the middle outward, she deftly worked on modifying the pattern to fit the evolving size of the piece. This looked like the easiest thing in the world to do, yet I challenge anyone to try repeating this! Any knitter or weaver in the Global North would know this: typically, one needs a diagram on paper and a series of detailed steps about rows, number of stitches and so on in order to realize such a seemingly simple shape and pattern. In other words, the artisan did not need a translation onto another support such as paper to be able to actualize a design in their mind. But here again is the incommensurability: most of the artisans I encountered are what in the west we would label as lacking literacy and numeracy skills. The artisans in particular were struggling with simple number operations. I witnessed this when the designers gave them paperwork. The forms required them to first weigh the thread they were given at the beginning of a project. At the end of the project, the artisans were tasked with weighing the remaining thread and subtracting it from the original weight to calculate how much thread they used. Most struggled with this seemingly simple operation. They were not used to numbers written on paper, and even less to paper-based additions and subtractions, and so these artisans, while able to undertake complex mathematical thinking and operations with textile, were unable to perform basic western mathematical operations.

The Values of Making

One can easily imagine the consequences of such an incommensurability: the work of these women is almost always devalued as *basic*, as providing for basic necessities such rugs, bags and so on, that are never credited as the result of complex thinking and mathematical genius. Their textile practices are seen as folk craft—as something that is colorful and cheerful, but definitely not a brilliant materialization of mathematics. The women themselves, because many did not have access to much school education, are de facto treated as unintelligent, even when their handiwork manifestly proves otherwise. Overall, many women, especially in newly formed and not-yet-fully established groups, had internalized this and downplayed their skills. The designers mentioned that quite a few women artisans completely lacked confidence in their ability to collaborate: filling out forms already appeared an enormous, if not unsurmountable challenge, and the idea of being responsible for using materials in specified ways and producing a certain amount of pieces that would meet specific production criteria felt even more overwhelming. The underlying issue was that a significant number of artisans had internalized the belief that their lack of school education meant that they would never succeed professionally. Only a couple of women were willing to travel to Lima to look at designs and shop for materials, for instance, while most were quite petrified at the idea of traveling such distance. Even traveling to the closest big city, Trujillo, to sell their wares at craft markets was daunting. Lack of confidence was high, and the idea that the newly formed artisan communities themselves could start developing their own wares often felt like an impossible dream. The designers thus not only produced designs and oversaw production: a large part of their job encompassed some form of social work and coaching, encouraging women one-on-one and organizing group discussion and sharing, seeking external public and private funding for computer training and to hire a psychologist to work on boosting self-esteem and confidence. All this work eventually paid off: three years after my visit, the designers reported that the women were much more empowered and active, creating their own lines and working to sell in local and national markets.

The question of the value of textile work and textile-making is thus profoundly shaped by the two incommensurabilities mentioned above: the lack of understanding, from a western perspective, of how textile signs communicate and of how textile objects are digital objects. The valorization of one's work as meaningful, satisfying and worthwhile—as something that mattered—from both an individual perspective and a social one was a constant concern for the women's group and for the designers, not only in terms of economic value of labor and wages, but also the value of work as a platform of transformation and empowerment. This final incommensurability surrounding value lies in the fact that handmade textile in the west is not recognized as a skilled form of labor. The work of Indigenous textile makers, in order to be recognized, often has to be articulated around the preservation of non-western cultural identities, and around artistic value. And while these two aspects are indeed central to contemporary textile craft, they gloss over the question of embodied mathematics and thus tend to fall prey to repeating neocolonial patterns. Too often indeed, handmade textile makers are pictured as part of a romanticized pre-industrial past that actually serves neocolonial logics, both for customers in the west looking for exotic products as much as for the textile production and distribution systems, which can use this romanticized vision to put a high value on these handmade commodities. The designers pointed out a set of particular pressures related to this romanticization, mentioning that, for instance, they were asked to use cotton rather than synthetic thread for production, but that nobody was willing to accept the higher price point that would result from this. Romanticization of handmade craft, in other words, could not jeopardize profits. The key challenge here is about how to use existing networks of power that establish the cultural and economic values of textile commodities, and to create new connections, and therefore new channels of production and distribution that could go beyond this impasse.

This particular struggle will also be the core of the next chapter, but for now I will conclude by focusing on how the designers navigated these tensions in order to establish durable networks of production that could eventually be used to empower women makers beyond the selling of high-value commodities on the global market. Let me rely again on Karen Barad's point about mattering: that practices of materialization work to define ontological status, and therefore the value of textile objects and the work that goes into producing them. For the designers, there were three parallel strategies of materialization that had to be developed. Finding a global outlet was a crucial first step towards materialization: the designers knew that only through finding economic partners in a position to order large enough amounts of textile objects could the whole enterprise gather enough attention to attract other business partners and qualify for private and public funding: proof of economic success had to be provided before getting access to funds, means and infrastructures for sustainable and durable development.

Working for the high-end global textile market involved several types of pressures: developing designs that would appeal to wealthy customers, combining exoticism and fashionability; working with requests for fast production turnarounds at a moment's notice; and training on the ground a small team to package the textile objects into luxury ones to be sold into high-end department stores in Europe. Once economic success was achieved, there was some room for the makers to further engage with developing wares for the local community and tourism trade—experimental materializations could be developed. There was a difference in the designers' mind between their work for the global market, which required using traditional techniques with designs that appealed to a rich customer base, and with local markets, which the designers saw as a way to empower the artisans themselves to develop their own new designs. Here in particular, they supported experimentation and innovation on the part of the makers, encouraging them to become their own designers, but also marketers that should go and meet their customers in order to figure out further designs. The final strategy was for the designers to work in close collaboration with the makers to experiment with design objects to be sold internationally. Here the focus was on producing ground-breaking designs using traditional techniques and materials in new combinations, working through many prototypes to participate in design and industry fairs and competition in North America and Europe. The resulting household objects were distributed through high-end design stores, appealing to a specific clientele of design aficionados. All three strategies were fraught with difficulties and were not straightforward, from finding designs that would appeal to particular audiences to creating the infrastructures through which these designs could be produced and circulated. One thing all these strategies had in common, however, was around maintaining a proper work–life balance for the makers.

What is it, ultimately, that makes textile work for these women something worth pursuing? The first answer I was given is that textile work can be done from the home—it was crucial for the women I interviewed to be able to find an economic activity that would not conflict with child-rearing. A few women recounted how much they emotionally suffered when they had to work away from home, and how the textile work they were doing enabled them to be there for their children. They enjoyed the work as well, describing weaving and weft-crochet as calming, meditative and creative activities that, at the same time, enabled keeping an eye and an ear out for what their children were up to. This experience of textile work is worth dwelling on, as it articulates the relationships between meaning and matter. In *Meeting the Universe Halfway*, Barad examines the meaning–matter relationship, explaining that discursive practices and practices of materialization both work on the ontic, on establishing the apparatus whereby meanings can be enacted and something can come to matter (both in the sense of materialization and as the becoming important for others). And the question of the meaningfulness of textile work requires in turn, defining proper practices of materialization. The designers explained the following: one needs to make work meaningful, which requires careful thinking about the kind of work required, and the kind of production demands (e.g., materialization practices) put on the artisans. One of the designers offered an example: they had worked with other communities in the past on reviving *peines*—comb-like objects made up of wooden sticks the size of toothpicks and woven together with threads to create patterns. *Peines* are common in archeological digs in Peru, and the tradition still exists in the Shipibo-Conibo communities of the Peruvian Amazon, where men make *peines* as gifts to express affection. The designer was interested in reviving the *peines* tradition with other Indigenous communities in Peru to promote Indigenous patterns. What the designer had to carefully think about was the production of the wooden sticks: if they were to be made entirely by hand as was traditional, the project would be very time-consuming and the cost of labor and cost of the objects would have to go up accordingly. If they were to use industrially produced wooden sticks, the making of the objects would become meaningless, and lose the kind of careful attention and affection that makes these objects unique in the first place. The designer talked about how this process highlighted the need for balance and the careful balancing out of the different aspects of labor: enjoyment and emotional involvement; costs and potential markets. These kinds of considerations were at the forefront of the designers' choices for planning and organizing the textile groups: it was important to balance out the need for the women to fit in their textile work in positive ways into their lives, which meant not doing it full-time, while establishing reliable production standards, expectations and goals. This required extensive and ongoing discussions with the different communities to figure out how to keep the work meaningful while managing demands from clients in the fashion and apparel industry. The meaning of textile-making and textile work were therefore key concerns for the designers and the women's groups and dictated processes of materialization. For the women makers, the possibility of continuing with a millennia-old tradition of textile work and reinventing it to gain socioeconomic power was key. And further, the idea that they could create and launch their own craft enterprise locally spurred fear and resistance at first, but an incredible amount of energy subsequently. Women reported feeling more valued in their families, being able to stand up for themselves and have a say in household matters and dynamics. That being said, the kind of profound existential dynamics at play in the use of pre-Columbian symbols and patterns, in the development of new designs and in the practice of embodied mathematics do not often surface. The key effort from a commercial perspective is to find a way to translate, reach and talk to external audiences. Often, this requires careful steps not to challenge western audiences and consumer markets, and not to show them the limits of their worlds and knowledge.

If we were to take stock of what the Quechua women's weaving groups in Northern Peru could tell the nineteenth-century male silk-weavers, it would be the following: that the immensely rich world of technical extensions, in order to fully engage and delink from the dominant matrix of power, has to develop a discursive-material apparatus, where objects can gain meaning, and non-industrial work comes to matter. In the reworking of craft for these diasporic textile groups, we see a profound reflection on developing one's place through temporal and spatial crossings. Both making practices and the objects resulting from it express by materializing and symbolizing such existential trajectories. Textile becomes an existential medium that crosses through many worlds and pasts. Let me continue such reflection on the making as existential mediation and transformation by turning to another category of makers, who are usually seen as subservient subject to the dominant matrix of power: the domestic woman as textile worker in pre-industrial France.

References

Allen, Catherine J. (1998). "When Utensils Revolt: Mind, Matter, and Modes of Being in the Pre-Columbian Andes." *RES: Anthropology and Aesthetics*, no. 33: 18–27.

Arnold, D. Y. (2018). Making textiles into persons: Gestural sequences and relationality in communities of weaving practice of the South Central Andes. *Journal of Material Culture* 23 (2), 239–60. https://doi.org/10.1177/1359183517750007.

Barad, Karen. (2007). *Meeting the Universe Halfway: Quantum Physics and the Entanglement of Matter and Meaning*. Durham, NC: Duke University Press.

Bourget, Steve, and Kimberly L. Jones. (2009). *The Art and Archaeology of the Moche: An Ancient Andean Society of the Peruvian North Coast*. Austin: University of Texas Press.

Bier, Carol. (2004). Pattern Power: Textiles and the Transmission of Knowledge. *Textile Society of America Symposium Proceedings*, January. https://digitalcommons.unl.edu/tsaconf/444.

Derrida, Jacques. (1977). "FORS." *The Georgia Review* 31 (1): 64–116.

Hemmings, Jessica. (n.d.). "Navigating Cultural Threads." https://www.jessicahemmings.com/navigating-cultural-threads/ (accessed 17 July 2023).

Ingold, Tim. (2010). "The Textility of Making." *Cambridge Journal of Economics* 34 (1): 91–102.

Latour, Bruno. (1999). *Pandora's Hope: Essays on the Reality of Science Studies*. Cambridge, MA: Harvard University Press.

Leon, Levy, and Nicole Caroline. (2018). "'La cultura chicha como recurso turístico de Lima.'" Universidad César Vallejo, Trujillo, Peru. https://repositorio.ucv.edu.pe/handle/20.500.12692/28495.

Mignolo, Walter D., and Catherine E. Walsh. (2018). *On Decoloniality: Concepts, Analytics, Praxis*. Durham, NC: Duke University Press.

Paternosto, César. (1996). *The Stone and the Thread: Andean Roots of Abstract Art*. Translated by Esther Allen. Austin: University of Texas Press.

Sack, Warren. (2019). *The Software Arts*. Cambridge, MA: The MIT Press.

Salmón, Dorian Espezúa. (2009). "¿Cultura chicha?" *Crónicas Urbanas*, no. 14: 99–110.

Santos, Boaventoura de Sousa. (2018). *The End of the Cognitive Empire: the Coming of Age of Epistemologies of the South*. Durham: Duke University Press.

Saunders, Nicholas J. (2013). *Icons of Power: Feline Symbolism in the Americas*. London: Routledge.

Saussure, Ferdinand de. (1999). *Course in General Linguistics*. Reprint edn. Chicago: Carus Publishing.

Smith, T'ai. (2018). "Textile, A Diagonal Abstraction: Glass Bead in Conversation with T'ai Smith—Glass Bead." *Glass Bead*. 2018. http://www.glass-bead.org/article/textile-diagonal-abstraction/?lang=enview.

Trever, Lisa Senchyshyn. (2005). "Slithering Serpents and the Afterlives of Stones: The Role of Ornament in Inka-Style Architecture of Cusco, Peru." Thesis. University of Maryland, College Park. https://drum.lib.umd.edu/handle/1903/3108.

Urton, Gary. (1998). "From Knots to Narratives: Reconstructing the Art of Historical Record Keeping in the Andes from Spanish Transcriptions of Inka Khipus." *Ethnohistory* 45 (3): 409–38.

Urton, Gary. (2003). *Signs of the Inka Khipu: Binary Coding in the Andean Knotted-String Records*. Austin: University of Texas Press.

Urton, Gary, and Primitivo Nina Llanos. (1997). *The Social Life of Numbers: A Quechua Ontology of Numbers and Philosophy of Arithmetic*. Austin: University of Texas Press.

Villavicencio, Maritza. (2017). *Mujer: Poder Y Alimentación En El Antiguo Perú*. USMP, Universidad de San Martin de Porres, Fondo Editorial.

Washburn, Dorothy K., and Donald W. Crowe, eds. (2004). *Symmetry Comes of Age: The Role of Pattern in Culture*. Seattle: University of Washington Press.

Part III

Transformative Entanglements

Chapter 5

REWEAVING THE INTERFACE

Domestic Textiles and Power

The idea of domestic textile-making seems quaint and out of touch today: who can even sew a button, let alone a garment? And yet, there is a revival of domestic textile practices: knitting and sewing studios have popped up in many cities, as have fabric stores and a lively scene on the internet for selling and exchanging both finished goods, tools and materials, patterns and notions. This revival of domestic textile craft in the west has several roots: awareness of the unsustainability of mass-produced textile in terms of labor exploitation and environmental destruction is one, as is the rediscovery of the creative and expressive potential in textile work, both for personal and social purposes (Black, 2017). Also notable, we have seen the progressive acknowledgement that domestic spaces not only kept women confined and at the mercy of a patriarchal order—they also allowed women to gather away from patriarchal surveillance and establish their own sphere of freedom and social bonding (Goggin and Tobin, 2009; Parker, 2010; Plant, 2016). We might have the impression that domestic textile work was only an excuse to gather together because it is so tedious and time-consuming. And indeed, how else to think of the many handmade textile ornamentations of the nineteenth- and early twentieth-century household? The lace curtains and doilies, the crochet blankets and so on evoke stifling atmospheres where the few spaces of physical and creative agencies for women were channeled as the reinforcement of the patriarchal order. But this is not the whole history of domestic textile in the west. In North America, notably, quilting has a long tradition of being a creative and expressive form (Knauer, 2019; Garber, 2013; Stalp and Eicher, 2007) of collective community building and remembrance (Rand, 2007). Quilting allows for silenced voices—Indigenous, African-American, women's—to be heard (Brown, 1989). It is also a material type of storytelling and community building, where making is as important as the finished product, and where, up until recently, distribution took place through a gift economy. The renewed popularity of quilting and sewing (Tamboukou, 2015) today has much to do with its adoption within artistic-activist circles as a way of giving palpability to collective action as well as individual experience. I argue in this chapter however that these transformative potentials of domestic textile encompass more than the telling of silenced stories: domestic textile-making is primarily about direct engagement with power. This might seem like a grand statement, and perhaps an overly general one, but I argue that domestic textile is an engagement with power in two important yet paradoxical ways: first, in that it actualizes power by materializing abstract dominant values of economic productivity, social hierarchy, patriarchy and so on; and in so doing, it establishes the subject position of women as being in charge of textile. Second, at the same time it places the textile maker and the making process in a state of suspension—a pause, but also a bracketing of sorts—where other latent potentials can emerge, where other connections can be layered on top of existing ones. To borrow from Rosi Braidotti, domestic textile work enables "transpositions" (2006)—ways in which seemingly stabilized identities and subject positions are actually troubled, and where the making engages in a process of becoming in Deleuze and Guattari's sense: becoming-other, becoming-worker, becoming-to oneself. In other words, domestic textile work is about subjectivation—both as power exerted via establishing subservient subject position and as creative becoming that seizes new opportunities to articulate new horizons of being. The quiet, repetitive work of domestic textile allows "creative links and zigzagging positions" (Braidotti, 2006: 7), movements that show how potentials for reinvention and resistance lurk even within the very dispositif of the dominant matrix of power.

This chapter therefore focuses on domestic textile work in France as paradoxical vectors of imprisonment, creativity and reinvention (Parker, 2010) that organize themselves around two overlapping, yet divergent processes: that of subjectivation and of making—of defining who one is according to existing power formations and, on the contrary, entering into states of suspension and indeterminacy. It investigates how textile can be a medium for transindividuation—for becoming-to and with others through the activity of making—despite also carrying at the same time dynamics of deindividuation, dehumanization, exploitation and inequality through the imposition of subaltern subject positions, such as that of the stay-at-home wife. It is through exploring the tension between subjectivation and making that we can better understand how textile functions as an interface that can be used for both the exercise of control and power at the same time as it offers new forms of bonding with and within communities and new modes of transformation and escape from subject positions. The definition of interface I use here is not the one associated with computer interface: by interface I refer to that which enables the encounter between two or more elements, processes, dynamics and so on. Defining textile-making as interface means tracing the encounters that it enables between dominant subject positions, flows of becoming, individual dynamics, collective processes, economic considerations, social hierarchies, technical transformation and so on. By dwelling on this paradox of domestic textile work, I hope to enrich existing analysis of the *dispositif* of power—how power functions through establishing heterogenous networks—by focusing in turn on the space and time of new combinations and relationships that emerges through domestic textile work. Western domestic textile work is particularly interesting as a critical site of analysis because it carries less of the mystique and romanticism that western perspectives often assign to non-western domestic textile work. By focusing on the western version and its ambivalence, I aim to show how the dynamics of resistance and transformation are often superimposed on dynamics of power, building flows and relationalities that point to an outside of the dispositif.

I argue then that domestic textile is an interface that enables both power over and power of invention, or to borrow from the Spinozist tradition, both *potesta*—power as control over something or someone—and *potentia*—power as the immanent capacity to act (Deleuze, 2001). In so doing, I want to point out how domestic textile work—usually seen as mundane, repetitive, best for passing time or ornamenting one's quotidian life, and therefore definitely not on the same level as writing a book or painting a work of art—is actually a powerful mode of transformation, both individually and collectively. In particular, I want to pay attention to the materiality of the making process as that which enfolds and layers these contradictory movements of control, escape and invention. Deleuze's concept of the fold (Deleuze and Guattari, 1987) here is particularly important in that it expresses how broader dynamics can be folded in at the level of daily making, and what can in turn lurk under the surface, first unsaid and untold, emerging through daily gestures that come to gain new meanings in one's sense of existence. Further, I see the materiality of textile-making—the same gestures repeated over and over again to produce cloth which is adorned—as a form of "refrain" to borrow from Deleuze and Guattari (1987). That is to say, domestic textile work, through its repetitive nature, delineates spaces of domesticity but in so doing, also points out what is outside these spaces, yet reachable through leaps, displacement, and new articulations.

In particular, I am interested here in adding to the kind of examination of the dispositif as focalizing on large-scale dynamics in specific locations and situations by paying attention in turn to everyday practices at the micro level. I want to understand how the repetitive and small gestures of domestic textile work delineate spaces of agencies and relationalities that in turn escape from and face dominant subject positions related to domestic work. I am referring here to the kind of cognitive, affective and material relations one can have with a transindividuating medium such as textile, relations that range from conscious to unconscious, personally significant or in turn so mundane as to be routine, habitual and banal, so apparently meaningless as to escape the grasping gaze of dominant power. In other words, rather than adopting the point of view of the dominant system controlling and exploiting everything, it is crucial in turn to focus on the interfaces of transindividuation that allow individuals to develop minute, normal, habitual practices that in turn provide for experiences that are not captured by a dominant order. To think about textile practices as interfaces that exist in complicated and paradoxical relationships with dominant socioeconomic powers requires focusing on the processes and components that assist a textile maker in delineating a sense of positionality and agency by offering potential connections to the world.

I base my analysis on the difference between subjects and makers. In critical communication and media studies, we usually focus on processes of subject formation—of how broader social, economic and political processes inhabit, activate and animate subjects by establishing relationships between how one should be and act in the world and how one experiences and understands oneself, by defining important values and life goals, by delineating both material and symbolic conditions and possibilities of existence (Foucault, 1977). Makers could be seen as a category of subject and indeed, as we have seen in the previous chapter, how one perceives oneself and is perceived by others as a textile maker is dependent on how one is valued and perceived as a productive member of society: meaning, again, is dependent on mattering and vice-versa. However, whereas the subject and the maker overlap, they also diverge in fundamental ways. Making means connecting disparate elements into a whole: economic, social, practical, material, symbolic, cultural and so on, that coalesce together as crafted objects. Typically, the maker disappears from general awareness as the objects they make stand out, and the temporality and space of making recedes from consciousness. But it is important here to reflect on this very time and space of making as, in the case of textile, ambiguous power. To put it simply: in being a maker, there is a potential to find power in the most powerless situation. The best example to think of here is that of *The Odyssey*'s Penelope, who weaves a funeral shroud during the day and undoes it at night to keep her suitors at bay during the many years her husband, Ulysses, is off on his odyssey. In this way, Penelope manages to keep a state of suspension by being not a subject (a woman in a patriarchal society, a queen to be married, an asset for male power) but a maker in charge of creating a set of connections that requires set boundaries: she must "finish" the shroud that pays homage to Ulysses' father Laertes, therefore fulfilling familial obligations and displaying her legitimacy as daughter and queen, all-the-while maintaining her "freedom" from marrying one of her many suitors by stalling. By undoing the shroud at night, Penelope lengthens the space and time of making as one of suspension, where connections that should be made are kept apart (Cocker, 2017). In so doing, she is not only resisting power, but also shows that making can be the moment when the routines of power can be suspended. Ultimately, the story goes, Penelope is found out and is only "saved" by Ulysses' timely return and thus her return to being a dutiful subject. But what is left of Penelope is her political cunning, her capacity to find ways to escape subjection, at least for a while, and to become a maker to claim a time and space of suspension of the machineries of political power grabs (Cocker, 2017). Of course, Penelope receives help and support: she is not completely by herself in resisting dominant power. Going back to Braidotti's concept of transposition, what we have with the myth of Penelope is the use of making to explore other potential modes of existence than the one assigned to her. What is the significance, then, of textile-making in understanding how one can navigate power relations and gesture towards—and perhaps even create—new spaces of agencies and new connections? How do we understand the space of uncertainties and latencies behind routine textile-making processes?

Marking Subjects

Quite counter-intuitively, let me start my investigation of domestic textile makers by looking at objects first. This focus on not only the visual but also haptic qualities of these objects ultimately helps to understand the dynamics of power in relation to textile makers. In that regard, I follow Paterson and Dodge's argument that haptic methodologies such as using one's own body and its haptic experiences is not a solipsistic experience but rather a "central investigative tool for generating valid empirical observation" that "necessitates a relational approach" and therefore can be used to map relationalities of power (2016: 12–13). I am originally from France, and some of my earlier memories of textile stem back from sleeping over at my grandmother's place, where I discovered for the first time heavy cotton sheets and wool blankets—a shock to the system for a kid used to Ikea's thin, weightless duvet covers. The weight of these old textiles, their surfaces that I found rough, itchy and uncomfortable, expressed more straightforwardly than anything else a deep generational gap: sensorial experiences point out the existential abyss that opens up with deep socioeconomic transformations such as the one that appeared with mass industrialization and mass consumerism. I was lucky enough to grow up in such an environment where old textiles endured as destabilizing and disturbing time capsules: one of my grandmother's final accomplishments was the cross-stitching of a set armchairs; my other grandmother was a devoted and prolific knitter. Such haptic experiences provided me with an early awareness of how modes of existence are materially enacted, and that paying attention to the sensorial yields important clues to how mediation can link small, mundane gestures to vast infrastructures of existence. Let me here further explore such insights through sensorial analysis of textile-making practices.

My analysis focuses on discarded textile objects, texts and documents. All these objects come from the same region of Auvergne in France, which I visit regularly. Auvergne has a long history of rural industry dating back to Roman times with large-scale production of pottery, knife-making, metalwork and textile-making, forestry, among others. The region is composed of towns and villages with the city of Clermont-Ferrand as the capital. Each of the towns and regions of Auvergne historically had their own industrial specialization: silk production and weaving, hemp and linen weaving, lace-making, gold embroidery, knife-making and so on. Industrial production was organized through the coordination of small groups of producers depending on time available: while some were engaged in industrial production full-time, it was more often the case that industrial work took place alongside agricultural work, offering income in the winter months for instance. Manufacturing was highly specialized as well: in textile-making, women were tasked with focusing on very specific techniques such as bobbin lace-making, and on the production of specific pieces. As we will see, such paid domestic textile work was not creative work by any means, but rather aimed at high productivity. Domestic textile production was important as well up until the 1960s, when cheap textiles that could be afforded by all entered the market and when lifestyle changes (urbanization, new educational opportunities, new employment opportunities) meant that textile-making practices were progressively abandoned.

The first set of objects I want to examine are domestic textiles including bed and table linens (Figure 5.1). I found these at a nonprofit second-hand store in the town of Thiers. The store had many such linens, donated when a grandparent or

Figure 5.1 Embroidered linen, date unknown. Courtesy of the author.

great-grand-parent died and their house emptied—heavy wood furniture, old magazines, books, everything. It is therefore impossible to trace when these textiles were actually produced, but given that the people who sold them were mostly from the postwar generation and stated they had belonged to their parents, one can guess that they were made between World War I and the 1950s. The first characteristic was that even though they were donated and some were damaged by humidity, these linens had been well taken care of for the longest time. They were perfectly laundered and folded: they were obviously handled as meaningful, valuable objects. The quality was there: the type of cloth used to make them is no longer found—heavy cotton, linen or hemp meant to withstand the test of time and boiling water and bleach. Today, these specific qualities, however, are not much valued: such textiles tend to be seen as too heavy, too bulky and cumbersome, requiring too much care, indeed. Most people do not find the need to invest in something that will last through time: it is more convenient to buy thinner fabric that is cheap and can therefore be discarded without a second thought when it becomes too used. These old fabrics are, however, in high demand for upcycled fashion—their unique sturdiness makes them ideal for garment-making and they do find a value here as rare materials no longer made. Indeed, the stock at the second-hand store I visited was high at the time because the town where it was located does not get many visitors and is somewhat off the map as a tourist destination. Yet, the store staff had mentioned that as the last generation of locals who inherited these fabrics was quickly disappearing, they were getting rarer and rarer.

Two important characteristics for these domestic textile objects appeared: first, unlike today's linens, they did not have a label although they were definitely machine-produced; and second, the person who purchased them left a mark of ownership in the form of embroidery work. Thus, the branding of these textiles fulfilled a different purpose than the one we are accustomed to now and which is focused on both symbolizing and materializing socioeconomic status and aspirations. Here, the branding is linked to social status, but in the sense of establishing a new family unit through two embroidered components: the initials of a bride and groom's last names, and some ornamentation. Both of these components feature handmade white-on-white intricate embroideries, most frequently featuring cutwork techniques involving relief stitching of lines and cutting of the fabric to create designs. Some of the ornamental cutwork involved many tiny symmetrical slits all along the edges of a tablecloth, for instance, while the embroidered initials' design featured elegant, elaborate calligraphy. We can think about these ornaments as contractual signatures, similar to a marriage certificate, and as celebration, so delightful are these designs. At the same time, they also stand for a specific commitment to time, one that is defined by the lifespan of husband and wife. The use of time-consuming techniques such as cutwork embroidery, as opposed to faster ways of marking textiles (think for instance, of affixing a label) denoted a commitment to a long living time indeed, but one that is meant to come to a final end. The linens, in that sense, are testaments to what was and never will be again. And indeed, the embroidered initials make these textile objects quite personal and provide a reason as to why they are subsequently discarded when their owners die: it would be difficult for a child to fully appropriate something that belonged so uniquely to the parents, to their union and their lives together.

Frequently part of a wedding trousseau, these textiles, when embroidered, functioned indeed as cultural techniques, both materially delineating and defining a new family space as well as symbolizing a family unit. In that sense, they linked together the mundane, the habitual and the sacred. Such domestic textile objects— bed linens, tablecloths, table runners, napkins, handkerchiefs—marked the start of and delineated a framework for a new set of family narratives, relationships, and memories that were to unfold over many meals and through many food stains, many days and nights. The few culturally significant types of textile objects left today in the Global North are typically associated with communicating the spiritual in daily life: a baptismal dress, for instance, a white wedding veil, or black clothes for mourning, all of which mark important life events and communicate these to the world. As Yuko Tanaka reminds us (2013), human life often begins with a newborn being wrapped in cloth and ends with a corpse being wrapped in a shroud. Textile historically marked important transitions, and allowed family members and groups to join in, witness and participate in an individual's existence. In that regard, it acted as a way of weaving existences together and therefore imbuing them with meaning; it existed as a *trace* of such new links. Overall, these textile ornamentations were markers of existence in both personal, collective and impersonal ways: marking a specific union between individuals, inscribing this union within social hierarchies but also ultimately signposting the boundedness of human existence.

At the same time, and from our contemporary perspective, these textiles also embodied gendered role division and identities along the lines of the bourgeois Catholic social order in provincial France. These textile objects withstood the test of turbulent history as they were also safely stored and cared for: their owners obviously had either many such textile objects to use, or the time, and maybe the staff, to be able to take care of them so that they were always immaculate. Historically, textile-making tends to be associated with keeping specific groups subservient and occupied. The classic image of the bourgeois woman being tasked with textile-making in order to be kept inside the family house comes to mind. In patriarchal societies, women who excel in domestic arts are often praised for fulfilling their subservient role as nurturers and peace-keepers of the household, and textile-making is often associated with this dynamic. But there is also a darker history of using handcrafted textile as a way to keep other marginalized groups subservient. Historically, both male and female prisoners were tasked with making textile as a way to keep them occupied and productive. Thus, textile-making, over the years, has been associated with soft and strong forms of control and subservience. But even such textiles that are the epitome of bourgeois patriarchal order and stability constitute multifaceted interfaces, in that they connect signs of social status with temporalities of making.

One thing particularly stood out as I observed these textiles: the embroidered mark was as much a mark of belonging as it was a trace of a painstaking making process. Examining them conjured up the ghost of the makers—the one that spent countless hours in precise embroidering and that was not entirely just a subject of the bourgeois patriarchal order, but an expressive, creative agent. The makers might have been the future wife working on her wedding trousseau, or perhaps she was hired help. The trace of making appeared as important as the content of the mark itself (i.e., the initials), perhaps because we are not used to the presence of makers anymore. Textile makers, after all, are always rendered invisible, and machine-making produces serial sameness. Yet, when looking at handmade embroidery work, the presence of the maker is undeniable. I remember once textile artist Dorothy Caldwell showing her personal collection of hand-embroidered textiles, among which were embroidery practice exercises done by a group of women at an embroidery school in India. The patterns and stitches were exactly the same, but as she pointed out, the individual character of each of the makers was undeniable: one definitely had a strong sense of humor, another was very serious, another playful, and so on. We often think of textile and needlework in particular as demanding perfect repetition of stitches, but even the most perfectly handmade embroidery had certain qualities that made it much more alive and interesting than machine-made embroideries. Such qualities only appear through close examination, and it is these often ineffable qualities that, in turn, can give us some idea as to how textile and textile-making acted as a medium of transindividuation.

Reading through the Lines: The Evanescent Maker

The linens thus transindividuate in that they delineate both the duration of life and its necessary end. In that regard, while they are definitely properties of a family unit, they are also impersonal reminders of time passing. The marks on these textiles conjugate disparate dynamics and processes, among them the ambiguous relationship between the domestic subject and creative maker.

Let me turn away from linens to printed educational materials: one book on textile techniques and 127 textile weeklies printed in black and white on newspaper. Those were given to me by an elderly man who, when house cleaning, found these documents that had belonged to his grandmother. He did not know much about his grandmother, having spent his school years at a boarding school away from his home and therefore was unable to give many details as to the kind of person she was. The book was the *Encyclopédie des ouvrages de dames* (Figure 5.2), written by Thérèse de Dillmont. This was a bestseller, translated into multiple languages since its first publication in 1884, and known in English as the *Encyclopedia of Needlework*. Dillmont was an Austrian embroiderer who had moved to France. The copy I received was printed by French thread company DMC (Dollfus-Mieg et Compagnie), whose cotton embroidery threads are commonly found today in pretty much any craft store. A written note on the title page reads that this book was given as a sewing prize to a student at the Jeanne d'Arc high school in Clermont-Ferrand in 1912–1913. At over 800 pages of very fine glossy paper, this pocket format book indeed features hundreds of sewing and needlework techniques, from hand sewing and machine sewing to crochet, macramé, knitting and many, many types of embroidery and lace-making. The note from the publisher states that that *Encyclopedia of Needlework* was featured at the 1893 Chicago World Fair as one of the top forty French titles deemed "the most useful for the education of women." My copy was in mint condition, as were the needlework magazines. These magazines spanned from 1910 to 1933, were carefully stored together in a portfolio, and included titles such as *Le journal de la broderie Lyonnaise*, and *Broderie piquée* (Figure 5.3). The magazines mostly featured patterns and ideas for needlework, featuring an endless and overwhelming array of house linens and clothing ornamentations: doilies, table runners, tablecloth, bed linens, cushion covers, collars, handkerchiefs, bonnets and hats, hems, blouses, dresses and countless garments for men, women and children. Indeed, turning the pages of these magazines gave rise to a somewhat claustrophobic feeling, given their

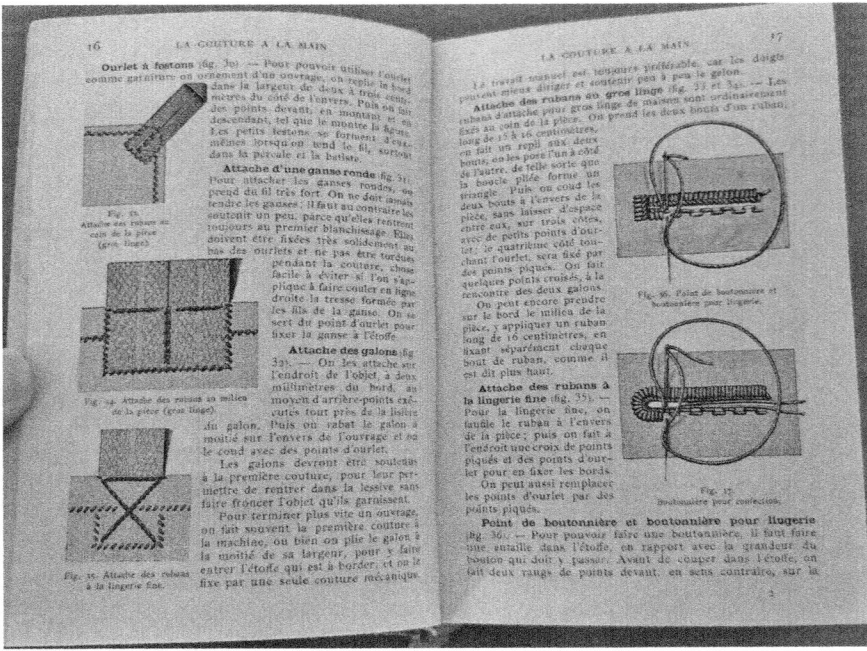

Figure 5.2 *Encyclopédie des ouvrages de dames.* Courtesy of the author.

relentless insistence that every and all corner of a household be filled with some kind of needlework. This call for endless decoration of the household reflects some of the ways in which textile work can be used as a way of control and discipline, imposing specific subject positions on women: respectable by accepting responsibility for household upkeep. Overall, these documents reflect the kind of discourse networks (Kittler, 1992) of gender roles in middle-class, pre-WWII France, and beyond, as demonstrated by the global success of the *Encyclopedia of Needlework*. Textile practices served as a medium through which different institutions could delineate the scope of women's role in the bourgeois middle-class sphere: state educational institutions through home economics curriculum and special prizes to top students, commercial institutions such as those providing needlework materials, and a whole publishing industry devoted to cultivating a stable and continued readership through an endless provision of new projects and new fashions. Textile practices thus served as *interface*, that is, as devices where the dominant discourse defining subject positions could encounter making bodies, and the finished textile objects thus acted as cultural techniques, delineating space but also roles, providing material markers as well as symbolic ones that overall defined the bourgeois household.

It would be tempting to stop the analysis here and consider this textile discourse network as one that cultivated subservient subject positions for women. Yet, this

Figure 5.3 Left: An issue from the newspaper *L'oeuvre* announcing the end of World War I; Right: Example of an embroidery magazine. Courtesy of the author.

would be incredibly limiting. The discourse network of textile practices delineates the scope and space of bourgeois women's work, but what about their engagement, in turn, with these time-consuming textile practices? At first glance, these documents did not reveal much about the person who received and used them with regard to their identity. I could see that the woman who owned these documents took care of them and kept them in excellent condition. There were, however, no personal notes or letters. Stuck in the pages of the magazines were precise and neat hand-copied and transferred patterns, indicating that only a few patterns were actually of interest to the maker in question. Indeed, whole issues of these monthly magazines felt untouched. As an indication of personal preference, the patterns that the maker focused on were mostly for embroidery work on household linens: napkins, tablecloths and so on, and overall mostly decorative work (letters and floral patterns). The question that cannot be answered is, what were the meaning and purpose of these particular projects for this particular maker? Were they given away as presents or kept for the home? While there is no information that could provide an answer to this question, the very act of picking and choosing which patterns to focus on and the precise copying of such patterns demonstrate a quiet confidence in one's skills, and determination.

Indeed, traces of transindividuation are not only found in personal reflections and recorded memories, but also in the use of materials and objects. In that regard, it is important to place the entire set of documents within the overall context of World War I. While none of the printed material published during the war or after made any mention of contemporary politics, the woman in question finished high school right before the war in 1913, and therefore spent her early adulthood during World War I. This particularly came to the fore with a set of findings amidst the pages of the magazines relating to the war. First, the only non-embroidery related item in the portfolio was an 18 November 1918 edition of Paris-published newspaper *L'Oeuvre* (see Figure 5.3, above), with a front-page celebration of the annexation of the Alsace-Lorraine region to France. The region had historically been a territorial struggle between France and Germany, and its previous annexation by the Prussian empire as a result of the 1871 war had fed national politics leading to World War I (1914–1918). Forty million soldiers and civilians, inluding 1.7 million French, died in that war. The north of France was decimated in the protracted *guerre des tranchées* where the French, British and Belgians fought against Prussian soldiers in a dirty trench wars for years on end. Needless to say, the war was both deeply traumatic for the French population, but eventually, with their victory, became a point of national pride and revenge over the Germans. Keeping a record of this historical event that marked the end of World War I and France's victory indicates the importance of nationalist sentiment and belonging to the imagined community (Anderson, 2006) of victorious France, but one cannot but imagine also the toll of the war in countless deaths and destruction.

And indeed, the relational dynamics between this particular woman and World War I was not straightforward, as two other documents from during the war revealed. Stuck in between two magazine editions were two folded pieces of paper that were used to transfer patterns. These two pieces of paper were cut from the same poster (Figures 5.4 and 5.5), which featured images and information about how to distinguish enemy German planes from an allied English or Belgian ones, and what to do in the hypothetical situation where one of these planes was to make an emergency landing in one's vicinity. The decision to recycle such wartime pieces of information into paper for copying patterns to make embroidered collars creates a break and radical bifurcation in the wartime discourse network. While the poster calls forth a specific kind of engaged civilian ready to do their bit for the sake of the nation, the recycling of the poster in turn deliberately preserves a feeling powerlessness in the face of war. One could even imagine what the woman must have thought—was she to subdue German enemies with her thread and needle? Such a small and mundane gesture also turns on its head the notion of domesticity. Here the domestic textile sphere is reclaimed as parenthetical moment of existence that folds away the omnipresent context of never-ending meaningless mass killing and destruction, and very real anxiety about male family members, friends and whole communities indeed compulsorily drafted to fight, that is, to lose limbs, to suffocate in poisonous gas and often die incredibly painful deaths. In that sense, the fact that the set of documents was kept void of

Figure 5.4 Poster about plane landings, WWI. Courtesy of the author.

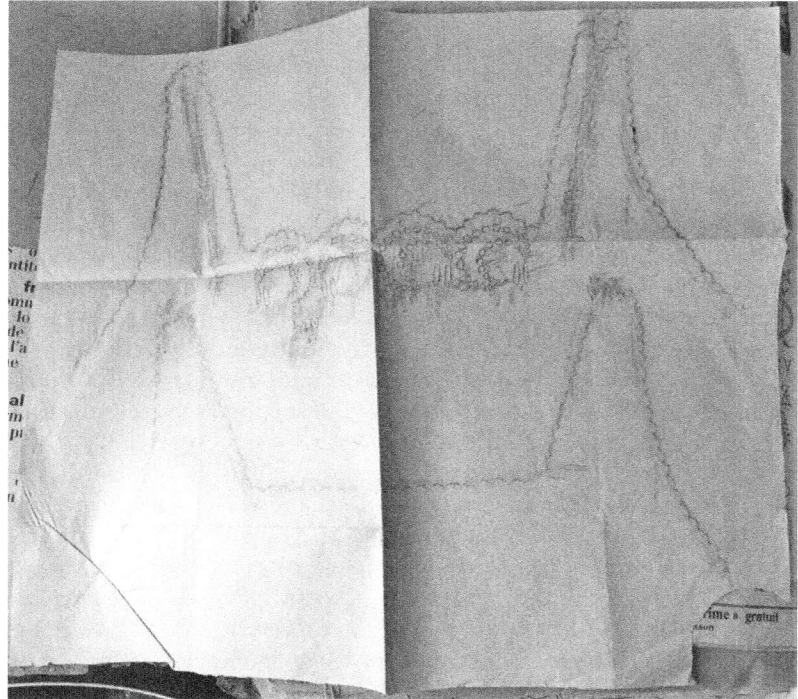

Figure 5.5 Back of the poster.

any personal recollection makes more sense: just like Penelope, the woman here turned to making as a strategy for creating space and time for not being subjected to the forces of history and nationalistic politics. The repurposing of such material—both crucial information about enemies and friends and propaganda about how civilians should act—into a renewed commitment to one's textile practice, and therefore to one's self creates a bifurcation in textile practices. Here, domesticity and craft-making cease to be an imposition by a patriarchal order, to become a claim for a space of agency while being within the patriarchal and military order. The space of individual individuation is not outside of dominant power, but *folded* within it. The reference to Deleuze is inevitable: the fold works with "interiorization, but a relative one, always in progress and never complete" (1993: 233). Spaces of internal freedom within dominant powers: this is indeed the repetition of Penelope's web, of the use of domestic arts and conformity to one's subject position as woman in order to create paradoxically (at least temporarily) a space of respite, of ambiguity, of things and of one's life not being automatically determined. The woman, in other words, operated an act of transposition by articulating together official statements and personal craft practice and in so doing, opened up a space where domestic textile became a vector of subjective resistance against the war.

Portable Technologies of Making

Let us turn to another textile object, and another woman and textile maker, to further investigate this specific notion of the transindividuating interface. Still in the same region of Auvergne, I was given a strange device that was completely falling apart. It was a handmade bobbin lace-making block (Figure 5.6). Bobbin lace-making is a traditional technique for creating lace ribbon: a pattern is pinned to a cushioned revolving drum, thread is wound up on bobbins and interlaced around needles placed at specific points. The resulting series of intertwined knots create a lace ribbon. Bobbin lace-making has a long history in Auvergne, particularly around the town of Puy en Velay, which still produces today the renowned Dentelles du Puy. There are several lace-making techniques using different tools (bobbin, needle, crochet needle and knitting needles), different treatment of material (cutwork, embroidery) and support (netting for instance, or only thread). Lace-making appeared in Western Europe during the sixteenth century, and early patterns were drawn from Renaissance designs. In the Puy en Velay region, it had a significant cultural and economic role, as it was common for women in the countryside to do this work. The work itself was managed and distributed, each local group tasked with making parts of an overall pattern. It was usually paid by the piece, thus encouraging productivity. The more complex the piece, the higher the lace maker was paid: an incentive for skill development. Because the market for lace-making was for religious and high-fashion purposes and therefore lace materially demonstrated wealth, religious commitment and social class, it encouraged complexity and intricacy of designs. Bobbin lace-made

Figure 5.6 Old bobbin lace-making block and lace-making patterns and tools. Courtesy of the author.

products from the region enjoyed an international reputation, sold all over France through a network of traveling salespeople and throughout the world via commercial and import offices. Their inclusion in world expos throughout the nineteenth century demonstrated that lace from the Puy region was not just about decoration, but about modern craft and technical skills that fit with notions of progress at the time (Association pour. . ., 1998). Hence, a small piece of intricate lace-work connected individual makers with a dominant western ideology and global politics around technology, development and progress. That a small piece of lace could be seen as participating in the technical imaginaries (Jassanoff and Kim, 2015) of the time is something that we saw in Chapter 3 about Jacquard silks. Far from being quaint and old-fashioned, lace-making as a source of technical excellence further showcased the specific roles of textile in formulating a specific kind of modernity, which has now been all but forgotten. Lace-making thus made rural women from the Puy region active in the project of nineteenth-century modernity, thus enabling them to define themselves as cultural and economic actors. In my encounters with lace makers from the region, the historical importance of lace-making as a skill and source of revenue for women was a crucial identity marker. As one of my interlocutors explained, even older women with declining eyesight could still use bobbins and pins: as the patterns are pierced by pins, they can be read haptically. Bobbin lace-making was therefore historically a transindividuation medium: it built individual economic autonomy, but also established shared group identities as skilled workers from a specific region. The practice of bobbin lace-making itself involved both individual work but also regular collective gatherings in the evenings: it fostered community among women who taught each other and passed down their knowledge to the new generations.

Representations in historical documents usually show elegant lace-making blocks covered in richly patterned fabric that embody a certain bourgeois aesthetics. But the particular object I was given was handmade with found materials and belonged to someone from the rural class. The handmade pieces of wood were mismatched and not tightly fitted together. The drum was stuffed with hay and several layers of scrap fabric. On either side of the drum, images of saints had been placed and secured with thick transparent plastic. A missing drawer compartment completed the object. This particular block is a multimedia center in its own right. Not only does the lace-making involve digital processes and logical, algorithmic thinking, as I'll discuss below, but the block is also a portable media and communication technology. I was told that the images of saints, attached on either side, were eventually sometimes replaced with images of movie stars, showing how different important cultural influences were carried around at all times, and fostered personal relations between an individual and their cultural and spiritual symbols, but also created habitual patterns. Of course, the images of saints could demonstrate obedience to the dominant bourgeois Catholic order, but the lace-making block contained other modes of communication as well. The drawer, I was told, not only contained needles and thread, but also letters, notes and other small personal trinkets. The block itself is lightweight and portable and was carried around as something to do in between other tasks in the fields. It could indeed be seen as an early prototype of smart portable networked technology, combining mass media, personal communication and a workstation in one object. Often when we look at textile, we tend to ignore the context of making and the small, daily practices and entanglements with a network of objects that constitute it. These micro-practices are indeed difficult to explore in the past, being evanescent and often seen as not meaningful enough. But these micro-practices and the habits that accompany them are the core of transindividuation, and give a space for an individual to navigate and combine complex and paradoxical processes, so much so that something such as textile practice can be both a medium of control and a space of some kind of intellectual freedom. The lace-making block is a tool of becoming: becoming-woman; becoming-economic agent; singularization of oneself at the crossroads of collective, shared, personal and even secret thoughts.

Looking at these textile objects and documents might not reveal much about the persons who used them, if only for one thing: their capacity to use these objects as interfaces to layer diverse and contradictory processes, dynamics and values and to in turn combine or articulate them or make them unfold on different strata so as to create frictionless paradoxes. These objects are transindividuating media, enabling a space of not only breaks, negotiations and tactics against the strategies of the dominant order, to borrow from de Certeau, but also to anchor daily habits, fostering a specific rhythm for one's life (Barthes, 2012). Again, the capacity for textile-making to create an interface where personal rhythms of life can develop and exist alongside the demand for productivity and broad dominant ideologies suggest that we need to rethink how power works, especially with regard to the relationship between domination and subordination. What is key here is understanding what is *not* controlled by dominant powers: in the case of bobbin lace-making, even if economic productivity pressures are exerted, the conditions of actual making—either collectively where community is created through collaborative work, or individually as a psychic space of escape—allows one to take charge of at least an aspect of one's life. In that sense, handmade textile practices and objects allowed not only for social, cultural and economic networks and therefore functioned as a plane of connections, but also fostered depths and folds, where processes can exist on different strata. To turn to Deleuze and Guattari, the critical political question becomes one of understanding that dominant power (i.e., the tripartite system of modernity, capitalism and colonialism) can connect and invade these strata, which it eventually achieved with textile through its transformation as a factory mass-produced commodity. Indeed, whereas capitalist production logics might not particularly be focused on individual processes of transindividuation, colonialism in turn was about control over bodies, minds and psyches, and a key move for colonial powers was to dismantle Indigenous textile practices and techniques because it allowed for complete deindividuation at both the collective and individual levels. Handmade textile practices and techniques mediate transindividuation processes in complex ways, thus uncovering a need to rediscover them as instances of transindividuation that allowed for new bifurcations and directions.

"Where Am I Going?": Creative Meandering

- *"Where am I going? I got myself stuck. . ."*
- *"Now look, you can get back on track here."*

I heard this and similar exchanges several times when observing bobbin lace-making workshops in Auvergne. The practice is being reinvented in the region. Of course, the Dentelles du Puy have always been in existence and sold in many tourist shops in the town of Puy en Velay; fulfilling their religious role, as the Puy is an important stop in the pilgrimage to Santiago de Compostela. However, most of these laces are done by machine at this point. Similar to so many other crafts, handmade bobbin lace-making progressively disappeared throughout the nineteenth century as machine lace-making was developed and general interest in lace progressively disappeared throughout the second half of the twentieth century. Today, lace-making is undergoing a revival that is similar to other textile practices like knitting and sewing (Figure 5.7). This is partly due to feminist activism that focused on reappropriating traditional women's practices as new forms of empowerment. The Stitch and Bitch movement, for instance, creates safe spaces for women and LGBTQs where they can meet, talk, and develop common projects. In addition, part of the revival of textile follows a more general revival of craft culture as a way of challenging the meaninglessness of consumer capitalism and finding ways of relating to human-made objects that are more sustainable, meaningful and

Figure 5.7 Bobbin lace-making equipment, June 2017. Courtesy of Wikimedia Commons User Krzysiu.

respectful of the environment. This stands in direct contrast with a discourse that often described needlework as tedious and repetitive, requiring one to repeat the same gestures (knitting, pushing a needle into a piece of cloth) over and over again. Overall, there is a broader realization that needlework does not need to be tedious and repetitive, although it does indeed involve repetition and attention to small details. There are two reasons for this realization: one related to the redefined status of bobbin lace-making today, and the other to the actual practice of bobbin lace-making.

First to the latter reason: while repetitive, bobbin lace-making, is not dummy work by any stretch of the imagination. Take a lace ribbon that requires six sets of bobbins and thread (twelve in total) in order to be made. The technique consists of using needles as anchors around which thread is intertwined. There are several types of intertwining that can be done, offering a rich expressive vocabulary of possible combinations, with bobbin pairs being interchanged to create a new direction for a thread. The maker has to go from the beginning to end of the pattern and must end with the same number of bobbins and thread. But there are multiple paths to get from beginning to end, and it is up to the maker to choose which path to take. What is fascinating as well is that these paths are not straightforward from either right to left (e.g., knitting) or top to bottom (e.g., weaving) but usually use combinations of going down and sideways. For bobbin lace makers, the key point is not to get themselves stuck somewhere where they cannot go back to another side and complete the pattern. While repetitive then, bobbin lace-making offers choice as to how to complete a design. Such characteristics make the practice quite versatile, which brings us to the other reason why it is undergoing a revival today, which is related to its newly acquired status as an "artistic" practice. As economic need for handmade bobbin lace pretty much disappeared throughout the twentieth century, several institutions (including the Centre d'enseignement de la dentelle du Puy) and lace makers decided to explore and promote bobbin lace-making as an art form. This meant freedom from the white ribbon and trim format and the capacity to create artistic designs, including whole landscape and intricate figures using color threads. As a result, the lace-making block with a roller was abandoned for a flat surface that enables the design of different shapes. Further, the choice to see how bobbin lace-making could fit within fine arts meant exploring new materials and new scales, including small decorative pieces, jewelry, landscape, all the way to large installation pieces made out of thick rope or wire.

The lace-making group I visited in the city of Thiers was made up of women in their late thirties to retirement age. These women would gather every week to work on their own lace-making project. The group leader also taught workshops to school children. Sometimes the group would work on a collective large-scale project, other times on individual projects. One woman was making small figures such as butterflies for birthday card decorations for her grandchildren. All the women talked about how creative lace making can be, and how it finds a place both in the intimate gift economy as a way to materialize feelings of care and love for family and friends, and as an artistic form in its own right, destined for exhibitions and dedicated social media groups and tags. Bobbin lace-making has found an international audience and following, they explained: women from Quebec to Japan were actively practicing it, developing their own regional styles and aesthetics. As one woman recalled, this new status as artistic form is a radical break from how it was perceived and practiced in the past. She recalled mentioning to her grandmother that she had taken it up as a hobby. Her grandmother was furious: how could her granddaughter do something for free when she should be paid for the work, and was not she, in that sense, lowering the value of lace-making and demeaning the practice? Here the clash between two modes of transindividuation is even clearer: whereas bobbin lace-making in the past was a source of economic revenue for women, and therefore a source of economic freedom and control over one's life and a mode for experiencing some kind of social power, it now offers a kind of transindividuation that is geared towards personal and collective self-expression. The change of status for the maker—from remunerated worker to unpaid artist—meant for the grandmother a complete deindividuation, whereas for the granddaughter it was an experience of creative freedom. Here we see how similar material practices diverge as they are abstracted into symbolic values: either as hard-earned economic agency and power or as creative power and caché. In this way, the divide between working hard for greater remuneration, and working for pleasure with no economic constraints shows the extent to which bobbin lace-making, as a transindividuation interface, has been radically transformed. Same techniques, new goals and new contexts define new possibilities for transindividuation, while they close off others. To go back to the question of the fold, then, the textile-making interface, when re-contextualized, makes the folding of the economic plane into the interiorizing space of self-definition impossible. Self-definition undergoes new connection and means something different—from shared economic power among women to individual creative fulfillment. With French women practicing domestic textile work, we thus see the troubling of the links between socioeconomic processes and lived existence, between material practice and the articulation of new subjectivities. What ultimately this case study recognizes is that the work of delinking from existing dominant power requires paying attention to the potentials that lurks in these layered assemblages.

To take stock of what the chapters have shown us so far: textile-making as the assemblage of humans and techniques leads to creative flights that in turn, engage with the question of the crafting of meaningful existences, and existences that matter. These creative flights not only refashion subjectivities for the makers, but as we see in the next chapter, for those receiving textiles as well. Let's now loop back to the relationships between textile and politics, and how the textiles of the Shipibo-Conibo gesture towards a politics of meaning and matter that open up towards a decolonization of co-existence.

References

Anderson, Benedict. (2006). *Imagined Communities: Reflections on the Origin and Spread of Nationalism*. London: Verso Books.

Association pour la promotion des dentelles de la Haute-Loire le Puy en Velay. (1998). *Dentelles En Haute-Loire: Les Jardins Tissés, Catalogue de l'exposition à La Chaise-Dieu*.

Barthes, Roland. (2012). *How to Live Together: Novelistic Simulations of Some Everyday Spaces*. New York: Columbia University Press.

Black, Shannon. (2017). "KNIT + RESIST: Placing the Pussyhat Project in the Context of Craft Activism." *Gender, Place & Culture* 24 (5): 696–710. https://doi.org/10.1080/09663 69X.2017.1335292.

Braidotti, Rosi. (2006). *Transpositions: On Nomadic Ethics*. Cambridge: Polity.

Brown, Elsa Barkley. (1989). "African-American Women's Quilting." *Signs: Journal of Women in Culture and Society* 14 (4): 921–29. https://doi.org/10.1086/494553.

Cocker, Emma. (2017). "Weaving Codes/Coding Weaves: Penelopean Mêtis and the Weaver-Coder's Kairos." *TEXTILE* 15 (2): 124–41. https://doi.org/10.1080/14759756.2 017.1298233.

Deleuze, Gilles. (1993). *The Fold: Leibniz and the Baroque*. Minneapolis: Univerisity of Minnesota Press.

Deleuze, Gilles. (2001). *Spinoza: Practical Philosophy*. Translated by Robert Hurley. San Francisco: City Lights Publishers.

Deleuze, Gilles, and Félix Guattari. (1987). *A Thousand Plateaus: Capitalism and Schizophrenia*. Minneapolis: University of Minnesota Press.

Foucault, Michel. (1977). *Discipline and Punish: The Birth of the Prison*. London: Random House.

Garber, Elizabeth. (2013). "Craft As Activism." *Journal of Social Theory in Art Education* 33 (1): 53–66. https://scholarscompass.vcu.edu/jstae/vol33/iss1/6.

Goggin, Maureen Daly, and Beth Fowkes Tobin, eds. (2009). *Women and the Material Culture of Needlework and Textiles, 1750–1950.* Farnham: Ashgate.

Jasanoff, Sheila, and Sang-Hyun Kim. (2015). *Dreamscapes of Modernity: Sociotechnical Imaginaries and the Fabrication of Power.* Chicago: University of Chicago Press.

Kittler, Friedrich. (1992). *Discourse Networks 1800/1900.* Translated by Michael Metteer. Stanford, CA: Stanford University Press.

Knauer, Thomas. (2019). *Why We Quilt: Contemporary Makers Speak out about the Power of Art, Activism, Community, and Creativity.* North Adams, MA: Storey.

Parker, Rozsika. (2010). *The Subversive Stitch: Embroidery and the Making of the Feminine.* New York: I. B. Tauris.

Paterson, Mark, and Martin Dodge, eds. (2016). *Touching Space, Placing Touch.* London: Routledge.

Plant, Sadie. (2016). *Zeros and Ones: Digital Women and the New Technoculture.* Rev. edn. London: Fourth Estate.

Rand, Erin J. (2007). "Repeated Remembrance: Commemorating the AIDS Quilt and Resuscitating the Mourned Subject." *Rhetoric and Public Affairs* 10 (4): 655–80. http://www.jstor.org/stable/41940329.

Stalp, Marybeth C., and Joanne B. Eicher. (2007). *Quilting: The Fabric of Everyday Life.* Oxford: Berg Publishers.

Tamboukou, Maria. (2015). *Sewing, Fighting and Writing: Radical Practices in Work, Politics and Culture.* London: Rowman & Littlefield International.

Tanaka, Yuko. (2013). *The Power of the Weave: The Hidden Meanings of Cloth.* Tokyo: International House of Japan.

Chapter 6

KENÉ, OR THE PROMISE OF UN-KNOWING

I am lucky to be part of a textile arts and craft cooperative in Toronto, and to brush shoulders with talented textile artists and designers. I remember entering the cooperative studio space one day and one of the designers—who had recently been hired for a collaboration with Peruvian Indigenous textile artisans—had spread out on our big printing table the samples that she had received from all over Peru: grasses, feathers, strands of alpaca, some as soft as baby's hair; bright woven pieces and among all of this, a curious set of embroidered textiles in bright colors that looked like labyrinthian maps. This was my first encounter with Shipibo-Conibo textiles and Shipibo-Conibo *Kené* practice (Figure 6.1). Of all the textiles spread on the table, only the Shipibo-Conibo ones provoked a unique yearning in me to decipher and read them, to comprehend their intricate lines in order to find

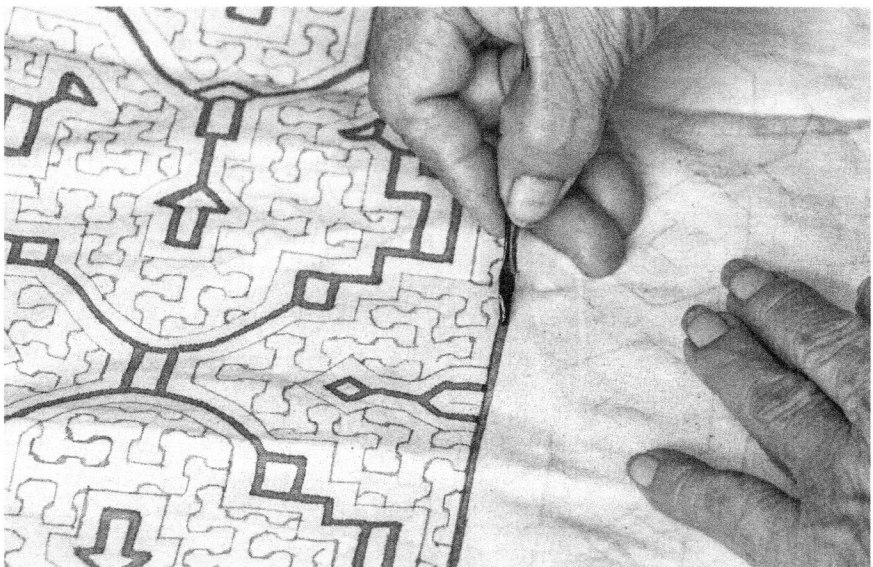

Figure 6.1 *Kené* – natural ink on cloth. Courtesy of the author.

their meaning. And yet, as I explore in this chapter, Shipibo-Conibo textiles are not texts. Encountering these non-texts that are nevertheless incredibly meaningful, I was confronted with the limits to my scholarly training. Rather than trying to fill that gap with the Eurocentric research arsenal at my disposition, this chapter is my attempt to delineate the limits of knowledge so as to open up to non-western forms of mediated communication, which go far beyond the question of text to the question of how to be in divergent worlds—at the crossroads between Indigenous worlds and the world of the dominant matrix. Shipibo-Conibo textiles now circulate globally, and therefore they now engage with and are appropriated by Eurocentric perspectives. Yet at the same time, they are not just appropriated: through them emerges continuous efforts from Indigenous actors to reach non-Indigenous actors using fragile and misunderstood assemblages that radically differ from those of the dominant matrix of power.

In this chapter, I look at how Indigenous textiles as media objects circulate on the contemporary global scene. I start by examining the paradox in establishing Indigenous textile objects as relevant to an audience for whom textile has lost most of its capacity for being meaningful—the capitalist subjects conditioned to see either textile as a fleetingly fashionable ornament, or as an investment to build a collection. I then show how in producing textile for an external market, Indigenous groups aim to establish a set of relationships with the world outside their communities, which transforms textile objects originally meant for domestic use into uneasy interfaces where Indigenous cosmovisions, values, rights and claims meet an outside marked by postcolonial and neocolonial capitalist logics of exploitation and appropriation, as we saw in Chapter 2. In such a context, it would be easy to see Indigenous communities as victims of global capital, either by being dispossessed by it or forced to adapt to its demands, and only surviving in the margins, in niche markets. The accusation here, as I further explore in the chapter, could not be more unfair and hypocritical because it both puts the burden solely on Indigenous makers for failing to resist an infrastructure of constant appropriation and exploitation, and overlooks the responsibilities of the western consumer. I want to turn the tables here, and to lay the burden of failure at the feet of not only the infrastructure of the dominant matrix, but primarily of the western consumer subject. Let it be clear: I am by and large, this subject. It is this subject—conditioned by narrow interpretive frameworks that establish a disconnection between meaning and matter, pitting transcendent and spiritual abstract thoughts against lived actual experiences—who continuously fails to reach an understanding of the capacities of Indigenous textiles, which their Indigenous makers, in turn, spend countless hours patiently crafting. In this chapter, I examine *Kené* textiles as media objects that work to open up a fraught space to initiate both an encounter between two radically different actors—the local, Indigenous maker and the western visitor and consumer—and a confrontation of modes of existence and being (Indigenous vs. capitalist ones) that are incommensurate. In these confrontations, there is an opening where the possibilities of relations not based on exploitation and objectification can arise and be experienced, however briefly. Dwelling on these moments of confrontation is a way to engage with Viveiros de

Castro's perspectival anthropology—to experience moments of doubt that allows for the preconceptions of others and their world to fall apart, and in turn to acknowledge "the virtual presence Another" "who, prior to being a subject or object, is the expression of a possible world" (Viveiros de Castro and Wagner, 2016: 47). I specifically choose to mobilize the concept of "perspectival" here to further explore what can be produced through the encounter between practices and cosmologies that have nothing in common. While the tendency is to find equivalents in the dominant culture to absorb Indigenous cosmovisions, I want to pay attention here to what at first might seem like limited interventions but should be understood as moments of equivocation, of establishing moments of not only suspension, as we saw in the last chapter, but of troubling of the dominant matrix of power. Viveiros de Castro's perspectival anthropology invites the researcher to continue the work of comparison between uncommon worlds, and to engage in a specific work of translation:

> Anthropology compares *so as to translate*, not to explain, justify, generalize, interpret, contextualize, reveal the unconscious, say what goes without saying, and so forth. I would add that to translate is always to betray, as the Italian saying goes. However, a good translation—and here I am paraphrasing Walter Benjamin (or rather Rudolf Pannwitz via Benjamin)—is one that betrays the destination language, not the source language. A good translation is one that allows the alien concepts to deform and subvert the translator's conceptual toolbox so that the intention of the original language can be expressed within the new one.
>
> Viveiros de Castro, 2004: 3

In this chapter, I recount some of the many attempts at translating Shipibo-Conibo textiles in ways that would make sense to the westerner, translations that typically have tended to try to fold these textiles into a western-centric understanding of the world. I then show how the very conceptualization of Shipibo-Conibo textiles as fixed spiritual meaning is the very problem at the core of translation: if anything, Shipibo-Conibo textiles shift, and have always shifted, following changes to the world around them, articulating materials with cosmovision. It only makes sense, then, to embrace their troubling indeterminacy in turn as a political gesture.

Shipibo-Conibo Textiles and Perspectival Anthropology

The Shipibo-Conibo (est. 35,000) traditionally live along the Ucayali river in the Peruvian Amazon. The combined pressure of mining, logging, climate change, pollution and need to access educational and health resources has meant that a significant number of Shipibo-Conibos (or Shipibo for short) have moved or been displaced from distant villages to the city of Pucallpa and even further, to Lima (Ontaneda, 2017). The Shipibos are well known for their cosmovision, including their healing and shamanistic practices, which are anchored in a deep knowledge of the Amazon ecosystem and the medicinal properties of local plants. Since the

1970s, a combination of policy changes allowing Amazonian Indigenous groups in Peru to claim land ownership (Pinedo, 2017; Postero and Zamosc, 2006; Rénique, 2009), and renewed interests in Shipibo culture from scholars and tourists have led to a renewal and reinvention of Shipibo identity and ways of life as clearly distinct from mainstream Peruvian society (Brabec de Mori, 2011, 178–79). Tourism in the region is not as developed as in Cusco, for instance, but Shipibo culture enjoys an international reputation. Most visitors come with an interest in Shipibo ritual practices (Hern, 2016), which were popularized in William Burrough's and Allan Ginsberg's *The Yage Letters* (1963). Descriptions of drinking ayahuasca, a brew of hallucinogenic plants, during ceremonies to attain a transcendental, mystical experience and understanding of self, Other and the world have proliferated ever since. Today, many foreigners come to participate in healing rituals led by *médicos* (shamans), which involve not only consumption of ayahuasca, but also of other medicinal plants and foodstuffs. Foreign tourism in the region therefore tends to be a specialized one that involves interest in spiritual issues, dissatisfaction with western ways of life, including never-ending material consumption, and desire to seek radically new experiences and ways of being in harmony with the cosmos. Shipibo medicine also has a deep appeal—as an alternative to western medicine, it is acknowledged by the scientific community (and further evidenced by reckless patenting of local Amazonian plants by the pharmaceutical industry), that the Shipibos have a sophisticated medical knowledge.

Shipibo ceramics and textiles (Odland and Feldman, 2010; Odland, 2016; Wali et al., 2016) offer a continuation of such experiences, as they are adorned with designs—or *kené* in Shipibo—that are commonly described as the visual translation of spiritual and intangible encounters. Only women engage in *kené* as a spiritual and artistic practice, and usually from a young age. Developing the capacity to dream and imagine designs (Belaunde, 2012: 81) often requires a ritual consisting "of placing a few drops of piripiri plant (*Cyperus* sp.) juice in (the) eyes and navel" of young girls (Belaunde, 2012: 82). This eventually allows Shipibo female artists to access designs in their thoughts, visions and dreams that they then translate onto skin, ceramics, and cloth. The finished designs are characterized by lines of various thickness forming a web of labyrinthine paths. *Kené* designs are quite unique and difficult to classify—there is no equivalent for them in the western world. What they mean is an ongoing discussion, and many anthropologists have attempted to decipher them, with at times confusing results that highlight the incommensurability of *Kené* when it comes to trying to make it fit within a western perspective on art and communication. *Kené* has been described as transcriptions of spiritual visions and therefore as the materialization of the intangible (Belaunde, 2012). It has also been said to represent the skin of the cosmic serpent that created the world, and therefore the paths that lead to other strata of reality (ibid.). More recently, *Kené* designs have been said to be transcriptions of healing songs, but this is a recent interpretation that is not widely shared among Shipibo artists (Brabec de Mori, 2011: 181). Perhaps they might be closes to semasiography, which, as John Durham Peters explains, "does not represent speech but communicates meanings via visual representations without designating an unambiguous vocal or linguistic correlate" (2015: loc. 4937). Yet, some designs components have names—for instance, piranhas, fish, bird and human, although these are conventions that can change from one group to the next. There have been propositions, both from anthropologists and their Shipibo interlocutors, that *kené* could be compared with writing. Yet here lies the main difference: a *kené* design expresses a changing multiplicity of references, some that are related to myths, others to emotions or desires, others to personal histories, others to communities, and others to the very specific context within which they appear (Belaunde, 2012: 85; Feldman, 2016: 51). It is agreed that *kené* designs are about transformation because they are the pathways to different worlds, different realities. They materialize the capacity to access other worlds and realms, of communicating with the non-humans, of traveling through different times and spaces. In that sense, they are the reverse image of writing and visual depiction, especially the kind of writing and depiction that finds its roots in precision of meaning and fixing things (e.g., a map, a travel journal, a visual sign such as "stop"). Further, *Kené* are not figments of one's imagination only; they are communication with other realms and other entities that have no equivalent in the west, and it would be a mistake to try to attribute to them a solely human authorship. To try to fit a specific *Kené* design into one of our western categories: myth, fiction, poem, map, prophecy, letter, order and so on is impossible. It encompasses aspects of these categories, but always escapes them. It involves both humans, non-humans, and more-than-humans. It refers to temporal relations that are not what the western world would think of as past, present, and future, and to different planes of reality.

To refer to Viveiros de Castro, *kené* is to discourse what Amazonian cosmology is to western ontology: its inversion. Here lies its relevance: it is the materialization of an Other, not as representation, but as expression of other modes and possibilities relating to other worlds. It is, for the foreigner, an undecipherable map to other modes of being in the world. Viveiros de Castro, addressing the problem of western anthropology encountering Amazonian people and their cosmology, states that: ". . . the problem doesn't reside in seeing the native as an object, nor does the solution reside in casting him as a subject. That the native is a subject is beyond doubt; but what the native forces the anthropologist to cast into doubt is precisely what a subject could be. . ." (Viveiros de Castro and Wagner, 2016: 47). The point of studying Amazon Indigenous cultures is about throwing into question and highlighting the limitation of the very concept onto which any capacity for knowledge and meaningfulness are based—the subject—in two ways. First, taken further to encompass not only anthropologists, but any Western visitor who encounters Shipibo culture, such a statement not only highlights the limitations of western epistemological framework—the assumptions about what the other is supposed to be, but also allows for casting into doubt the western subject itself, thus severing the ties between dominant modes of subjectivation and the self. Second, if encountering the "native" forces us to reconsider what a subject is, then encountering Indigenous modes of expression means casting into doubt what communication, and by extension what meaningful relationships with the world, is about. *Kené*, because it is so visible, tangible and material, is the medium through which one can engage with such casting into doubt. For all their incomprehensibility to the western subject, *kené* designs are nevertheless impactful—they challenge preconceptions and apprehensions of what spiritual communication is about. But more than this: *Kené* is outside and functions entirely differently from the western discursive apparatus for meaning-making, and therefore it troubles one's interpretative framework and how one perceives and engages with the world. It is this very troubling of *kené* that allows for openness to take place because it dismantles common western discursive apparatuses. The question, in turn, is about how this interface of openness and encounter between incommensurable worlds and modes of being, and the space of equivocation and doubt that it opens up is both colonized and deterritorialized.

Kené *in the Global Market*

The development of Shipibo textiles as a commodity for external markets is a fairly new development, as traditionally *kené* designs were for domestic use only, adorning skin, clothes, ceramics and houses. At the Shipibo women's craft group Maroti Xobo in Pucallpa, members gather to embroider or paint on textile, and sell their pieces to visitors: small, medium and large-scale wall hangings, either painted or embroidered; smaller painted or embroidered pieces such as patches; clothing; and bags (Figure 6.2). In terms of materials costs and prices, Maroti Xobo experiences the same tension as traditional textile makers elsewhere: as their pieces are handmade, they are pricier. The priciest are the ones made with local

Figure 6.2 A Shipibo arts and craft stand at Maroti Xobo, Pucallpa. Courtesy of the author.

hand-spun cotton woven on a backstrap loom, on which the artists paint *kené* designs using local natural dyes and pigments. Shipibo embroideries are also renowned, and usually feature *kené* designs in bright colors. The higher price point is a turnoff for the local market, and so most purchasers of medium- and large-scale textile pieces tend to be visitors. The selling of textile is important to Shipibo women, and it is estimated that 80 percent of them derive some income from their craft (Shipibo Joi, 2011), which helps covers basic food, educational and health needs for their families. The production of textile for outside of the community fulfills important needs: it provides for a source of income and there is hope that this will translate into social mobility and better conditions of life; it offers an incentive to younger generations to train and continue with *kené* rather than assimilate to mainstream society; and it plays a central role in showcasing Shipibo culture and cosmovision on the international scene.

However, problems of cultural and economic appropriation accompany Indigenous textiles as they enter a global market. This appropriation involves the following: first, a visitor will record the designs and copy them back in their home country, so that they can be found on garments for the psychedelic scene in the North America (e.g., Burning Man), for instance, or on apparel destined for the spiritual, hippie and yoga markets. Others purchase a large quantity of Shipibo textiles and then sell them in stores or online at a higher price. There have been a few instances of foreigners asking to be trained in Shipibo embroidery, who then start their own businesses selling their embroideries, mostly online (Bauck, 2017). Etsy is the main online platform where one can see the circulation of Shipibo textiles on the global market. While there are some sellers that state that they are working in collaboration with Shipibo artists through commissions and giving back a percentage of the sale, the vast majority of online sellers are located in Europe and North America, and do not claim any form of collaboration, giving back to the community, or awareness of fair-trade practices at all. But many of the descriptions of Shipibo or Shipibo-inspired items on Etsy will claim a kind of magic power in the items being sold, a link to some kind of cosmic energy, a way to tap into some kind of spiritual understanding. Some of the western makers claim that their embroidery practice is a spiritual one as well—the textile objects they sell are thus imbued with a capacity to communicate with some mystical spiritual realms. It is interesting to note here that the interface of openness through *kené* discussed earlier turns into a polysemic vagueness around some kind of access, through the mere purchase of exotic designs, to undefined well-being and spiritual power. Through such particular work on establishing equivalencies, the ontological incommensurability between two worlds (the west and the Indigenous Amazonian world) is transformed into commodity fetishism, with the original makers—the Shipibo women and their communities—being completely erased in the process and the actual Shipibo cosmovision being transformed into personal well-being. The interfaces of openness therefore are captured and colonized through both distribution and communication networks that redistribute meaningful potentials—for other modes of existence and relating to the world and to others—as personal consumption of commodities. It is interesting to note as well that this process pits makers against makers and is not primarily about big fashion companies stealing designs to mass produce them. Rather, we can note the radically different forms of engagement and relationalities between makers and artisans cast as micro-entrepreneurs inhabiting niche fashion markets, and Indigenous artists and artisans. The former engages in commodity production for personal consumption through cultural appropriation, the other is, at this point in time, much more indeterminate and by and large open to experimentations with alternative networks and apparatuses, as will be discussed shortly.

We therefore find in Shipibo textiles destined for external markets a common dynamic of cultural and economic appropriation (Varagur, 2016; Abbott, 2016; Larsson, 2015), of not only the design, but also rituals and cosmovision. This is further enabled by the impossibility, for the vast majority of Shipibo makers, to gain direct access to the networks of distribution, production and communication that organize the circulation of Shipibo textiles worldwide. Most Shipibo women do not have computers, let alone high-speed internet access. In addition, most of them, like all Shipibos, are in a situation of poverty and thus cannot afford the services of marketers and lawyers. As it is, Shipibo people, like many Indigenous groups, do not receive much in terms of institutional support (local and national) for protecting their intellectual property, even though they are encouraged to market their art and craft. If we were to map out the network of cultural appropriation of Shipibo textile, we would therefore see two dynamics at play. The first one would be the transformation of an interface of potential communication—Shipibo textile—into a commodity for personal consumption, thus separating the spiritual from the sociopolitical context, the item from its network of makers, the cosmovision from the actual relations and acts of engagement and composition that make it alive and meaningful. The second one is control, by mostly western actors, over networks of circulation of Shipibo textiles, which encompasses: 1. the infrastructure of material distribution (shipping, mailing, customs, online payment systems, etc.); 2. the online networks that allow for an imposition of a discourse that circumscribe the meaningfulness of Shipibo textile to an individual act of consumption leading to some kind of vague individual empowerment; and finally 3. the legal infrastructures that Indigenous groups cannot access and that enable such appropriation to take place. From this situation, it thus seems that Shipibo textile arts for the external market are stuck in a dynamic of appropriation and colonization.

Delineating the Space of Un-knowing and Potentials

And yet, I would like in turn to challenge such conclusions, because as interfaces that put in contact Shipibo culture and non-Shipibo audiences, Shipibo textiles are much more open to potentials and experimentations of what it means to encounter an Other. In that regard, I want to move away from a focus on how westerners deal with Shipibo textiles, to what Shipibo artists and makers and those that support them—from NGOs to other artists, designers, and so on—are doing. This is not to deny the intractable forces of capitalist appropriation, but to further understand the kind of experimentations that Shipibo artists and their supporters are developing. My analysis follows ethnomusicologist Bernd Brabec de Mori's assertion that: "An 'orthodox' western understanding of most processes of change makes the Indigenous people appear very passive, likewise reacting to the intruding forces of the globalising world. However, a deeper understanding of the Indigenous structuring of time reveals that their role is much more active" (2011: 186). There has been a rise in an essentialist discourse around Indigenous identity, so much so that for instance, Shipibo cosmovision is commonly assumed to be an ancient tradition that has remained unchanged throughout time. Such romantic visions of Indigenous people abound in the western imagination, especially for people in search of spiritual answers. Furthermore, mobilizing an essentialist version of indigeneity has been a successful strategy "to claim rights to space, land or natural resource wealth (Fabricant, 2013: 167). It is however a mistake to settle on an essentialist understanding of Indigenous cosmovisions as fixed and unchanging. In the case of the Shipibo, Brabec de Mori explains that the emergence of a discourse centered on a "singular" and fixed Shipibo Indigenous identity, as opposed to the plural cultures and "histories of various sub-groups" (2011: 180) serves several actors, including "natives, missionaries, NGOs, researchers, and tourists in a surprisingly consistent mutual agreement" (ibid.). In practice, the materialization of such discourse around a singular and fixed Shipibo identity includes: 1. a displacement of rituals outside of the "ayawaska (*sic*) complex"; 2. a transfer of the once "marginal and feared" ayahuasca rituals to the center of Shipibo culture, including the new practice of having participants consume ayahuasca rather than only the *médicos*; 3. a simplification and standardization of *kené* designs and their meanings; and 4. the association of *kené* designs with healing songs (ibid.: 181). As Brabec de Mori states: "this combined multimedia package was thus declared a millennial tradition and explained as "the ancient tradition of the Shipibo" (181). Brabec de Mori further explains, this preoccupation with tradition and authenticity is intrinsically a western imposition—original authenticity as a concept does not even exist in most Amazonian societies, which have a completely different understanding and experience of time and of the relationships between past, present and future. In particular, for the Shipibo: "the past is flexible and un-fixed, and just like the future, has an immanent presence that is often not felt directly but located in... remote strata of realities that only specialists such as *médicos* can visit, access, manipulate and use to transform everyday life through rituals" (185). Brabec de Mori goes on to argue that this understanding of time allows Shipibos to be quite creative and "innovative" in their use of rituals and culture, concluding that: "the structuring of time and distance in Shipibo understanding allows for complete freedom in maintaining, transmitting, creating and changing of 'tradition'. (...) History is in the making" (186). An anecdote reported to me illustrates this tension: I was told of a westerner commissioning a Shipibo textile artist with an embroidered piece, but specifying that only local materials should be used—local, hand-spun and hand-woven cotton and thread, hand-dyed with local dye-stuff. While there are painted textile pieces using local dye stuff and hand-woven cotton, Shipibo embroideries typically use bright synthetic colors, for reasons I will further explain in a moment. The resulting piece was, in the eye of the westerner, an authentic Shipibo textile that went back to some kind of original roots when Shipibo arts was unsullied by external forces. For the Shipibo maker on the other hand, the constraints imposed were entirely artificial. Here again, we find a misalignment of expectations and understandings surrounding what constitutes true Shipibo arts and craft: on the one hand, the western presumption of the spiritual as sacred, and therefore unchanging and rooted in some kind of pure origin. On the other hand, a fluid and unfixed approach to transformative cosmologies and new encounters with other worlds, based on playfulness and practices of composition and recomposition, that is, of creative linkages with actors, elements and processes that are heterogenous.

It would be very tempting at this point to mobilize postmodern theories to explain how contemporary Shipibo culture as presented to the external world is a construction, a collage of different interests, values and preconceptions that manage to construct a single narrative around a so-called authentic Shipibo culture in order to better market it to tourists and visitors. This understanding of Shipibo culture as a made-up narrative, however, would be a profound misunderstanding of the kind of complex dynamics of composition that are at stake in making Shipibo culture in the present. As more and more anthropologists of Shipibo culture are showing, Shipibos, just like any other group, adapt and react to changes, especially the changes brought about by contact with the external world and with other Shipibo groups. Brabec de Mori and others recall for instance that the widespread adoption of ayahuasca resulted from intercultural contacts among Shipibo groups through forced migration and settlement into Catholic missions in the twentieth century. Similarly, it would be a mistake to see *kené* as something that was unchanged until recently: Shipibo artistic practices have evolved, both in the production of new designs and in the adoption of new aesthetics and new materials. For example, the quality of lines for *kené* designs has changed: there are at least two different styles in existence, with the older one being more angular, and the newer styles being more curvaceous. Shipibo embroidery textile artists in turn use and sometimes combine these different styles in order to produce different aesthetic effects. In terms of materials, Shipibo textile artists have embraced the use of synthetically dyed embroidery floss and textiles. Their aesthetic preferences go towards bright and neon colors that are in high contrast with one another, and such colors cannot be found in the natural dye palette (Figures 6.3, 6.4 and 6.5). Shipibo makers have begun to find new applications for *kené* designs, particularly garments. They now sell t-shirts and pants with *kené* designs that are often perceived by visitors as the proper kind of apparel to take part in ritual ceremonies. These garments have very little in common with the traditional Shipibo garments but find a place in the reinvented rituals mentioned above. Interestingly as well, some Shipibo artists have moved away from the abstract geometric lines typical of *kené* designs in favor of pictorial representation.

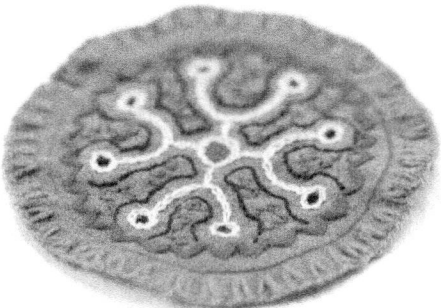

Figure 6.3 Example of *Kené* embroidery. Courtesy of the author.

Figure 6.4 Example of *Kené* embroidery. Courtesy of the author.

Figure 6.5 Example of *Kené* embroidery. Courtesy of the author.

Such integration of pictorial representations is a shift toward finding new ways to communicate with visitors and foreigners and it would be wrong to view this trend as either disingenuous or imposed by market demands. Rather, it would be more accurate to see these changes as an effort to find bridges between radically different modes of existence: that of the Indigenous Shipibo and that of the western visitor. The *Kené* textile object emerges again as an interface, but while in the previous chapter the textile interface helped dis/re/connect personal and collective experiences and economic and social patterns into maker subjectivities, here the interface itself becomes a troubled object of encounter between two subjectivities and two cosmologies—Indigenous and western. Viveiros de Castro's perspectival equivocation that opened the chapter comes to the fore here: westerners should acknowledge that the changes in *kené* textile are not indications that Indigenous subjectivities have been invaded or polluted by western culture. Rather, one should look at these textiles as challenging the western romantic perception of Indigenous identity as authentic and unsullied and as troubling these preconceptions. A small *kené* embroidery patch, like the ones pictured in Figures 6.3, 6.4 and 6.5, are not just mere tourist trinkets, they are the interfaces of an encounter between radically different cosmologies, which translate the efforts, on the part of the Shipibo maker, to find ways for partial connections and understandings. More specifically, as interfaces, they work to produce new prehensions that are not based on western preconceptions of what both western and Indigenous people and cosmologies are. I use the term prehension here in reference to Whitehead, especially how Andrew Murphie further explores it (2005). Prehension involves sensations, perception and sometimes cognition in how one approaches an Other, be it animate or inanimate, technological or biological. Typically, the prehension of something in the present is indebted to the past, so that for instance, the prehension of thirst-quenching when I am given a glass of water is based on my past memories of and embodied knowledge of what it feels like to drink water on a hot, dry day. At the same time, these past experiences allow me to project myself to, in this case, a very close future, where I know I am about to feel hydrated and refreshed. Prehension is what allows for the past and the future—memory and projection of something to be—to be articulated in a present moment. The creative and political challenge is to refashion prehension away from faulty assumptions about what the Indigenous cosmologies and subjects are, and by extension, what the western cosmology and subjects could be. Indeed, we all have experienced faulty prehensions such as the popular example of jumping in fright at the sight of a snake, which reveals itself to be, on second viewing, a piece of rope. What this means in the case of the *Kené* textiles pictured in Figures 6.3, 6.4 and 6.5 is that they challenge sensorial and cognitive habits. And paying further attention to my reaction to *Kené* designs that I opened this chapter with is useful here. It is clear that *Kené* textiles triggered in me a type of prehension related to deciphering, reading, learning, interpreting. At the same time, the designs were troubling because they short-circuited in the present the knowledge I possess from past experiences of reading and interpreting, all based in a western media environment, so that I ended up feeling like something very important was escaping me. And in so doing, the failure of my habitual prehension challenged my taken-for-granted projections into a future where I can fit any piece of media and information into the western interpretive frameworks that I have used all my life. In earlier versions of this chapter, I referred to Barthes's punctum to try to explain the feeling of a usual prehension such as reading and interpreting being so profoundly troubled (Barthes, 1981). But this analogy is not accurate: it is not a piercing that brings back a personal memory and allows for the past to haunt and shape the present, rather, it is a moment in the present of uncomfortable suspension and powerlessness that points out a much larger, richer and unknown world of meaningful encounter. Whereas Barthes goes to the recovering of the past, *kené*, as I experienced it, is about being opened up in the present to media otherness, and therefore to the otherness of media-making and media-makers. It is important to note that prehensions establish relationships that are co-constitutive, and that the troubling of prehension therefore asks about what kinds of other relationships are possible. Prehension, then, becomes political: and textile in particular becomes the means of establishing new politics of encounter where Indigenous cosmologies and subjects are not inevitably folded into the dominant matrix. These are not, however, lone political gestures.

Back to the Basics

Understanding the *Kené* textiles such as the ones I have encountered in Pucallpa—where Shipibo artists work with foreign audiences and customers—as experiments in prehension makes it possible in turn to understand the other strategies that Shipibo have developed in order to develop modes of encounters at the crossroad of divergent worlds. It makes sense here to refer to Chapter 2 that examined Quechua textiles in the context of mass tourism in the Cusco region. As I showed in Chapter 2, the strategy developed by Quechua makers involved a multifaceted discourse network, where explanations about the importance and signification of Quechua textiles was further reverberated through the use of traditional dress and showcasing Indigenous ways of living and making. Altogether, this discourse network delineated Quechua textiles as central material objects that exist in ambivalent and fraught relationships with the mass tourism market. Indeed, while all kinds of appropriations and devaluations of Quechua textiles take place continuously, without traditionally made Quechua textiles, such mass tourism market would quickly disappear. In Chapter 2 then, we saw how discourse and materials were made to work together: specifically how discursive strategies were central in making Quechua textile matter in specific ways. With Shipibo textiles, the strategies that are being developed are different. In contrast to the developing industry around the ayahuasca complex as yet another form of spiritual tourism, we see some Shipibo actors making tremendous efforts to bring things back to the ground, so to speak, and working with materials and embodied experience. This involves for instance, developing ways to enable visitors to experience Shipibo cosmovision through lived experience—sharing the daily life of a village, being educated in the Amazon ecosystem and so on. Overall, the efforts lie in combatting the view that only ayahuasca and the rituals around it are only what matters. Instead, the idea is to work on experiences on the ground that will enable visitors to gain something else from Shipibo rituals and cosmovisions that go beyond personal experiments with psychedelic drugs. For this reason, it would be more appropriate to consider these changes and experiments, including ones around Shipibo textiles, as practical ways of doing the kind of perspectival anthropology that Viveiros de Castro advocates. Let me in turn describe some of these efforts, with the following caveat for the western reader: these efforts, as small and mundane as they might at first seem, operate something very important: they bring back the question of matter, of materialization, of groundedness, to the tendency for the western visitor to focus on the abstract, the psychedelic, the intangible meaning of Amazonian cosmovisions. The mistake that westerners make with Shipibo textiles and cosmovision in general is to try to fold them into the immaterial world of spiritual visions, to recreate the old western division between nature and culture. The Shipibo textile are obviously material—they resist the tendency towards pure abstraction, or rather, they show that the tangible and the intangible are linked together, that matter and meaning are intertwined.

The propagation of Shipibo textile demonstrates, at least in Pucallpa, an incredibly wide variety of ideas and experiments that are often prevented from happening because of lack of support and infrastructure, from fashion education for instance to financial investment. Here again, the question of matter resurfaces as the necessary infrastructure through which other modes of encounter, and other types of cognition and prehension could be developed. There is a general desire from Shipibo artists to explore new avenues for dissemination of *Kené* designs, through collaborations to open new markets and through learning new skills in textile and fashion design. This is very similar to the efforts developed by Quechua women's groups in Northern Peru that we saw in Chapter 4. Neoliberal multiculturalism plays a dual role in this, much like what we saw in Chapter 2: the idea that Indigenous groups should become entrepreneurs capable of marketing their identities and ways of life has led, on the ground, to collaborations with foreign designers and artists, thus providing some economic opportunities. However, collaborations such as these carry with them some important contradictions: the development of products that the makers themselves will never see or use (e.g., high-end western style furniture); and the presumption that through projects that are short in duration, Shipibo makers will become savvy global textile designers and marketers. The problem is that while these collaborations showcase Shipibo art, they do so momentarily for a very remote and rarefied audience. These collaborations generate a lot of hope in terms of enabling Shipibo makers to make economic gains, but by and large they are usually one-offs and at best sporadic, offering no long-term economic stability. What they highlight in turn for Shipibos is the need for long-term collaborations, but these would involve a fairly profound rethinking of textile objects away from commodities that have to fit into the dynamics of the mainstream fashion and design market. Overall, there is strong desire to rethink how *Kené* can best communicate with a desire to develop new applications other than wall tapestries and clothing, but the infrastructure that would allow for such engagements, which recalls the development of new Indigenous textile objects in Chapter 4, is not there yet.

My encounters with NGO workers supporting Shipibo communities also highlighted how, much like the fight against the abstraction of ayahuasca from its Amazonian context, there are plans afoot to bring *kené* designs back to the ground as well, to their materialities. One example is a proposed project for a "Natural Dyes in the Amazon" workshop open to non-Shipibo artists. The project aims to fulfill several goals: first, to offer a way for non-Shipibos to experience more than the finished *kené* designs, that is to say, to experience the environment and world that shape Shipibo cosmovision. Second, the project offers a way for Shipibo artists to be exposed to other artistic and design practices. Third, it aims to strengthen the use of local materials for artistic practice, especially for younger generations, thus strengthening identity building through contact with the Amazonian environment. Finally, this helps promote knowledge of Amazonian plants and materials, as many local dyes and pigments have medicinal properties as well. In all, the transitions toward mobilizing Shipibo craft, especially textile, as an interface for forging new relationships, reveals attempts to establish new and different networks to mobilize different dynamics and actors away from purely capitalist relationships of appropriation. Based on some feedback in academic circles, such projects overall might seem too prosaic with regard to understanding Shipibo's cosmovision and media. Indeed, the idea that in order to understand Shipibo cosmovision one might want to spend some time along the Ucayali river collecting mud for pigments is at odds with our western academic habits of living purely in remote, abstract and highly intellectual spheres. While not many of us critical scholars would think of philosophizing in the mud, if we were to go past our ignorance, we might yet be able to understand how the material and the abstract, the elemental and the cosmological after all are inseparable, and that only through engaging with the Amazonian environment in material ways can we ever hope to gain an understanding of Amazonian cosmovisions. If we western scholars were to acknowledge our blind spots, then we would need to start with the basics indeed, and get to learning them before we could even hope to grasp the complexity of Shipibo modes of expression. Learning to deal with how to make materials for expression and to understand their place in the environment is a solid beginning and one indeed, as I will explain in Chapter 7, that can be the most transformative and revolutionary.

References

Abbott, Jeff. (2016). "Opposing Corporate Theft of Mayan Textiles, Weavers Appeal to Guatemala's High Court." *Truthout*. August 14, 2016. https://truthout.org/articles/opposing-corporate-theft-of-mayan-textiles-weavers-appeal-to-guatemala-s-high-court/

Barthes, Roland. (1981). *Camera Lucida: Reflections on Photography*. London: Macmillan.

Bauck, Whitney. (2017). "Guatemalan Artisans Are Going After 64,000+ Etsy Products for Copyright Infringement." *Fashionista*, August 22, 2017 (accessed April 25, 2019). https://fashionista.com/2017/08/guatemalan-artists-etsy-copyright-infringement.

Belaunde, Luisa Elvira. (2009). *Kené: Arte, Ciencia y Tradition En Diseno*. Lima: Instituto Nacional de Cultura.

Belaunde, Luisa Elvira. (2012). "Diseños Materiales e Inmateriales: La Patrimonialización Del Kené Shipibo-Konibo y de La Ayahuasca En El Perú." *Mundo Amazónico* 3: 123–46.

Brabec de Mori, Bernd. (2011). "The Magic of Song, The Invention of Tradition and the Structuring of Time among the Shipibo, Peruvian Amazon." In *Yearbook of the Phonogrammarchiv at the Austrian Academy of Sciences*. Edited by Gerda Lechleitner and Christian Liebl, 2:169–92.

Burroughs, William S. and Allen Ginsberg. (2001). *The Yage Letters*. 3rd edn. San Francisco, CA: City Lights Publishers. [Original published 1963.]

Fabricant, Nicole. (2013). "Good Living for Whom? Bolivia's Climate Justice Movement and the Limitations of Indigenous Cosmovisions." *Latin American and Caribbean Ethnic Studies* 8 (2): 159–78. DOI: 10.1080/17442222.2013.805618.

Feldman, Nancy Gardner. (2016). "Chapter 5: Evolving Communities: Aspects of Shipibo and Andean Art, Textiles, and Practice in Contemporary Peru." *Fieldiana. Anthropology*, no. 45: 51–59.

Hern, Warren M. (2016). "Yushin Huemena: Visions of the Spirit World, Art, Design, Medicine and Protective Spirits in Shipibo Ritual." *Tipití: Journal of the Society for the Anthropology of Lowland South America* 14 (1): 1–14. http://digitalcommons.trinity.edu/cgi/viewcontent.cgi?article=1218&context=tipiti.

Larsson, Naomi. (2015). "Inspiration or Plagiarism? Mexicans Seek Reparations for French Designer's Look-Alike Blouse." *The Guardian*, June 17, 2015. https://www.theguardian.com/global-development-professionals-network/2015/jun/17/mexican-mixe-blouse-isabel-marant.

Murphie, Andrew. (2005). "Differential Life, Perception and the Nervous Elements: Whitehead, Bergson and Virno on the Technics of Living." *Culture Machine* 7 (January). https://culturemachine.net/biopolitics/differential-life-perception-and-the-nervous-elements/.

Odland, Claire, and Nancy Feldman. (2010). "Shipibo Textile Practices 1952-2010." *Textile Society of America Symposium Proceedings*. http://digitalcommons.unl.edu/tsaconf/42/.

Odland, J. Claire. (2016). "The Making of 'Shipibo: La Pelicula De Nuestra Memoria.'" *Fieldiana. Anthropology*, no. 45: 35–49.

Ontaneda, Constanza. (2017). "Shipibos Displaced in Lima: Insurgent Citizens as Authorized Indians in Peru." *Latin American and Caribbean Ethnic Studies* 12 (1): 25–47. https://doi.org/10.1080/17442222.2016.1273856.

Peters, John Durham. (2015). *The Marvelous Clouds: Toward a Philosophy of Elemental Media*. Chicago: University of Chicago Press.

Pinedo, Danny. (2017). "The Making of the Amazonian Subject: State Formation and Indigenous Mobilization in Lowland Peru." *Latin American and Caribbean Ethnic Studies* 12 (1): 2–24. https://doi.org/10.1080/17442222.2016.1270537.

Postero, Nancy Grey, and Leon Zamosc. (2006). "The Struggle for Indigenous Rights in Latin America." *Journal of Latin American Anthropology* 11 (1): 208–10. https://doi.org/10.1525/jlca.2006.11.1.208.

Rénique, Gerardo. (2009). "Law of the Jungle in Peru: Indigenous Amazonian Uprising against Neoliberalism." *Socialism and Democracy* 23 (3): 117–35. https://doi.org/10.1080/08854300903290835.

Shipibo Joi. (2011). "Welcome to Shipibo Joi." *Shipibo Joi* [blog]. August 29, 2011. https://shipibojoi.wordpress.com/2011/08/29/hello-world/.

Varagur, Krithika. (2016). "Mexico Prevents Indigenous Designs From Being Culturally Appropriated—Again." *HuffPost Canada*. March 17, 2016. http://www.huffingtonpost.com/entry/mexico-prevents-indigenous-designs-from-being-culturally-appropriated-again_us_56e87879e4b0b25c9183afc4 (accessed 17 July 2023).

Viveiros de Castro, Eduardo. (2004). "Perspectival Anthropology and the Method of Controlled Equivocation." *Tipití: Journal of the Society for the Anthropology of Lowland South America* 2 (1), 3–20. https://digitalcommons.trinity.edu/tipiti/vol2/iss1/1.

Viveiros de Castro, Eduardo, and Roy Wagner. (2016). *The Relative Native: Essays on Indigenous Conceptual Worlds*. Translated by Martin Holbraad, David Rodgers, and Julia Sauma. Chicago: HAU.

Wali, Alaka, J. Claire Odland, Luisa Elvira Belaunde, Nancy Gardner Feldman, Daniel Morales Chocano, Ana Mujica-Baquerizo, and Ronald L. Weber. (2016). "The Shipibo-Conibo: Culture and Collections in Context." *Fieldiana Anthropology* 45 (1): 1–100. http://www.bioone.org/doi/abs/10.3158/0071-4739-45.1.1.

Part IV

COSMOMEDIA

Chapter 7

COSMOMEDIA: A TALE OF TWO INDIGOS

Have you, reader, ever made color? By this, I do not mean squeezing and mixing paints out of tubes or opening a packet of colored dye to throw in a bucket of water. Color is everywhere, but we seldom stop and ask ourselves where human-made colors come from: we take color as a given, but rarely look at it as media technology (Kane, 2014). The technologies for making color vary greatly depending on the medium, of course: there is a world of difference between producing color for a digital interface and producing it for textile. Up until the invention of synthetic dyes and colors in the nineteenth century, making color for textile entailed extracting materials from the environment, including mud, minerals, plants, insects and mollusks (Cardon, 2007). It further required experimenting with these materials and other chemicals in order to see which mixture produced lasting color (Garcia and Bernard, 2006; Garcia, 2016), that is, color that once applied is both steadfast and lightfast. And indeed, it would be difficult to imagine textile as medium without color to create a multiplicity of expressive combinations and encodings. Color on textile is difficult to achieve and requires knowledge of botany, chemistry and entomology (Boutrup and Ellis, 2018); technical skills in developing recipes for dye applications (Vejar, 2015); and craft, that is, tacit knowledge borne through repetition of the same gesture and intimate knowledge of one's materials. By definition, textiles are meant to be used and washed and reused, and creating a color that does not disappear too fast is indeed a struggle.

With dyeing, color penetrates into the textile fiber, rather than coating the surface, like in screen-printing, for instance. Dyeing can happen at all stages of the textile-making process—from dying fibers, threads, or finished cloth. Natural dyestuffs are very common: where I live in Ontario, goldenrods that grow as weeds in the summer give beautiful and deep yellows, and black walnuts found everywhere in fall give rich browns. In the home kitchen, avocado pits and skins give romantic pinks, while onion skins give rusty oranges. In Central and South America, cochineal parasites give an intense red. There is an immense variety of colors—from black to red, beige and orange—to be derived from different muds. Natural dyes tend not to work well on synthetics as opposed to protein or cellulose fibers such as wool, silk, cotton, hemp, linen, but also the more recent modal and rayon fabric. Often, the fibers will need to be pre- or co-treated with chemicals in order to be able to receive the natural dye: a process called mordanting involving minerals such as aluminum sulfate or substances rich in tannins such as gallnuts or myrobalan, which can also be used to give different hues to the same dye. Further, one can use modifiers: squeeze a few drops of lemon on a cochineal-dyed fabric and you will see the color turn from deep red to bright pink. Add some iron to any dye bath and you will get greys and blacks, depending on the concentration. Natural dyes can be layered on top of each other to produce colors that are difficult to achieve otherwise, for instance, layering yellow and blue dyes in order to obtain greens. The Bayeux tapestry made in the eleventh century used such techniques to achieve a rich foliage green. Somewhat paradoxically, greens are hard to achieve with natural dyes, even though natural dyes often involve leaves. Over time, the yellow dye in these Bayeux tapestries faded, so that now only blue dye from woad remains.

Which leads to the central object of this chapter: the dye color that has been the most cherished and valued the world over is blue, and especially the blues derived from indigo. Indigo blues provide some of the richest traditions and testaments to the importance of color for human expression. They have many different histories because there are actually over 750 plants in the world that contain indican—the compound for indigo dye. There is no one single point of origin for indigo dyeing— rather it was discovered in multiple places over the world, in Central and South America, Asia, Europe and Africa. Only a handful of plants contain indican in large enough quantities to derive some strong dye color from it. The most common of these plants historically and up to the present day is Indigofera tinctoria, originating in Southern Asia. It was the most commercially exchanged indigo the world over up until the invention of synthetic indigo in 1865. In South America, Indigofera suffruticosa or anil is the plant that is most used to produce blues, including, when mixed with clay, the famous Mayan blue. These two types of indigo grow in warm and tropical climates. Colder climates have different sources of indigo. In Europe, woad, which contains indican in a smaller percentage, was the main source of lighter blues until the arrival of Indigofera tinctoria from India. In China and later Japan, Polygonum tinctorium was the plant commonly used to produce natural indigo. These two indigo plants—Indigofera tinctoria and Polygonum tinctorium—will be my focus here because while they both provide some of the richest blues found the world over, the kind of technologies, media practices and systems of distribution and valuation that revolve around them are so vastly different that they enable diverging sets of relationships between people and environments and indeed, radically different ways of making worlds. Following from the previous chapter, I argue that the Japanese tradition of creating blues from Polygonum tinctorium is at its core a form of un-knowing in that it is requires the human maker to give up on any sense of control over the dyeing process, and requires instead that one enters into a composition with other non-human and more-than-human actants and entities.

I follow Yuk Hui's argument in the *Question Concerning Technology in China* (2016) that the key issue in exploring media technology and the making of worlds is to challenge the tendency to assume monotechnologism: a modernist, western-centric view that technology is only meant for control and profit. In this chapter, I examine how indigo dyeing, particularly the Japanese tradition of Indigo (*Aizome*) is built on an understanding of technology and media as relational and transformative vectors requiring a deep attunement between humans and non-humans. In so doing, I want to show how it is never about technology, but rather technologies, and their accompanying media practices and forms that constitute expressive relations through time and space that are different than the one experienced in the dominant monotechnological system. I examine in particular the material, technical and chemical processes that enabled the capture of Indigofera tinctoria within the modernist, colonial and capitalist matrix. Against this history, I turn to the significance of indigo blue in Japan as cosmotechnics and ecosophical media, that is, as forging not only new relations but also collaborations with the world in ways that inscribe human expression within environmental dynamics.

Cosmotechnics and Ecosophical Media

Let us consider the broader picture for a moment. Until the invention of synthetic dyes, all dye colors were derived from the environment, and we could think of dyes as media that organize the transition and continuity between nature and culture. Dyes as media mobilize both techniques (the extraction and transformation of materials) and communication (the application of transformed materials for expressive purposes that then have actual effects). Techniques in general are about the extraction of materials and their transformation into usable susbstances. Communication, as we have seen in previous chapters, involves abstracting systems, both symbolic and digital in the case of textile, to materialize effects, both close and at a distance (i.e., through space and time). Dyed textiles, as a medium, transform bodies and selves, leave testimonies and transmit memories—they unleash myriad modes of existence and relations, both actual and potential. Communication thus becomes a question of the politics of a meaningful life together. Techniques, on the other hand, are about the politics of environmental relations, because they are anchored in the extraction and transformation of materials from environments—at least that is how they are anchored to colonial capitalism. But if we hope to go beyond this dominant matrix of power, we would do well to reflect on what Yuk Hui calls cosmotechnics: the argument that technology should be seen as technologies, multiple and diverse, and "characterized by different dynamics between the cosmic, the moral and the technical" (2016: 54). The challenge lies in understanding how a set of relationships with the world— abstract and material, personal and collective, practical and symbolic, ethical and expressive—can be built through the articulation of technologies with specific media processes and practices. The recent turn towards environmental and elemental understanding of media—turning towards water, fire and air, for instance, as media themselves (Peters, 2016) that unfold with and allow for the shaping of media techniques and objects—fits with this new understanding of mediation: as the crafting of relations that necessarily engage the human with the non-human in the process of articulating modes of existence as ways of living in or at the crossroad of specific worlds.

The stakes of the relationship between technologies and media are important because they enable *worlding* (Haraway, 2016). Worlding, as Palmer and Hunter (2018) further elaborate is "a particular blending of the material and the semiotic that removes the boundaries between subject and environment." This definition of worlding, anchored in the humanities, can be expanded to an ensemble of processes whereby living and non-living entities and meaning-making processes as well as relational practices and habits emerge and come together, not as a perfect machinery, but as a system of productive echoes, resonances and dissonances, transformation and hybridization. Worlding is a process and never a finished state of affairs, and has come to the fore today as a critical response to the Anthropocene (Altvater et al., 2016; Viveiros de Castro and Danowski, 2016; Kolbert et al., 2017; Scranton, 2015). In realizing the existential need to break away from the destructive processes of the matrix of capitalism, colonialism and modernity, there arises the need to not just retreat from the world and from nature, but rather to build mutually supportive environments. Worlding in that sense enlists technologies and media to further delve into fostering relationships among living and non-living entities. It would be a mistake to see worlding, and the kind of relational technological and media practices that accompany it to have to be radically new, as if the past was one big mistake. Rather, as I want to show in this chapter, worlding involves reappraising old and long existing practices that have been forgotten and pushed to the margins. Worlding is a political project in the sense that it radically puts into question general western assumptions around linear progress as the technical and scientific subsumption of the environment to human determination, in turn fundamentally decentering the place of the human as controller, master and ultimately destroyers of environments. On the contrary, humans can be part of complex processes of worlding, composing with dynamics, affects, entities and beings through relations that are mutually beneficial and empowering, as Ana Tsing so powerfully demonstrates in *The Mushroom at the End of the World* (2017). Worlding is also not about a return to an unsullied state of nature, but rather a recognition first of all that technologies play a central role in establishing relationships between humans and entities, environments and other beings. In that sense, making natural dyes, particularly indigo, is a kind of worlding because it requires a very specific attunement between different entities and human components to transform a set of materials into a mode of expression. Second, technology, like science, needs to be profoundly rethought to take into account and care for the lives of humans and non-humans alike (Stengers, 2018; Bellacasa, 2017).

Worlding finds an echo in the work of Félix Guattari, especially in the *Three Ecologies* (2008). For Guattari, writing in the late 1980s, the global environmental crisis caused by "world integrated capitalism" obviously required intervention in the techno-scientific and techno-economic systems that exploit and destroy the environment, but not only there. Rather, critical interventions to formulate ecosophies (ethical relationships with and through worlds) rather than just ecologies (sustaining natural environments) required moving away from capitalist, colonialist and modernist logics as they permeate all aspects of human and non-human lives. Protecting natural environments was not enough: ecosophy engages with different levels of existence and their relationalities, hence the need to develop ecosophies of the social and the psyche. Social ecosophy involves new modes of being together and new values that break away from, for instance, neoliberal conceptions of humans as economically and existentially competing with each other, but also addressing questions of systematic racism, neofascism, human exploitation, misogyny and so on. Further, Guattari calls for a "putting into being" (*mise en être*) that would move away from dominant processes of subjectivation and toward more experimental processes that foster new ways of feeling, thinking and being. This ecosophy of the psyche includes new understanding of conscious and unconscious processes (dreams, affects, fantasms and so on) as well as new relationships with one's body and physical engagements with the world. Here, we could think of practices of biosensing, of working with affective energies, capacities for dreaming as the opening of potential spaces and ways of reconciling with past and future as component of this ecology of the psyche. The three ecosophies are not separate and the point indeed is to organize political, critical and existential interventions at all levels, from the global system of production to individual habits. Guattari's work offers multiple sites of intervention where the dynamics that flow through human and non-human actants and entities are worked on in the making of life and existence. As I further show in this chapter, the Japanese indigo dyeing tradition allows for an exploration of the three ecosophies (environmental, social, psychic) and their mutual imbrication.

Combinations and Recombinations: Indigo Dyeing and the Making of Worlds

Indigo blues have (and still are in many cultures) the most revered and valued blues. Indigo blues are part of many cosmologies in South America, Asia, and Africa—linking the human with the spiritual: the blues reach out to the sky, but also to water, life. It would be impossible here to trace the many cosmologies that feature indigo, some of which are powerfully described in Michael Taussig's *What Color is the Sacred?* (2009). Indigo blues are life, and by this I refer not only to spiritual values, but also to sensorial qualities as well as physical properties. Indeed, while it is meaningful and revered as a color, indigo was by no means reserved for special occasions. Indigo blues are found in many cultures and groups: the Black Hmongs in Northern Vietnam, the Miaos in China, the Yorubas in Nigeria, the Tuaregs in the Sahara and so on. In the west, indigo is inseparable from denim. Indigo is durable, and it also reinforces fabric: it is inseparable from everyday workwear. Yet, indigo blues produced by artisans all over the world have this special quality of luminous liveliness that no synthetic color possesses. This is particularly evident when comparing natural indigo dyed fabric with synthetic indigo, even though the chemical compound is the same: although synthetic indigo produces bright blues, they are harsh and inert compared to the ineffable qualities of natural indigo blues. True indigo blues are more than blue—they radiate: even the darkest, almost black hue is the color of space in between stars. The process of producing indigo and using it for dyeing itself is so miraculous as to be akin to giving birth, as mentioned in the introduction of this book, in reference to Yuko Tanaka's *The Power of the Weave* (2013), and as detailed below. Such life is not particularly human life, but the life of a cosmological assemblage, where plant, materials, chemical processes, fibers and human expressive techniques all come together to produce lasting blues.

Indigo blues might be magical and spiritual colors, but that does not mean they are separate or abstracted from a material environment. Rather, these blues involve a specific series of technologies (the extraction and transformation of materials) and media (abstraction through codes and materialization as effects at a distance). The technical processes involve extraction of indican from indigo plants, and the transformation of indican into indigotin that can dye textile fibers. The media processes involve applying indigo to create aesthetic effects, from variations of blues to color combination, but also the creation of patterns and figures. These representational and non-representational aesthetic effects subsequently gain cultural and socioeconomic meanings and values as they circulate within communities and across communities.

Here are further details around these technical and media processes that are involved in the making of indigo blues.

1. Extraction: while fresh-leaf indigo can be directly used to produce light blues, the darker blues can only be attained through extracting indican from the plant and oxidizing it to transform it into indigotin. There are historically two ways to achieve this: water extraction or composting. Water extraction involves several steps where leaves are rinsed, submerged in water, then either/or both heated and fermented, then alkalized, oxidized and filtered. The remaining indigo is then dried into a powder or pressed into cakes. This method was used in India, while other places, particularly Japan, use a compost method, wherein the leaves are chopped, sun dried, and then spread inside to compost, getting turned over and watered on a regular basis over the winter. The resulting product of concentrated indigo content is loose, compared with the water extraction method. As well, Japanese indigo tends to have lesser concentration of indican than the Indian Indigofera Tinctoria.

2. Transformation / Indigo reduction: indigotin is not water soluble. In order to become soluble and to adhere to textile fibers, it has to undergo a unique process that no other natural dyes require. There are two ways of transforming indigo into a dye: either through microbial or chemical means. The microbial method is the oldest, and consists of adding substances to an indigo vat in order to raise the pH of the vat (alkalinity), and substances to create microbial activity, or fermentation. Typically lime or soda ash from wood burning can be used to raise alkalinity, alongside wheat bran, rice bran, but also sake in Japan, for instance. The chemical or reduction method is a more recent

invention from the mid-nineteenth century (Balfour-Paul, 2011: 129–30) which involves ammonia to raise alkalinity and sodium hydrosulphite to provoke the indigo reduction. It should be noted that these chemicals are harsh and toxic and have serious environmental and health impacts. In response, the past decades have seen the development of chemical indigo vats involving environmentally friendly ingredients such as calcium hydroxide (or pickling lime) for alkalinity and overripe fruits for the reduction (Garcia, 2016), although this method tends not to be used for large-scale indigo dyeing.

3. Dyeing: once an indigo vat is properly fermented or reduced, the dyeing process can take place. There are many techniques to create visual effects using indigo, and they all require some kind of resist techniques so that only part of whatever is dyed receives the indigo. Resist techniques can involve tying fabrics or threads so that the dye cannot penetrate the fibers, applying a resist paste that can be made of rice powder, or clay, or lime, or wax; pressing fabric in between carved wood blocks, and so on. There are many names in different cultures for these processes, among which are: *ikat* all over southeast Asia (where the threads are bound together and dyed before weaving to create patterns on either or both the warp and weft); *shibori* in Japan (tying, see Figure 7.1); *bandhani* in India (tying); *katazome* in Japan (rice resist); *Ajrakh* in Pakistan (block-printing with lime resist); *batik* (wax resist) in Indonesia and so on.

4. Designs: such resist techniques enable different codes—both abstract and representational—patterns or unique designs. These range from very fine *ikat* variations to bold rice-resist designs, from free-hand designs with rice resist to pattern repetition with block-printing.

The many aesthetic effects that can be achieved with indigo, their histories, practices, cultural significance and meaning are so vast and varied the world over as to fill many libraries (Legrand, 2013).

The extraction and processing of indigo is key to understanding the dual and contradictory histories of indigo as a colonial and capitalist medium on the one hand, and as a cosmological medium on the other. This might at first seem to make no sense: after all, the extraction and reduction of indigo happens regardless of the different chemical and microbial processes used. But in actuality, technologies of extraction and transformation mobilize specific non-human entities in political ways. The decision of which entities to call into action fundamentally expresses how one thinks and acts in the world. In other words, the choice of materials and technical processes already expresses cosmovision and ethical principles about how to relate with non-humans actants and entities. Natural indigo is unique because it is the result of complex chemical processes resulting from many non-human entities and materials coming together. The making of the reduced indigo vat without using either synthetic indigo or harsh chemicals is indeed quite fussy, as is the fermentation vat (Figure 7.2). Indigo dyeing, in other words, is quite hard to achieve and requires quite a lot of practice in learning how to build and maintain

Figure 7.1 Example of Japanese Shibori with indigo, Hiroyuki Shindo's collection. Courtesy of the author.

an indigo vat. The uncontrollable character of natural indigo has been fully recognized by many, including the British textile artist and socialist thinker and activist William Morris, who famously wrote in a letter to a friend that "it would be a week's talk to tell you all the anxieties and possibilities connected with the indigo subject" (MacKail, 2013: 325). Here are some examples in which the process can go wrong, taken from my own five-year experience with indigo dyeing:

1. The reduction does not take place. This can be due to several factors: the water is of poor quality, too alkaline or not alkaline enough; the reducing agent, especially when using fruits, is not high enough in fructose; the temperature of the room is not warm enough; the vat was too agitated or nor agitated enough; and so on. Try again.
2. The dye result is of poor quality and uneven: the vat has not properly reduced (see above); the water is of poor quality and deadens the blue; the cloth is

Figure 7.2 Indigo vats at Hiroyuki Shindo's workshop in Miyama, Japan. Courtesy of the author.

covered with chemicals and other impurities and has not been properly scoured; the dyer introduced too much oxygen when adding the cloth; the dyer lost patience and did not dip the cloth several times for several minutes in order to build a solid color; the cloth was not submerged evenly in several or one of the dips; the cloth caught some residue either at the bottom of the vat or on top that resulted in uneven oxidization; and so on. Try again.

3. The cloth dyes, but it is not the right hue, and does not get deep and bright enough. This is because the indigo content is too low. Perhaps the leaves were of low quality, or the plants suffered and therefore did not develop as much indigotin as hoped; perhaps the reduction has not fully taken place; perhaps temperature changes in the room have changed the speed at which the indigo penetrates the fibers; and so on. Try again.

4. The finished dyed cloth develops green and yellow streaks after it dries. This is because the reduction process is still happening; or because the cloth was left in the sun for too long; or because it was not rinsed enough with good quality water; or perhaps was not washed well; or perhaps there was too much ozone in the region where the dyeing took place; and so on. Try again.
5. The dyer manages to obtain solid blues with no variations on cloth but cannot control the process so that the same blue can be achieved repeatedly. This is actually a sign of lack mastery of indigo, and as Franco-Malian indigo artist and designer Aboubakar Fofana states, one needs at the very least ten years of thorough training in order to master the capacity to reproduce different hues of blues (2021). Try again, for many years to come.

Again, natural indigo dyeing is both magical and incredibly difficult: there is nothing quite like pulling out a piece of cloth submerged in the indigo vat and seeing it, in contact with oxygen, slowly turn from yellow to green to turquoise to the purest blue. There is also nothing quite like the disappointment of waiting for a dyed piece to dry and reveal its glaring imperfections that cannot be hidden or recuperated and realizing that one has produced an expensive and time-consuming rag. The difficulty of the indigo process lies in the fact that there are so many elements that go into the making of a properly reduced vat: from quality of materials to chemical reactions to environmental factors like the weather. There are two ways to deal with this state of affairs: one is to find ways to control this instability, the other is to embrace it as an interface of communication with non-human actants and entities. In other words: one can decide to discipline and control the indigo process so that it can be made reliable at large and mass scales, or one can embrace indigo as the coming together of elemental mediations, to borrow from John Durham Peters (2016), that enable the development of a cosmovision. In this second version, control is abandoned in favor of attunement and composition: unlearning and un-knowing are embraced. Such process is delicate because it relies on a series of material, elemental mediations that do their work at their own pace: the soil that grew the indigo plant in the first place, the combination of air and water that allows the leaves to decompose, the rice bran that feeds the bacteria that reduces the indigo, the oxygen contained in water or air that turns the indigo blue.

Colonizing Indigo

To further understand this, let's briefly look at the histories of two strains of indigo: Indigofera tinctoria and Polygonum tinctorium: the indigo first cultivated throughout the Indian subcontinent and the indigo historically cultivated in the cooler climates of China and Japan. The processing of Indigofera tinctoria to extract indigotin marks that first step in making this particular type of indigo susceptible to being embedded within a system of production and distribution across the globe, in this case the European colonial system. The dark indigo blue fabrics first arrived in Europe from Asia via the Silk Road. Darker shades of blues were impossible to achieve with natural dyes derived from European plants: woad provided some indigo content, but in much lighter concentrations, resulting in a range of light to mid blues. It is hard to imagine the immense psychological, cultural and aesthetic impact of the arrival of a new color, especially on new and exotic fabrics such as cotton and silk. Nevertheless, the heavy and continuous importation of Indian and Chinese silk and cotton from Roman times onward is testament to the importance of textile in creating intercultural exchange, as seen in the first chapter of this book.

Indigofera tinctoria is processed through repeated washes of water with other chemicals to extract the indigotin, which is then dried into a powder that can be pressed into cakes. As Elena Phipps notes, the material form of indigo as cakes made it much more transportable than fermented balls of woad leaves, which "were difficult to transport because they required consistent levels of moisture and temperature" (2013: 128). From the get-go then, techniques for extracting indigo were evaluated for their capacity to be transported across distance, first starting with the commercial trade networks from the Indian subcontinent to Europe and especially England through the East India Company (ibid.), but expanding worldwide with the colonization of the Americas and the discovery of Indigenous indigo plants there. The transportability of processed Indigofera tinctoria opened the door to including indigo within the global colonial trade system, which involved transportation capacities across distance, but also mass production of materials such as indigo through land grab, ruthless exploitation and enslavement. In short order, Indigofera tinctoria went from an expression of cultural craft and sophistication to a mass-produced and traded commodity that materialized key aspects of colonization. As Phipps summarizes:

> Concomitant with the intensive cultivation practices necessary to sustain such large quantities of indigo exports was a long history of abusive labor practices.... Indigo was also intimately connected to the growth of slavery, which ... supplied much of the labor force needed to grow the crop, especially in the Americas. In the last quarter of the eighteenth century Bengali farmers in India were compelled by contracts with the English East India Company, which virtually governed the region, to grow indigo in their most fertile ground.... The resulting famine and widespread resentment under the oppressive British plantation system led directly to the Indigo Revolt of 1859-1860...
>
> Phipps, 2013: 128

This history of indigo then is a history of appropriation of a foreign color to transform it into an important economic and cultural element in the colonial-capitalist machinery, into a commodity that embodies a key paradox of the colonial-capitalist system: that something that allows for many kinds of cultural expressions and rituals was so thoroughly appropriated and colonized to become inseparable from systemic violence at both levels of production and distribution. It is important to note that this mobilization of indigo was due to the techniques for extraction of indigotin, which resulted in a material that could travel long distance, and could therefore be part of the networks of empire, in Innis's sense (2007). The techniques of extraction and the systems of distribution over the globe enabled an association between indigo-dyed fabric and mass production and circulation of textiles. This kind of new colonial network has to be distinguished from the Silk Road on a number of levels. First, everything was managed through the western colonial powers organizing this new global trade. Second, while the Silk Road was characterized by the movement of exotic commodities from afar coming into Europe, both luxurious like silk or richly ornamented like cotton, the mass production of indigo in colonial time, especially in the eighteenth and nineteenth centuries, saw indigo blues used not for aesthetic purposes but for practical ones. As Taussig observes: "By the eighteenth century, thanks to indigo, naturally lightfast and fadeproof, blue had become the uniform of work and authority" (2009: 144). From Napoleon's soldiers to police officers around the world, and later, with the invention of denim, rural and industry laborers around the world, blue became the uniform color of colonial empires and their social ordering.

But the capacity to transport indigo as cakes of solid, shelf-stable blocks is not the only intervention that allowed for such control and colonization of a color that was anything but western. The original fermentation vat was temperamental as described above, and efforts were made over the years to develop other methods for reducing indigo and to develop inorganic vats, where reduction was undertaken through the use of chemicals (Balfour-Paul, 2011: 129–31). Commonly used chemicals were ferrous sulphate and zinc dust, and today sodium hydrosulphite or thiourea dioxide. These chemicals allow for fairly quick and easy reduction of the indigo and were thus deemed suitable for the production of mass quantities of indigo dyed cloth. All of these chemicals, it should be noted are extremely harmful to humans exposed to them in large quantities and are well known to pollute environments. The discovery of synthetic indigo—which produces completely reliable blues—and its mass production starting in 1897 further enabled the development of mass production of blue cloth. The resulting effects are still found today as denim is one of the most mass-produced textile items, especially for the fast fashion market. The health consequences and environmental pollution can be visibly seen in denim production locales like Xintang, China, where the contaminated waste waters from the dyeing of blue jeans can be seen mixing into the local river system from satellite (Rickets, 2021).

The history of indigo in the west, then, is the history of control and appropriation of what Michael Taussig calls "the crossover color par excellence" (2009: 156), of exotic blues and fabrics that were subsequently appropriated into the service of mass commodity production and the enrichment of western powers, particularly the UK and the United States. Appropriation of indigo meant appropriation of nature (Descola and Sahlins, 2013), of the plants and spaces and laborers within which Indigofera tinctoria could be grown, appropriation of techniques for extracting indigotin as a portable item capable of being distributed throughout the world, and continuous technical and scientific efforts to find reliable ways of producing blues. As Taussig argues, the magic that surrounded indigo then disappeared: the miraculous ways in which it works and fails to work, which are the results of many small and big reactions in the indigo vat.

Indigo and Collectives of Humans and Non-Humans

Today, we see a resurgence of natural indigo: the growing realization of the unsustainability of synthetic dyes combined with fast fashion has led to the rediscovery of natural dyes. Natural dye specialist Michel Garcia (2016; Garcia and Bernard, 2006) invented an environmentally safe set of recipes for the chemical vat, using fructose and pickling lime that is easy to set up, and in so doing spurred a renaissance of indigo dyeing for amateurs and artisans alike. Today's environmental crises have led to a renewed interest in finding alternatives to the synthetic dyeing practices dominant since the industrial revolution. The renewal of local and natural dye practices, both through historical rediscovery and scientific innovation has enabled a rediscovery of natural indigo beyond and before its colonization. Of course, no natural indigo practice will be sustainable if high levels of consumption through fast-fashion continue. Consequently, there have been sustained efforts to think through how to encourage more meaningful relationships with textile, starting with an appreciation of the efforts, many materials and labor required to produce a sustainable garment. But indigo still presents a problem: it is still difficult to master, and the best and most beautiful blue hues and patterns can only be achieved by trained and skilled artisans. In resisting efforts at being reasonable, indigo points out another way of relating to dyeing, one that requires careful attention to the elements and entities that are involved in the dyeing process in the first place.

    In that regard, it is necessary to revisit the role of the human actor in the making process. Typically processes of making, or *techne*, are divided into two models: one where the human maker is central and in charge of the entire process of extraction and transformation, and the other where the human maker becomes just a cog in a complex machinery. In other words, the divide with regard to the question of technology is between craft and industry, between holistic and prescriptive technologies as Ursula Franklin argued in *The Real World of Technology* (1999: 10–11). As she explains, the craftsperson in the holistic model controls all aspects of the making process, from selection of materials to choice of techniques for production and finishing. In the industrial prescriptive model, however, the making process is rationalized by being broken into discrete units so as to maximize efficiency. The worker has to submit to the speed of the automated assembly line, and is only in charge of repeating the same gesture over and over again, when she is not replaced altogether by another machine. In *The Question Concerning Technology* (2013), Heidegger makes a similar argument when he talks about the creative aspect of *techne* as *poiesis*—as bringing forth. For Heidegger, *techne* as *poiesis* is a way of revealing—in the same way that, for instance, the chalice is revealed through gold being worked. By contrast, Heidegger reflects on more recent developments that see *techne* as a means of realizing an instrumental will, whereby the process of extraction and transformation reduces the world to standing reserves, just like the dam reduces the river to a standing reserve of energy. Such enframing of the world is ultimately depleting and betrays the more creative possibilities of *poiesis*. The human factor in all of this is quite crucial: ultimately the decision lies in whether to go toward *poeisis* or instrumentality, something that we see today still in the opposition between craft objects made with attention and care for social equity and environmental protection, and mass-produced objects, which only feed into networks of consumerism and profit-making. So the question is the following: is craft only human mastery, or does it include more than that? Here we can turn to Tim Ingold, who argues that we need to distinguish between hylomorphism—the imposition of form onto materials (2010: 91), and textility, the weaving of materials, which he describes as "the way in which materials of all sorts, energized by cosmic forces and with variable properties, mix and meld with one another in the generation of things" (91–92). By invoking textility and the figure of the weaver, Ingold defines another version of *techne*, one that does not extract but rather is about relational productions that can combine together force and pliability, strength and malleability, for instance. The fermentation indigo dye vat can be seen, in the same way, as a combination of not only different elements, but also different energies. If we look at indigo growing and dyeing in Japan and contrast it with the processes developed in the colonial context, we have to acknowledge that the traditional distinction between craft and industry is not sufficient, in that the process of Japanese indigo dyeing is much more distributed among a complex network of actants, with the human actants being of course important, but by no means in complete control.

Polygonum tinctorium grows in the spring and summer, and as with all plants, its health (and the quantity of indigotin it contains) is dependent on soil, weather, water and absence of disease or pests: the energies of the elements (earth, fire, water and air) are already present from the beginning and influence the range of possible blues. The collected indigo leaves are sun-dried and then composted in big piles indoor over the winter months and are ready for dyeing in the early spring. The Japanese indigo vat as mentioned above works through bacterial activity rather than chemical assist. This is somewhat akin to sourdough and other food fermentation practices, in that there is a need to provide the conditions to create a healthy bacterial culture, which includes temperature and the "feeding" of the bacteria. The fermentation vat requires time—while bacterial activity can be encouraged through heating, it still takes place on its own temporality. But time and temperature are not the only key elements here. When talking to indigo dyers about the most important aspect of a successful vat, a common answer was water: the quality of water determines the success of the dyeing process. City water is usually processed and often "hard," resulting in dull blues. Fresh and unpolluted spring water is usually considered best, and many indigo dyers in Japan choose the location of their dyeing studios based on the quality of water available. Here, indigo forces us to understand water as a complex medium: the past of water—

what happened to it, which chemicals it encounters, which filtration system it went through—determines how the indigo will react to fabric.

Typically, Japanese indigo vats contain a mix of rice bran and wood ash for lye (a strong alkaline solution), which can be warmed up through fire in the colder months. The signs of active fermentation and proper indigo reduction are the same as with the chemical natural indigo vat: the development of a red to yellow to green sheen and of an indigo flower, which shows that the oxygen has been pushed out of the vat. A pH test can also show if the vat has reached the ideal alkalinity. But to really know when a vat is ready takes knowledge borne of experience. Sight of course plays an important role to see the color and quality of the vat—to judge the quality of its sheen, for instance. But other senses are involved as well: indigo dyer and textile artist Hiroyuki Shindo puts a drop from the vat on his tongue to test its condition. There is also a smell to the reduced indigo vat which gives information as to what is going on. Haptic sensation is also a good indicator: over time the feeling of the vat liquid against the skin of one's hand gives an indication as to where the vat is. These can be small, barely perceptible differences—whether the reduction process is coming to a halt and the vat is getting close to needing a rest, whether it requires more or less heat and so on. Only through developing knowledge through the senses can the indigo dyer yield consistent results. It is useful therefore to reconsider the making process as a distributed one, where the human actant is not only in relation with other non-human actants and entities, but where the human actant is broken down and reconfigured along a chain of communication: the vat indeed calls forth different kinds of sensorial reactions that are impossible to fully translate verbally. When dipping cloth in the indigo vat, the decisions as to how long to submerge the cloth, how much to massage the cloth so that it takes in indigo, how many times to repeat the dipping process are all impossible to fully explain: it is a kind of synesthetic sensorial knowledge based on non-verbal communication with the long chain of non-human actants and entities.

While seminal, the oppositions within *techne*—between craft and industry, *poiesis* and instrumentality—reveal critical limitations in the case of indigo. Indeed, the indigo dyer is never fully in control of the vat, but rather attunes herself to the variety of entities that come together to make a live indigo vat. Of course, this kind of technical situation of being at the mercy of external entities is not uncommon in craft processes. As textile researcher Yoshiko Wada argues, in that sense indigo dyeing is akin to putting one's pottery into the kiln: at some point, the human maker has very little agency apart from firing the kiln and hoping that the reaction of the elements being put together in the kiln—fire, glaze, clay, air, humidity—will come together to produce a perfect pottery object. In that regard, indigo dyeing is not just about technique, it is about communication with the non-human. And just like communication with humans, this type of communication is without any promises of messages being fully received. It is communication without control, *techne* without instrumentality, but without the human in charge of revealing anything. It is the coming together of non-human entities that creates something that links the human to the non-human and to, indeed, the cosmos.

Japanese Indigo and Natural Dyes as Cosmomedia

What happens, then, when the uncertainty, unpredictability of the vat was embraced, not as a given state of affairs, but as a sign of the need for a set of ethical and spiritual practices around indigo? Let us turn for a moment to Taussig's recounting of the poetry and ritual practices (2009: 150–52) surrounding the indigo vat for Indigenous groups the world over, which celebrate how the indigo vat is akin to giving life. For the reader who has never seen one, an indigo vat is indeed a mysterious entity. A properly reduced vat will have blue foam sitting on top, a sign that oxygen was pushed out of the vat and that the reduction is happening. The surface of the liquid will be purple and coppery in color, shining almost like a mirror. Beneath this film, the liquid will range from yellow to green to red and rusty. There will be sediment at the bottom, mud-like and that should not be disturbed during the dyeing process. As mentioned above, a piece of cloth carefully submerged and massaged in the vat will first emerge yellow and green, and slowly oxidize in contact with either air or water. Repeated dips will deepen and darken the color, and with very good quality indigo, until it is almost black. But to get to this level of dyeing, where indigo is not just a dye but the result from a miraculous process of giving life requires a kind of relation that encompasses ethics (Bellacasa, 2017), cosmovision, sensations, and a sense of poetry. Making indigo blurs categories about what the human and non-human can do, and it becomes a symphony of many different processes both microscopic (what happens in the vat, for instance) and planetary (the air that will oxidize the indigo).

In Japan and elsewhere, many indigo masters will argue the same point: the indigo vat needs to die, at some point. Theoretically, nothing can prevent one from putting more indigo and reduction materials into the vat, or re-using an old vat to create a new one. This is something that is done regularly. Yet, for most indigo masters, the life of the vat should be respected, even if the further it is used, the less indigotin the vat contains, and the lighter the blues and the harder it might be to repeat the same color effects for the dyer. Franco-Malian indigo artist Aboubakar Fofana talks about this at length in his social media posts: the life of a vat has to be respected as a way to pay homage to the nature of indigo as a precious, live substance. Weaver and natural dyer Fukumi Shimura echoes this, comparing the life of the indigo vat to that of a human being. She says, of the last stage of the vat that it produces a very pale blue, adding: "If it were a sound, it would be the faintest of whispers; if a scent, the perfume of a stranger passing by" (2019: 33). This lightest of blues is but a trace of what was, but also the very color of an early morning sky, the birth of a new day. The indigo vat mobilizes worlds, creates resonances and in the course of its life, requires constant care, and care for the vat becomes care for all the non-human entities and processes that participate in the making of the vat. The practice of indigo is the practice of celebrating the encounter with the cosmos, of the coming together of many temporalities and indeed lives at a specific moment in the dipping of the fibers into the vat, and the giving of permanence of these fleeting encounters as the cloth turns blue. Indigo is transportation: for the dyer, it means being recombined with the non-human, and developing tacit modes of composition with a cosmos. The finished cloth is a gathering together of multiple sensations, the permanence of fugitive moments, different scales of temporalities and space coming together. In so doing, environmental factors, non-human entities, cultural aesthetics, human sensations and affects come are orchestrated together, creating indeed, ecosophical communication.

It should be clearer by now that Japanese indigo resists capitalist commodification: it is incredibly time consuming to produce as the fermentation of the leaves takes place over winter months. It contains lesser quantities of indican, thus lowering productivity. It can never be scaled up to mass production, being more adapted to small scale, high-quality textile production such as high-end Japanese apparel and textile arts. The indigo culture in Japan stretches back centuries, and operates on an understanding of cultural techniques that is radically different from the west. In order to understand the Japanese indigo culture and how indigo functions as medium within this context, it is necessary to understand the broader context of natural dyes and textiles in Japan. While Polygonum tinctorium was introduced to Japan from China, along with silk and cotton fabrics, Japan underwent two and a half centuries of isolationist foreign policy from the fifteenth century until the mid-nineteenth century. And while foreign textile goods from China and India (through the Dutch East India Company) were imported even during that time, by and large, most textile needs, practices and production, including dyes, relied on homegrown materials. There are actually two sets of textile traditions in Japan. One is the high-end textile production for the nobility, using fine fabrics, especially silk. Kyoto established itself early as a center of high-end textile production, partly because of the high quality of its water. The other textile tradition was developed by folk or common people, and is characterized by use of local fibers, narrower range of colors using local dyes and a keen awareness of cloth as a rare and precious material. From the high-end textile tradition come many different techniques of using natural dyes in a wide variety of colors, including a dizzying array of resist dyeing techniques, from binding threads before weaving (*Kasuri*) to resist dyeing through folding and binding cloth (*shibori*) to applying rice resist paste to create designs and patterns and painting directly onto the fabric. Most of these techniques demands intensive training, and some of take up to twenty years of training to master, such as *kyo-kanoko shibori*, which involves using threads to bind fabric before dyeing, resulting in tiny dots that compose complex patterns. Such techniques are still surviving today, especially as traditional kimono wear is enjoying a revival of sort in Japan. The town of Arimatsu, in Aichi prefecture sees a high concentration of traditional *shibori* artisans dating back to the early seventeenth century, and its yearly *shibori* festival attracts thousands. Natural dyeing is still very much alive in Japan and part of the curriculum in textile arts programs. The natural dye tradition in Japan is very much local with the use of native plants to produce a vast array of colors. Today, the work done by the Yoshioka company in Kyoto provides magnificent testimony of the role of natural color in Japanese culture. The Yoshioka company not only produces incredibly bright colors out of natural dyes—something which is incredibly difficult to achieve—but also has documented in several publications and exhibitions what I would call a cosmological grammar of color, cataloguing local natural dye plants, the colors they produce, and how they can be combined and layered with other colors to reflect the characteristics of seasons and places (Yoshioka and Fukuda, 2000).

Natural dyeing therefore has a long history in Japan, and the textile arts in general have received more recognition for their cultural importance than in the West, where they tend to be seen as craft, as opposed to high art. Indeed, there is a longstanding acknowledgement in Japan that textile does act as medium for artistic and spiritual purposes. In *The Power of the Weave* Yuko Tanaka (2013) speaks powerfully about how the high-end kimono acted both as representational media and existential marker articulating nature, the human and the cosmos. The kimono often represents in its imagery such relationships, often giving, through abstract patterns, a sense of the rhythms of life (both human and non-human), and through color combinations that correspond to seasons and moments of the day, but it also requires a human wearer to map this relationship into actual existence. Wearing a kimono is not like wearing any kind of garment: it is supposed to transform the body into part of an expressive assemblage. Textile in Japan therefore has a long tradition of being a cosmological medium, and this is rooted in part in the recognition that natural dyes in general were labor intensive, required skills and a specific attunement to the environment.

Japanese folk textile traditions, on the other hand, were articulated around a different set of concerns and constraints, which formulated different cosmotechnics. First, silk was unaffordable, and cotton—which was imported until the sixteenth century and then grown in central regions—was expensive for most and therefore precious. The local fibers used in remote regions involved hemp, ramie, banana leaves, and wild wisteria. In areas with not enough fibers, paper made out of *kozo* (mulberry) was cut into thin strips and turned into a strong yarn—a technique referred to as *shifu*. There were many techniques and traditions around the weaving of local fibers, most of the surviving ones documented by anthropologist and textile artist Nobuko Hiroi and Goro Nagano in their phenomenal *From Base to Tip: Bast-Fiber Weaving in Japan and Its Neighboring Countries* (Nagano and Hiroi, 1999), unfortunately not translated into English. Cloth was rare and time consuming to make in a time before mass industrialization and mass consumption. Being labor-intensive and yet much needed for everyday life, the relationships to cloth that emerged in Japan for common folks, from what we can gather today, involved aesthetics borne out of preservation. The tradition of *boro* comes out of poverty and hardship: the decay of cloth had to be slowed down as much as possible, and cloth had to be reused and recycled (Tuzuki, 2009). These necessities transformed cloth into a medium of cultural transmission, where used materials were pieced together, reinforced, layered into new cloth and so on. There was a kind of visual and aesthetic grammar that arises from it through stitches evolving into embroidery patterns and technique known as *sashiko*. As mentioned in the introduction, this haptic form of cultural expression melds together the visual with the intimacy of skin contact, producing a mode of cultural and personal memory that embeds itself into the rhythms of daily life, from being awake to sleeping.

The relationship between textile fiber and indigo in Japanese folk cultures is also important. Common people were historically forbidden from having access to bright colors. Originally, indigo as well was a forbidden color reserved for the nobility, but the growing cultivation of Polygonum tinctorium in Japan made it more accessible. Thus, indigo was one of the few colors available to common people, and therefore became a central component of the kind of textile cultures that emerged. Garments repaired and pieced together were dipped in indigo in order to create a unified look. As well, resist dyeing techniques were also used to create different aesthetic effects. The opening of Japan to the world and access to mass-industrially produced goods meant the dismantlement of major aspects of Japanese textile production, art and craft. While high-end textile-making has survived to today, including major innovations such as in the work of Issey Miyake, for instance, folk textile traditions however have only more recently come back to the fore for Japanese textile arts, fashion and design (Wada, 2013). *Boro* and traditional folk wear and textile are highly sought after both in Japan and the rest of the world both as collector objects and materials for creation. Traditional bast fibers and *shifu* indeed offer the potential to highlight the different radiances of indigo, so much so that in my conversation with Japanese textile artists, fiber was as important as water to understand the potentials and importance of Japanese indigo. Of course, silk offers some incomparable qualities when it comes to indigo and natural dyeing in general, making colors shine. But while most artists still work with silk and cotton when dyeing with natural indigo, older local fibers are generating strong interests. Textile artist Shihoko Fukumoto has for instance reworked old hemp, wisteria and *shifu* garments into her tapestry work. This is what she says of her work with natural folk textiles:

> These cloths take indigo dye astonishingly well, and the deep, strong color brings out the cloth's qualities. . . The more I confront this cloth, the more I ponder the question of how to fully achieve this undertaking with the minimum of dye work—for I believe the less work goes into it, the greater the meaning of the creation, and the stronger the presence of old cloth.
>
> Fukumoto, 2018: 144

For Fukumoto, the indigo work establishes a dialogue with Japan's past, but not only that. Her tapestries made of preserved old bast-fiber cloth evoke and make present again past nature–human relationships, but also the cosmovision that accompanies them. Using cloth that is and feels handmade, where one can sense the efforts that went into twisting fibers into threads and feel the handwoven, slightly irregular qualities of the textile, and dipping it in indigo to obtain a range of blues aligns together human *techne* with a cosmological order, or ethos. In her work with wisteria cloth, Fukumoto works with a wide range of shades of blues, from dark to light blue that turns grey against the creamy white of the wisteria cloth: this gradation feels in turn like the receding imprint of waves on a white beach, like early dawn and eventually like the deep blue of deep space. Fukumoto's indigo work indeed often works with the theme of deep space, using resist techniques over large-scale works to create the impression of many star-lights reaching out from a timeless void. In her work with traditional folk textiles, she brings this cosmological scale down to earth—through the cream to beige colors of the natural cloth—and to the human-technical—through the handmade cloth. The work calls forth cosmotechnics: it links human to nature and to the supernatural. One type of pattern that figures often in her work is the partial dyeing of a straight piece of cloth, with the dyed part sometimes shaped as a long straight rectangle and other times ending on a bias. At a distance, these dyed strips cut through the undyed cloth, but up close, one can see the ways in which the dye bleeds slowly and gently into the fabric on the edge of the strip. This bringing together of contrasting sensation brings forth paradoxical temporalities and space and is therefore more than simply paying homage to the Japanese tradition of handmade cloth but to indicate how non-human elements—both cosmological and natural—can come together through human technique. In this regard, her work stands as a proclamation of technologies that are radically different from western dominant technology as separate from nature and characterized by complete human control. Fukumoto presents us with a way of thinking of textile work as a specific kind of cosmomedia.

Again, in Japan, traditional cosmological explorations are always embedded in nature, and traditional forms of cultural expressions are always an expression of relationalities with nature, at the symbolic, the technical and the material levels. Take for instance the silk kimonos by Fukumi Shimura, one of Japan's living national treasures. In *The Music of Color* (2019) and *Colors of the Shimuras* (Shimura and Shimura, 2009), Shimura speaks at length about the layering of these three planes of relationalities with nature as a weaver and natural dyer specializing in *kasuri*—the Japanese version of *ikat*, which consists of binding threads to achieve resist-dyeing effects before they are woven. *Kasuri* requires an incredibly precise technique as the length of the warp and weft threads and the placement of the binding has to be carefully plotted in order to create the desired final patterns. She explains in several publications how the collecting of natural dye materials is always a profound spiritual experience based on an attunement with changing landscapes and the sensorial qualities of each seasons, but also with dynamics of life and transformation. For example, Shimura recalls the decisive moment at which to collect cherry tree bark in order to have a dye obtain the color of cherry blossom:

> Powdery snow was still falling when I visited the foothills of Mount Ogura one year. There I met an old man who gave me one of the branches he was pruning from the sakura trees. Back in my studio, I simmered it into a dye that turned the fabric such a beautiful pink it seemed to fill my room with the fragrance of the blossoms. At that moment, I experienced what it was like to smell a color. Not as an actual scent, of course, but because all our senses seem to be connected at some deep level, elements of beauty perceived through one sense resonate subtly

across the rest as well. (. . .) When I received words that plans were afoot to trim the sakura near Omi ahead of the September typhoons, I practically flew to the scene to receive some prunings. However, the dye I got from them did not have the same 'fragrance' as before. The color was the same gray-tinged pink, but it lacked the previous batch's radiance. Pondering this difference, I realized that plants, too, have their cycles. In late winter, when I had received the branch from Mount Ogura, the sakura had been preparing within its trunk to bloom to the tips of every bough. *That color was the very spirit of the sakura*, I thought.

Shimura, 2019: 15

Shimura highlights the following: first, captured at the right moment, the invisible life flowing through the cherry tree as it comes out of winter is the decisive factor to obtain radiant color. Dyeing, then, is a permanent record for a moment of living transformation. Second, this kind of cosmological communication requires a mobilization of the senses: it is about an attunement that expresses itself as synesthesia (in this case, color and scent). As she further explains, then, these cosmological relations and exchanges resonate and reverberate through the dyeing process, including the indigo dyeing process. In Shimura's work, one can see the multiple ways in which indigo blues are mobilized: to recall the surface of a lake in winter, to call forth, in combination with bold bright colors, the memory of a summer music festival, to evoke the haziness of rain and moonlight. Fukushima's work builds on synesthesia to create a form of elemental communication in that seeing colors evokes rain, light, different seasons. This elemental communication, in turn, creates unique moments of transindividuation. What we see in Shimura's reflection on the making process from collecting dye materials to the final kimono is a continuous process of communication with non-human actants, processes and entities. This communication with non-human entities found in nature does not posit separation between human and non-human actants, but rather a distribution of the human throughout a cosmological landscape. The human maker is called forth by different entities and energies through the senses, developing an awareness and a capacity for understanding environmental and energy changes. These tenuous moments of connection allow for the appearance of color as the capturing of transformative energies. In Shimura's work, color combinations woven into rhythmic patterns allow for that deep resonance with natural energies to be redistributed back to the human in the form of unconscious, sensorial associations that evoke memories. These memories—of a lake, of a music festival, of a wood block print—are not individual memories, like a Proustian moment, but rather distributed, impersonal, yet deeply moving memories. When I look at Fukumi Shimura's summer festival kimono, I experience echoes of joy and celebration, and nostalgia for a past that I never experienced. I have never been to a traditional Japanese summer music festival, yet it resonates through me. This kind of transindividuation is quite unique, and I argue can only happen with the use of natural dyes such as a bright indigo and the ability to capture their liveliness. Indigo indeed goes through several lives: as plant encountering the elements, but also as entity encountering and being transformed by other live entities in the indigo vat, and as color on a garment that will be passed down, transformed and eventually fall apart. Indigo shines through these many lives, articulating them together as resonances and echoes that blur the line between human, organic and inorganic memories.

Japanese indigo is about non-human mediations. It speaks directly to the material turn in media theory found in the work of John Durham Peters (2016), Jussi Parikka (2015) and Sarah Kember and Joanna Zylinska (2014), but it includes many material mediations both superimposed and in succession rather than their focus on one element at a time. With Japanese indigo, elements such as water and air carrying the traces of their past encounters now are put together with living beings such as bacteria, and technical beings such as cloth. In my experience, it provides, as part of natural dyeing, a direct experience and engagement with cosmotechnics and with elemental mediation. It is critical thinking in action. In that sense, poring over a poorly dyed indigo cloth, in my experience, means understanding the long chain of what is going on with one's environment. This not only concerns pollution (for instance ozone or water pollution, or the many chemicals that are used to coat fabric and prevent dyeing), but also how the different materials record past encounters—a good or poor summer weather for growing indigo, alkaline substances that made the water too "hard" and dull natural dyes. Indigo opens up temporalities that are not human and, in that way, it is an exercise in precarity as Anna Tsing understands it, that is, as "a state of acknowledgement of our vulnerability to others" (2017: 29), which are not just other human beings, but other non-human elements and entities. Indigo dyeing asks one to acknowledge one's indebtedness to a cosmos, and it is through this very experience of being in debt, at the mercy of so many elements, that so much creativity can be unleashed. In acknowledging one's debt to the cosmos, one invites the world-making activities of non-human beings and entities to come to the fore, and to come together in a complex orchestration to produce radiant blues. The technical object—the cloth—is surrendered to the elements and beings in the indigo vat. Such reversal from the dominant technological model, and the immense beauty that it creates make indigo an important media practice of the Anthropocene: being at the mercy of the elements, contrary to beliefs in total collapse, means rediscovering new modes of life-giving.

References

Altvater, Elmar, Eileen C. Crist, Donna J. Haraway, Daniel Hartley, Christian Parenti, and Justin McBrien. (2016). *Anthropocene or Capitalocene?: Nature, History, and the Crisis of Capitalism*. Edited by Jason W. Moore. Oakland, CA: PM Press.

Balfour-Paul, Jenny. (2011). *Indigo: From Mummies to Blue Jeans. by Jenny Balfour-Paul*. London: British Museum Press.

Bellacasa, María Puig de la. (2017). *Matters of Care: Speculative Ethics in More than Human Worlds*. 3rd edn. Minneapolis: University of Minnesota Press.

Boutrup, Joy, and Catharine Ellis. (2018). *The Art and Science of Natural Dyes: Principles, Experiments, and Results*. Atglen, PA: Schiffer.

Cardon, Dominique. (2007). *Natural Dyes: Sources, Traditions, Technology & Science*. Illustrated edn. London: Archetype Books.

Descola, Philippe, and Marshall Sahlins. (2013). *Beyond Nature and Culture*. Translated by Janet Lloyd. Reprint edn. Chicago: University of Chicago Press.

Fofana, Aboubakar. (n.d.). "Live Feedback Friday – Aboubakar Fofana – Zoom." Accessed March 17, 2021.

Franklin, Ursula. (1999). *The Real World of Technology*. Toronto: House of Anansi Press.

Fukumoto, Shihoko. (2018). *Fukumoto Shihoko: Japan Blues*. Bilingual edn. Tokyo: AKAAKA Art Publishing.

Garcia, Michel. (2016). *Couleurs Végétales: Teintures, Pigments et Encres*. Aix en Provence: Édisud.

Garcia, Michel, and Annie-France Bernard. (2006). *Plantes Colorantes et Teintures Végétales: Le Nuancier Des Couleurs*. Aix en Provence: Édisud.

Guattari, Felix. (2008). *The Three Ecologies*. Translated by Ian Pindar and Paul Sutton. London: Bloomsbury Academic.

Haraway, Donna J. (2016). *Staying with the Trouble: Making Kin in the Chthulucene*. Durham, NC: Duke University Press.

Heidegger, Martin. (2013). *The Question Concerning Technology: And Other Essays*. New York: Harper Perennial Modern Classics.

Hui, Yuk. (2016). *The Question Concerning Technology in China: An Essay in Cosmotechnics*. Falmouth: Urbanomic Media Ltd.

Ingold, Tim. (2010). "The Textility of Making." *Cambridge Journal of Economics* 34 (1): 91–102. http://www.jstor.org.ezproxy.library.yorku.ca/stable/24232023.

Innis, Harold A. (2007). *Empire and Communications*. Toronto: Dundurn Press.

Kane, Carolyn L. (2014). *Chromatic Algorithms: Synthetic Color, Computer Art, and Aesthetics after Code*. Chicago: University of Chicago Press.

Kember, Sarah, and Joanna Zylinska. (2014). *Life after New Media: Mediation as a Vital Process*. Reprint edn. Cambridge, MA: MIT Press.

Kolbert, Elizabeth, Edward O. Wilson, and Thomas E. Lovejoy. (2017). *Living in the Anthropocene: Earth in the Age of Humans*. Edited by John W. Kress and Jeffrey K. Stine. Washington, DC: Smithsonian Books.

Legrand, Catherine. (2013). *Indigo: The Color That Changed The World*. Illustrated edn. New York: Thames and Hudson.

Mackail, J. W. (2013). *The Life of William Morris*. North Chelmsford, MA: Courier Corporation.

Nagano, Goro, and Nobuko Hiroi. (1999). *Base to Tip: Bast-Fiber Weaving in Japan and Its Neighboring Countries* 織物の原風景: 樹皮と草皮の布と機. 京都: 紫紅社.

Palmer, Helen, and Vicky Hunter. (2018). "Worlding." *New Materialism* [blog]. March 16, 2018. https://newmaterialism.eu/almanac/w/worlding.html.

Parikka, Jussi. (2015). *A Geology of Media*. Minneapolis: University of Minnesota Press.

Peters, John Durham. (2016). *The Marvelous Clouds: Toward a Philosophy of Elemental Media*. Reprint edn. Chicago: University Of Chicago Press.

Phipps, Elena. (2013). "Global Colors: Dyes and the Dye Trade." In *Interwoven Globe: The New Worldwide Textile Trade 1500-1800*, 120–35. New York: Metropolitan Museum of Art.

Scranton, Roy. (2015). *Learning to Die in the Anthropocene: Reflections on the End of a Civilization*. San Franciso, CA: City Lights Publishers.

Shimura, Fukumi. (2019). *Music of Color*. Tokyo: Japan Publishing Industry Foundation for Culture.

Shimura, Fukumi, and Yoko Shimura. (2009). *Colors of the Shimura*. Kyoto: Kyuuryuudou.

Stengers, Isabelle. (2018). *Another Science Is Possible: A Manifesto for Slow Science*. Translated by Stephen Muecke. Cambridge, UK: Polity.

Tanaka, Yuko. (2013). *The Power of the Weave: The Hidden Meanings of Cloth*. Tokyo: International House of Japan.

Taussig, Michael. (2009). *What Color Is the Sacred?* Illustrated edn. Chicago: University of Chicago Press.

Tsing, Anna Lowenhaupt. (2017). *The Mushroom at the End of the World: On the Possibility of Life in Capitalist Ruins*. Reprint edn. Princeton, NJ: Princeton University Press.

Tsing, Anna Lowenhaupt, Nils Bubandt, Elaine Gan, and Heather Anne Swanson, eds. (2017). *Arts of Living on a Damaged Planet: Ghosts and Monsters of the Anthropocene*. Minneapolis: University of Minnesota Press.

Tuzuki, Kyouiti. (2009). *Boro: Rags and Tatters from the Far North of Japan*. Tōkyō: Aspect Corp.

Vejar, Kristine. (2015). *The Modern Natural Dyer: A Comprehensive Guide to Dyeing Silk, Wool, Linen and Cotton at Home*. Illustrated edn. New York: Harry N. Abrams.

Viveiros de Castro, Eduardo, and Déborah Danowski. (2016). *The Ends of the World*. Translated by Rodrigo Guimaraes Nunes. Malden, MA: Polity.

Wada, Yoshiko Iwamoto. (2013). *Memory on Cloth: Shibori Now*. 2nd edn. New York: Kodansha.

Yoshioka, Sachio, and Denshi Fukuda. (2000). *Japanese Color Dictionary* – 日本の色辞典. 紫紅社.

CONCLUSION: THE SHAPE OF THINGS TO COME

This book was written during the pandemic, and it is only as I write these words that the province I live in—Ontario—seems to be getting a semblance of reopening, despite a massive sixth wave of infection. Obviously, textile has suffered: many of the groups that I presented saw their income from tourism disappear and many, as already marginalized groups with little access to health care, were the first to be hit by the pandemic. Some organized themselves online, with e-stores and fundraisers. How they, and textile-making, which is such a communal activity, are going to fare now is an open question. I recently was able to organize a small indigo demonstration for graduate students in Science and Technology. We had spent the entire the year, because of the pandemic, talking very abstractly about bodies, technologies, life. And only in this last class did we get an opportunity to engage all our senses in exploring the world around us through the medium of color. I have to say, teaching natural indigo dyeing is a favorite of mine, because while people listen to what I am saying, their eyes are glued to the indigo vat. The vat, while silent, is the main teacher here, the one that everybody pays attention to and listens to carefully. The vat unites all of us, accommodates all of us, organizes us into a community. The vat was, as I will further explain below, a pluriversal medium, capable of not only containing us class participants, but the many histories and potentials for indigo as well.

In this book, I tracked and was guided by textile when it exists as an outsider medium, that is, a medium outside of the dominant matrix of capitalism, modernity and colonialism, which distorts textile-making from the making of worlds to the destruction of the world. The physical and material consequences of this are more than obvious at this point in time. I wanted to show in this book a more insidious process: that the dismantlement of non-industrial textile-making erased a unique medium of communication that should be understood as pluriversal, and that pluriversal communication is key to addressing today's issues of neocolonialism, exploitation and destruction of environment. Textile, as we saw in the first chapter, was always plural, developed in parallel by groups the world over, wherever suitable fibers were available. But for all its plurality, textile was also a global means of exchange, and textile objects and techniques crossed through different worlds, and profoundly transformed those worlds, spurring not only new aesthetic and cultural tastes, but also new imaginaries. If the pluriverse, to refer to the Zapatista slogan, is "a world where many worlds fit," then a pluriversal medium is not only a medium that allows different worlds to flourish, but also one that allows them to exchange with each other. In other words, a pluriversal medium is a medium that allows for this world where all other worlds fit to exist, and for this to happen, it not only requires exchanges in the present, but also with the complex and violent histories that have led us to this particular point in time. This is not to say that textile before its colonization and capitalist mass industrialization was not without inequalities and physical violence, as we saw in particular with the question of domestic textile work and women's textile work, nor that it was without political power play, as we saw in Chapter 1. But textile before its colonization and mass industrialization, was often a medium for both developing local cosmologies and exchanging with other cosmologies, something that we do not find in today's mainstream contemporary media, which are the media of dominant power. Make no mistake, this lack has led to crisis. In the span of only twenty years, the most hyped media revolution of our time—the digital, networked revolution—went from promises of democratic participatory communication and free circulation of information and knowledge, to a dystopia of large-scale automated manipulation, propaganda and cultivation of ire and envy built on ever-increasing surveillance, commodification and exploitation of all aspect of human and biological life. All of this is supported by legions of underpaid workers and hardware made up of toxic materials extracted in brutal conditions, and whose cycles of planned obsolescence are becoming shorter and shorter. It is even more distressing that this monumental failure of our dominant and seemingly most promising media systems comes at a time when the need has never been greater to come together as communities worldwide to face threats of climate change, forced migration, species extinction, large-scale pollution, growing inequalities and rising fascisms. Like many of my colleagues, I feel an overwhelming sense of powerlessness as time goes by and things get worse, as we continue the work of critical theory, of dissecting the mechanisms of global destruction while such destruction continues. If anything is to be learned from looking at textile as a pluriversal medium, it is the following: that such sense of powerlessness has to be unlearned in that as much as textile has long existed at the forefront of colonization, unsustainable exploitation and corporate greed, this is not its only history. This is not to say that something like textile is the medium that will fix our problems. Rather, non-industrialized textile-making offers insights and practices of how to exist at the brink of and through destruction, of how to continue to find new ways to bind to each other and to the increasingly damaged worlds we encounter. While the creative capacities and achievements of the Lyon silk-weavers who heralded inventions such as the Jacquard mechanism have been countered by mass commodification, the women doing domestic textile work can teach us a thing or two about endurance, resilience, and seizing opportunities for reinvention. Indigenous textile practiced in Peru has much to say about how to extirpate oneself within the dominant matrix of power as an abyss that renders many forms of existence impossible. In turn, Indigenous textile-making shows that we can cross such an abyss, tactically diverting and reshaping production, discourse and distribution infrastructures. In so doing, it shows how to practice existing at the crossroad of Indigenous and non-Indigenous worlds. Such practice is destabilizing, precarious and creative, and textile in that sense acts as a message that opens the door to a plurality of critical practices, to new forms of politics and engagement without words, but filled to the brim with potential meaningfulness. Decolonial practice and thinking is hardly something new: it has existed for a long time, done by many across the globe, either at the center or at the margins of the dominant matrix of power, under many guises, one of them being the making of textile. And looking at some of the politics and discussions that take place in textile circles is revealing of a politics that expresses itself materially. For instance, I witnessed many debates in the past few years about which dyes are actually appropriate: natural dyes come to mind as being environmentally friendly, but they require large amounts of water. Thus, synthetic dyes that require very little to no water might be more appropriate depending on the context. Also, using avocado pits and skins for dyeing seems like a good upcycling idea, but given the unsustainable state of the avocado industry in Mexico, their use is not such a virtuous act overall. In these discussions of water and avocado garbage, the exploration of global politics, economics and the question of how to act meaningfully and in ways that matter in damaged and fragile environments takes on a very material turn rather than lofty discourses. The lovely pink of avocado skins should thus become a rare color in some part of the world, like Canada where I live. If avocado skins and pits are to become rare and precious, then an economy of color will emerge: dyed pink threads will be few and far between, and will be cherished as precious communication from afar. They will be carefully woven with other colors to highlight their rarity and beauty. How could they, for instance, be in dialogue with the much more common bright to rusty oranges extracted from onion skins? Textile-making is one of these rare cultural and artistic field, where artists are more and more thinking of limiting the kind of materials at their disposal as they engage in environmental communication with the worlds they live in and care for.

Looking at non-industrialized textile revealed long histories: what existed before the dominant matrix of power, what this dominant matrix subsumed and destroyed, what remains and is currently being imagined and implemented. Textile is a vector of power. Beautiful textiles are contagious—for any textile maker, the desire to achieve beautiful color, enticing patterns, intricate weaves and so on is irresistible. At the same time, textile-making is by default cosmotechnical: it always is a series of encounters with the world and reflects relational choices. What I find especially important in the cosmotechnics of textile is the capacity to create new connections, new potentials, to foster spaces of indeterminacy, of not knowing, of not being in control, that are not vague, but rather allow for the flourishing of new imaginaries and practices about how to relate to the world. I hope to have made clear that such textile practices in and of themselves will not solve the current challenge we face in the Anthropocene. Rather, my analysis rested on three aspects of textile as medium that work and deal with power, be it power experienced as control, or power as potential for newness and creativity: cosmotechnics, mediation and mattering/meaning.

The first aspect is the technological level of extraction and/or transformation. I started with a conceptualization of technological processes as cosmotechnics (Hui,

2016), in that they actualize an ethics of relations with the world. And through Hui, I inscribed my approach within the philosophy of technology of Simondon (1969; 1989) and Stiegler (2013): the idea that to be human is to be technological, and that technology is what enables human relationships with the world, both at the material level and at the symbolic level. Further, against the monotechnological model, based on absolute control for purposes of exploitation, textile-making shows how the relationship with materials and non-human beings, entities and processes can be and has long been a transformative collaboration. With the case of indigo, we saw how some textile techniques embraced an intimate yet distributed relationship between human makers and materials, where the humans orchestrate a series of material conversations and transformations with the support of environmental entities such as water, air and so on. And at the same time, the humans are never in control—they at best can be diplomats dealing with non-human entities and processes (e.g., the clarity of mountain water filtrated through rocks) that are much more powerful and intractable. This technological process works closely in and with environments, and thus stands in stark contrast with the technological model of absolute control over materials, and where the environment only exists as either infinite resource or dumping ground. Further, it is clear then that material processes participate in the formulation and communication of ethical values and that we can therefore understand seemingly small and simple making gestures as actually value statements. In other words, we go from material to mattering, to rich, empowering alliances that show a world filled with creative potentials. The key is that such communication takes place without words, and without what we usually understand as signification. Nevertheless, it proclaims specific ways of being with others, human and non-human alike. I use the term communication in this specific instance not as a catch-all, but to point out that these proclamations through making are also fragile—that they can be in turn denied, derided, easily made innocuous, just like verbal statements and proclamations can be rejected, ridiculed and so on. In that regard, the awareness that communication can take place without signification opens up a whole new range of inquiry into non-human forms of communication. I am thinking in particular of endeavors such as the Fibershed model (Burgess and White, 2019), which seeks to reintroduce local cloth production, from the cultivation of fibers, the betterment of natural dyes' local ecosystem in North America all the way to finished textile clothing and products. Fibershed focuses on regenerative practices that are carbon beneficial and help rebuild the environment. In developing local fibers, such as cotton, wool and dogbane, Fibershed engages with farmers and sheep farms, but also with Indigenous knowledge and practices all to create durable and functional home textiles and clothing, with traditional natural dyes practices that serve as a basis for technical and scientific innovation. In so doing, the collaboration between humans and non-humans becomes even more extensive, organized around core principles of soil regeneration and being carbon beneficial. While such practices are indeed part of regenerative development initiatives, they are also built on ways of communicating with the environment, ways of declaring inclusion of the non-humans as deserving voice and respect for their agencies.

What emerges, then, is that giving voice to the non-humans and organizing communication with them in ways that leads to transformation and even transmutation as organic materials become technological objects, as humans become technical conduits, takes place without the recourse to discourse. Hence why these forms of communication are usually absent from mainstream communication studies and only starting to come to the fore with the inclusion of Indigenous epistemologies: communication between humans and non-humans takes place without human verbalization, but nevertheless establishes pacts, diplomatic relations, collaborations and in so doing transformations.

Two key insights emerge from this notion of communication without words: first that we can understand meaning/mattering beyond signification as the formulation of horizons and conditions of existence; and second, that the circulation of meaning and matter refashions and blurs the past, present and future by bringing about transformative effects. Here, we go into the aspect of textile as mediation, that is, as the interface where meanings formulated through making and technical hybridization of human and non-humans come to matter through space and time. To put it simply: there is a world of difference between a pre-Columbian symbol that is made through backstrap weaving and the same symbol woven via a power loom in a faraway country. The challenge for us is that the symbol might look the same, but it declares and embodies radically different modes of existence. Such tacit and invisible communication for the majority of us not used to haptically reading textile is actually key to understanding its transformative power. Such is the task for decolonizing communication and media studies: in order to fully understand meaningfulness of textile symbols, we need to go beyond the surface of expression toward the question of matter. In that regard, it is even more pressing to turn toward Deleuze and Guattari and subsequently Guattari's exploration of meaning beyond signification. I did my best in this book to undertake the kind of a-signifying analysis they call for while avoiding much of the conceptual jargon they use. In *A Thousand Plateaus* (1987) and *Anti-Oedipus* (1983), Deleuze and Guattari express a deep frustration with the overall reliance on structural linguistics to understand the constitution of meaning, which they find quite inadequate to the task of understanding the politics of meaning-making, that is, how meaning-making practices articulate modes of existence. Deleuze and Guattari reject traditional linguistic frameworks, particularly Saussurean semiology, that see the constitution of meaning as a play of difference between abstract signifiers—the ideas and concepts associated with a sign. Whereas Saussurean linguistics cuts itself from the real to focus on the realm of abstract play on concepts, Deleuze and Guattari are more interested in looking at expressive systems—language for instance, but also money, music, film, etc., that work through both material systems and systems of abstraction, becoming planes where material, technical political, economic and social processes are mobilized to work on existence itself. Guattari subsequently formulated a framework—a-signifying semiotics—to map the different processes through which systems of expression encompasses material resources and abstract informational codes to have existential effects—to establish and actualize horizons of possibilities about the world, the self and each other (Guattari, 2018).

A-signification operates in multiple ways and through multiple combinations of materials, concepts and codes, including both classical linguistics codes such as grammar, but also non-linguistic ones such as DNA, musical notation, computer codes and so on. Subsequent explorations of the a-signifying framework, such as Gary Genosko's (2016), have focused on the questions of a-signs that are operation of power. This opens up a consideration of what I would call connectors—the specific objects and moments, both abstracts and material, that assemble a broader machine of existence by connecting for instance, material to networks, users to tools, human beings to political power. Connectors do the complex work of in turn abstracting-extracting and actualizing, enabling the crossing of heterogenous elements and the assembling of meaning and matter. The a-signifying framework is key to understanding the formulations of conditions of existence that take place through movements across seemingly heterogenous planes that then go through movements of connection and disconnection, folding and unfolding: biological, social, technical, cultural, ideological, habitual, micro and macro. The study of meaning/mattering then, needs to be much more than the study of signs on the surface, and requires plunging into dynamic, heterogenous process of transmutations, whereby materials are transformed and are given new agencies and in so doing actualize ethics of relationships between humans and non-humans, where abstract values are translated into daily practices of making that shape a rhythm of existence. Which leads to the second aspect of mediation: that meaning/mattering is never fully fixed and that indeed, by being primarily a phenomenon of transmutation, it opens the door to transformations. By this I do not mean that it is unstable, or vague. Meaning/mattering in non-industrialized textile is constructed of course, or rather co-constructed through collaborations among humans and non-humans. It is assembled as an interface that connects different spaces and temporalities. Again, this might also feel like a truism: meaning/mattering travels through space and time, but what textile means and how it matters enables deep transformations for textile makers and users, that is, the ability to find modes of transindividuation that do not only happen in the present, but through reinventions of the past and the future.

I started this book with the example of *boro*, and how it is a form of cultural transmission that works through lengthening the life of cloth and therefore the presence of past cloth caretakers into the future, but also through embracing inevitable decay and death. *Boro* conjugates temporalities: the *future* for past cloth owners as they pass down repaired textile objects; the *past* for the present-day users; and for all *past, present and future* users, the requirement for caring for and embracing decay and eventual death by practicing lengthening the life of textile. Encountering indigenous women textile makers in Peru also reinforced how textile acts as a paradoxical interface, offering an unbroken continuity of textile-making across millennia, but also enabling connections to other distant and foreign pasts, in the case of Moche archeological remains, to make possible the formulation of economic and social imaginaries in the present and future.

The continuous reinvention of textile-making makes it possible to cross through the abysses of colonization, including historical erasure of groups and cultures. By way of further illustration of how such an approach can serve deep political and social transformations, let me turn to the Baltimore Natural Dyes Initiative at the Maryland Institute College of Art (MICA). Artists and instructors both, Valeska Populoh and Kibibi Ajanku (2021) explained that the cultivation and use of natural dyes and in particular indigo by students and instructors enabled the creation of a common space where, in turn, difficult questions about the US legacy of colonization, enslavement and racism could be addressed. As they highlight, the history of indigo in the United States is one of linked to the cruelty and mass trauma of slavery. But for Kibibi Ajanku, indigo is also what connects her to the West African tradition of her ancestors; and her learning to dye with indigo in West Africa and developing an indigo textile practice has been a profound way of defining personal and collective modes of existence that reconnect with a past that was erased and make it possible to engage in healing practices. The power and import of such an experience—being able to address with others the very wounds that continue to separate, polarize, antagonize and victimize—cannot be overstated at this point in history, and I would argue is something that has not been fully understood by communication and media scholarship focused on the circulation of signs.

Mediation takes place in complex ways through textile, in its capacity to foster new linkages with past histories, thereby forging new futures. Textile-making defines modes of being(s) and not just subjects of power formations; it allows for the emergence of individual and collective modes of existence, including memories and imaginaries, and it does so by folding and unfolding in space and time. To plunge one's hand in the indigo vat is to experience and conjure, if one wants, multiple histories, and to actively formulate how they stand and continue to exist in the present. It also enables us to be mediated in turn, to be part of broader assemblages of potentials and becoming, to experience temporalities and agencies that we, as humans, do not and will not ever possess. I hope that reflecting on instances of a medium working through the temporal dimensions of transindividuation by way of practical engagement and communication with non-humans expands how we think about communication in relation to the making of worlds. The dominant matrix of power has long worked through negative externalities, in turn rationalizing, downplaying, rejecting or ignoring its most damaging aspects or insincerely promising future corrective or alternative. Such logic is becoming more and more untenable, as the accumulation of past and current environmental, social and psychic damage has taken over our present and spells out the impossibility of a future under the current dominant logic of power. The necessary need to delink from the dominant matrix of power has led to the development of renewed critical practices, particularly through non-human existence and intelligence (Tsing, 2017; Haraway, 2016); design (Escobar, 2018 Costanza-Chock, 2020); speculation and futurism (Keeling, 2019); and technological hacking (Renzi, 2020). All of these turn to the question of transindividuation in the Anthropocene through new environmental, social and psychic relationships: the need to engage in an ethics of recognition of the non-humans, the invention of tools and means to mediate multiple relationships and create new infrastructures that promote collaborative and empathic relationships, the formulation of future imaginaries based on a profound upheaval and refashioning of technology and science, the exploration of how alternative ways of making creates solidarity and fosters community building. The case of textile adds to this rich literature that has flourished in recent years and explores in turn practices that flow from one ecology to the next, from the environmental to the social to the psychic. In so doing, from a critical perspective, it asks us to think beyond our tendency to define sites of analysis as bounded enclaves: discourse rather than technologies; human communities rather than non-human lives. Instead, textile points at what traverses through these different aspects and sites of analysis, what always exceeds them and propels a constant work of suturing and piecing together paradoxical and disparate dynamics. The textile makers—be they the dyers, weavers, users caring for and repairing cloth—emerge as these transmutable figures, working alongside non-humans, traveling through space and time, continuing millennial ways of making, transmitting culture and exerting mathematical genius, developing cutting-edge intelligent technologies, while often managing domestic spaces. What I hoped to show therefore is a way to think through the heterogeneity of assemblage, their multi-layered and distributed agencies, by highlighting practices of traversing rather than just tracing, delineating and so on. In other words: to delink from the dominant matrix of power, deep transformations require rhythmic repetition that enable travel back and forth through existential territories and layers. And through these travels, through the folding and unfolding of existential layers, emerge potentials. In terms of critical use of assemblage theory then, I hope to have shown how a seemingly simple gesture like sewing actually sutures together complex assemblages. Further, the lack of control from human actants over the complex assemblages (Bennett, 2010) with multiple and distributed agencies does not mean passivity or powerlessness, but the capacity to compose with, to assist and participate in transformation and transmutation.

But all this amazing potential at the levels of technique and mediation cannot be fully realized and actualized without a system of exchange and distribution. By this, I not only mean an economic infrastructure that regulates the monetary value of textile objects and textile work and distributes them to specific markets, but the system of valuation that establishes the equivalencies between the world of the maker and that of the customer and user. Such equivalencies assign cultural meanings to objects as they circulate outside of their context of making, often through a romanticization of the handmade that erases its more revolutionary transformative potentials. They also establish a value for non-industrialized textile work, usually seen as keeping traditions alive in the case of Indigenous women's work, or increasingly by recognizing textile arts as "high art." Note that in so doing, these equivalencies empty out the radical transformative work of textile.

We ought to resist equivalencies that make us blind to alternatives and other modes of making, being and experiencing that have actually always been there. As I explained in the book, we should move from equivalencies—the work of bringing otherness into the fold of our familiar epistemological and ontological frameworks—to equivocation, that is, bringing what is other to trouble our epistemological and ontological habits to open up spaces of indeterminacy that can constitute the basis of transformation. It is necessary to acknowledge that the political work of transformation as it happens through textile does not often fall into how we think about radical politics. Let me explain this further: in my observations of textile makers (most of them women), I saw both the radical formulation of ways of existence and loud claims to equity, and to building lives where care and labor were two facets of the same thing. At the same time, I saw none of the political discourses that one might expect: discourses that one sees in the media and academia on decolonization, Indigenous rights, Indigenous philosophy and ways of lives were mostly absent. This does not mean that these ideas were not prevalent in crafting ways of sustaining oneself through textile practices—on the contrary they were always already engaged with, but through creativity, new designs, ways of organizing and distributing the work among the collective, through gathering together and talking about daily worries and so on. It would be a mistake, as I indicated in Chapter 5, to consider that because the radical political discourses are not particularly prevalent in the way we expect in the west, that radical politics are not taking shape. The task then is to challenge our collective blind spots to the habitual, the mundane, the seemingly small and modest gestures. In turn, textile show us how we can practice an ethics of care, of unfolding to and through the world and being folded in and extended in the world.

The final critical work then is to challenge how the relationship between dominant power and resistance has been conceptualized and studied. The field has long struggled with the dichotomy between seemingly all-powerful dominant strategies of power, and the seemingly small and limited tactics of resistance from minorities (De Certeau, 2002). In turn, this has led to widespread discouragement and cynicism, in that tactics of resistance never measure up to the overwhelming global capacities of dominant power. But as the dominant matrix of power continues to crumble through its self-destructive logics, tactics of resistance are a means of enduring, of slowly building the structures and modes of being together. It would be a mistake to try to measure the success of tactics of resistance by comparing them with the impacts of the dominant matrix of power. Rather, we can think of some of these practices as planting seeds, waiting for rain to come. I hope to have shown that those capacities have always been there, and that the dominant matrix of power can only function if it can keep these capacities invisible. Textile as it has existed outside of the dominant matrix is a key instance of a haptic media that can bring us closer together at the same time as it can project us into new horizons, toward new relations. In turn, we need to navigate un-knowing—that profound uneasiness of seeing our western categories of what counts as media, what counts as expression, what counts as important, completely dismantled. In a time that asks for quick fixes and research deliverables, arguing for un-knowing is not an easy ask, but one that is necessary in order to start from the basis of expression: the practice of encountering worlds.

References

Bennett, Jane. (2010). *Vibrant Matter: A Political Ecology of Things*. Durham, NC: Duke University Press.

Burgess, Rebecca, and Courtney White. (2019). *Fibershed: Growing a Movement of Farmers, Fashion Activists, and Makers for a New Textile Economy*. Illustrated edn. White River Junction, VT: Chelsea Green Publishing.

Certeau, Michel de. (2002). *The Practice of Everyday Life*. 2nd edn. Berkeley, CA: University of California Press.

Costanza-Chock, Sasha. (2020). *Design Justice: Community-Led Practices to Build the Worlds We Need*. Cambridge, MA: MIT Press.

Deleuze, Gilles, and Felix Guattari. (1983). *Anti-Oedipus: Capitalism and Schizophrenia*. Minneapolis: University of Minnesota Press.

Deleuze, Gilles, and Félix Guattari. (1987). *A Thousand Plateaus: Capitalism and Schizophrenia*. Minneapolis: University of Minnesota Press.

Escobar, Arturo. (2018). *Designs for the Pluriverse: Radical Interdependence, Autonomy, and the Making of Worlds*. Durham, NC: Duke University Press.

Genosko, Gary. (2016). *Critical Semiotics: Theory, from Information to Affect*. London: Bloomsbury Academic.

Guattari, Felix. (2018). *Molecular Revolution*. London: Bloomsbury Academic.

Haraway, Donna J. (2016). *Staying with the Trouble: Making Kin in the Chthulucene*. Durham, NC: Duke University of Press.

Hui, Yuk. (2016). *The Question Concerning Technology in China: An Essay in Cosmotechnics*. Falmouth: Urbanomic Media Ltd.

Keeling, Kara. (2019). *Queer Times, Black Futures*. New York: New York University Press.

Populoh, Valeska, and Kibibi Ajanku. (2021). "Reflections on the Baltimore Natural Dye Initiative." Presented at the Natural Dyes in Northeast America Conference, Toronto.

Renzi, Alessandra. (2020). *Hacked Transmissions: Technology and Connective Activism in Italy*. Minneapolis: University of Minnesota Press.

Simondon, Gilbert. (1969). *Du Mode d'existence Des Objets Techniques*. Vol. 1. Paris: Aubier-Montaigne.

Simondon, Gilbert. (1989). *L'individuation Psychique et Collective: À La Lumière Des Notions de Forme, Information, Potentiel et Métastabilité*. Paris: Editions Aubier.

Stiegler, Bernard. (2013). *What Makes Life Worth Living: On Pharmacology*. Oxford: Polity.

Tsing, Anna Lowenhaupt. (2017). *The Mushroom at the End of the World: On the Possibility of Life in Capitalist Ruins*. Reprint edn. Princeton, NJ: Princeton University Press.

INDEX

The letter *f* following an entry indicates a page with a figure.

Printed in Dunstable, United Kingdom

70628554R00125